MULTICULTURAL EDUCATION IN ALL-WHITE AREAS

For Bapuji

and in loving memory of
Ba (14 March 1920 - 31 December 1991)
and
Motabhai (14 February 1946 - 25 March 1992)

Multicultural Education in All-White Areas /

A case study of two ESG projects

KISHOR PATEL
*Formerly advisory teacher for multicultural and anti-racist education
and one time teacher fellow at the University of East London*

Avebury

Aldershot · Brookfield USA · Hong Kong · Singapore · Sydney

Published by
Avebury
Ashgate Publishing Ltd
Gower House
Croft Road
Aldershot
Hants. GU11 3HR
England

Ashgate Publishing Company
Old Post Road
Brookfield
Vermont 05036
USA

British Library Cataloguing in Publication Data

Patel, Kishor
  Multicultural Education in All-white Areas
  I. Title
  370.193410941

ISBN 1 85628 969 9

Library of Congress Cataloging-in-Publication Data

Patel, Kishor, 1952–
  Multicultural education in all-white areas / Kishor Patel.
        p. cm.
  ISBN 1-85628-969-9
  1. Multicultural education--Great Britain 2. Whites--Education-
-Britain. I. Title
LC1099.19'6'0941   1994   94-22707
370.19'6'0941--dc20   CIP

Printed and bound by Athenæum Press Ltd.,
Gateshead, Tyne & Wear.

Contents

Foreword

Jagdish Gundara

Teachers and other educationalists have been engaged in working on the issue of cultural diversity and its implications for education in Britain for a number of decades. The impact of much of this work is difficult to quantify in terms of the educational achievement and outcome of children in schools. The problem partly lies in the way in which there is very little agreement on the theoretical and conceptual issues in this field.

Kishor Patel's book very eloquently points to the complexity created by the usage of multicultural and anti-racist perspectives. These debates which were seemingly resolved in the late 1980s still reverberate in this book, partly because both terms are still used. The book therefore engages at length with the pros and cons of these different paradigms. The thrust of his argument is that the soft-edged multicultural approach tends to reinforce racist ideas, which anti-racist strategies are more adequately able to deal with. At a time when xenophobic and racist ideologies have acquired a new lease of life in Europe, it is important to take what the author suggests seriously. This is a field in which Britain could have been in the forefront due to the work many teachers, schools and local authorities have undertaken. Yet, the conservative restoration has dealt a body blow to the growth of more equal and safer schools in this polity.

The strength of this book lies in the fact that it deals with classroom practice and curriculum development. It focuses on curricular work in predominantly all white schools and also limits its analysis to three subject areas.

The underlying assumption of the author is that racism is a major problem; it is appropriate that there is an analysis of these issues in mainly white schools. The author worked as an advisory teacher in two Educational Support Grant projects and is able to deal with issues of curriculum development and intervention as a participant/researcher. He represents the perspective of a black researcher who has worked in Tyneside and London and points out that the deficit models of multicultural education have compounded issues. He demonstrates the immense contribution the black community has made in all aspects of British national life.

The curricular focus is on English and Mathematics as core subjects within the National Curriculum and Home Economics as an aspect of the curriculum. The book contains some interesting examples of the ways in which curriculum innovation was undertaken within classrooms in these subject areas.

The assumption underlying the enactment of the Education Support Grants is that issues of inequality would be addressed within them, although in the period 1985-7 only about £1.5 million were spent in over 50 local education authorities. This is a minuscule amount of expenditure to address curricular issues and establish teacher networks based on innovative ideas generated by various projects. Given the financial constraints these initiatives can, however, be successful if the head teachers support the initiatives being undertaken in various schools. The model of action research used in these projects was a cooperative one and based on the researcher and teachers working together. This method of research seems to be useful because teachers and students and schools can directly benefit from the involvement of such research work. The problem of resistance to change in various schools is also highlighted, thus enabling future projects to devise prophylactic methods in embarking on curriculum innovation in the future. The extremely strong institutional pressures to marginalise work in tackling racism in the classroom and within schools merits urgent attention at the national level. If this book assists such a process, the author's efforts would have been well rewarded.

There is a useful analysis of pupils' experience of racism and the variation of pupil responses to it over the period of stay in the school. The restriction of important curricular issues to the personal and social education area of the curriculum tends to reinforce the pupil's own view as to the lack of teacher and school commitment to initiating meaningful changes. The entrenchment of negative attitudes towards the use of languages other than English is also part and parcel of the exclusionary and marginalisation processes. The hardening of attitudes towards different religions could also have dangerous consequences for younger people, particularly in predominantly white inner city schools where the paucity of interfaith understandings can exacerbate conflicts.

One of the issues not discussed in the book is the level of teachers' competence to deal with these complex issues in British classrooms. It is likely that the policy of the Government to merely train teachers within schools, would leave them even less well equipped to counter the diverse range of problems in schools. This, combined with tokenistic curricular changes, would lead to greater pressures for separate schools by different communities. This is in itself a worrying feature because it would lead to little intercultural understanding through shared learning and experiences and would impede the development of a shared and common value system within the public domain. It could also fail to strengthen a civic culture in which there are clear understandings and commitments to rights and responsibilities within a system of greater equalities.

In sum, this book makes a valued contribution to a crucial and ongoing educational debate.

Jagdish Gundara
Head
Centre for Multicultural Education
Institute of Education
University of London
July 1994

Abbreviations

ARE   Anti-racist education

DFE   Department for Education

ESG   Education Support Grant

GM   Grant Maintained Schools

LEA   Local Education Authority

LMS   Local Management of Schools

MCE   Multicultural Education

NCC   National Curriculum Council

SCAA   School Curriculum and Assessment Authority

Acknowledgements

In a work such as this, the gestation period of which spans nearly a decade, it is difficult to remember all those people who, in one way and another, gave advice, prodded, cajoled, helped and hindered throughout the working document to the finished product you have before you. As with most pregnancies, scores of people offered advice - some from totally inexperienced parents to others who had delivered several babies and spoke with hindsight and experience.

I would like to thank my brothers and sisters for their kind support and understanding, particularly Kiritbhai for lending me his PC. I would like to say a big thank you to Lesley Loughran, Samantha Mitchell and Nilesh Patel for help with diagrams, graphs and word processing; to Ken MacKinnon for using his "magic box" to do the number crunching for Chi square analysis; to Tia Khan for making valuable comments on earlier drafts of this book.

I would also like thank the directors of education of the two local education authorities concerned, senior advisors, advisors, senior teachers, advisory teachers, head teachers, heads of departments and classroom teachers with whom I had the pleasure of working during my time on the Education Support Grant projects. I would particularly like to acknowledge my debt to all the children who gave so much of themselves during the research, and putting their faith in the unknown.

Most of all I would like to thank Tara, Krishen and Anoushka, without whom the gestation period would undoubtedly have been extended by another five years.

Preface

મલમલ સમાવે મુઠીમાં કારીગરો એવા હતા

કાપીજ કાંડા તેમના ઉદ્યોગને ધક્કા દીધા

The Gujarati couplet above tells the story of how the British decimated the livelihood of a whole village in India in order to protect and promote the British textile industry. This was achieved quite simply by severing the hands of all artisans - expert weavers of silk - at the wrist.

1 Introduction

A special feature of Education Support Grant projects concerning multicultural and anti-racist education in all-white schools is that they can be seen to be reversing the trend which has preoccupied the field of "race" and education during the past three decades.

Education Support Grant projects are of particular interest to me because I have been fortunate enough to have worked on two such projects in geographically distinct areas. My role as co-ordinator and advisory teacher on these projects gave me a particular practitioner perspective on the issues and problems in the implementation of multicultural and antiracist curriculum development in all-white schools.

My role as teacher governor, and now as parent governor, gives me a special interest in the direction that education is taking in this country. The Education Reform Act 1988 introduced the National Curriculum, which has been described as a mono-cultural curriculum[1], has meant that multicultural education and antiracist education work is not being undertaken in many multi-racial schools, let alone schools in all-white areas.

In 1987 there were some seventy Education Support Grant projects on "race" and education in all-white schools. By 1989 there were a further fifty. In both phases projects were funded for a period of one to five years. The projects ranged from establishing a multicultural centre[2] to school twinning: from initial teacher training to intervention models in schools and curriculum areas.[3]

Preliminary examination of the relevant literature revealed that the research was mainly of a descriptive nature. Most of this is confined to anecdotal sketches in educational journals such as *Multicultural Teaching*. It appeared as if an investigation into the problems and issues of implementing Education Support Grant projects was required.

It became apparent that a realistic understanding of the issues around implementation would entail an analysis of specific subject areas - that is small scale projects within the larger projects. When the literature review relevant to the Education Support Grant projects was undertaken, it became evident that there was a wide gap in our knowledge of these projects.[4] We only had a very patchy and incomplete picture of Education Support Grant projects and the issue of implementation was not considered or covered by other researchers. Neither was a distinction made between multicultural education and antiracist education; most educationalists, researchers and teachers accepted these distinct approaches as interchangeable.[5]

The literature that was available was not able to provide the links between policy and practice of multicultural education and antiracist education in all-white schools. As the literature review reveals, there is plenty of material on multicultural education and antiracist education in multi-racial schools, though there is a dearth of material regarding multicultural education and antiracist education in all-white schools. Thus, the present book is important in two respects: one is that it helps to fill the gap in our knowledge about the implementation of multicultural education and antiracist education through Education Support Grant projects in all-white areas. The second point is the contribution it can make to the changes currently occurring in the implementation of the National Curriculum following the Dearing Report and the recent publication of the new streamlined National Curriculum, in terms of multicultural education and antiracist education in all-white schools.

One possible approach to analyzing the issues around implementation of Education Support Grant projects in all-white schools was a descriptive analysis of the two projects. It was decided, however, that such a longitudinal study would be impractical given the various constraints such as the duration of the two projects, a period of eight years for both projects.

It was thus necessary for the present book to focus on how Education Support Grant projects, concerned as they are with curriculum development, were being implemented, rather than merely describe them. Most of the relevant literature assumes that curriculum development will be undertaken by teachers without analyzing the issues surrounding the process of implementation.

It became apparent at an early stage that an understanding of institutional racism in British society was a prerequisite for locating the Education Support Grant projects within the wider educational field. This stems from three main observations: first, the racist language used by white children to describe negative aspects of each others behaviour in terms of "race." For example, phrases often overheard by the researcher were ones that used racist language as a term of abuse even when the pupils were all white - phrases such as "You're working like a nigger" levelled at pupils who were traditionally seen as "swots". Second, the racist name-calling experienced by the few black children in these all-white schools; and third, the racism experienced by the researcher as a black teacher. Further, before one can present an antiracist perspective, one must have an informed and sophisticated understanding of racism, which is a very complex issue. Also, I would suggest that one cannot be antiracist if one does not understand the nature of institutional racism.

The fields of multicultural education and antiracist education have largely been confined to multi-racial schools and the effect of the schooling system on black children who were seen as a problem by educationalists in terms of underachievement and use of extra resources.[6] Where pupils are concerned, the focus has been on two main areas - one, preparing white pupils for life in a multi-racial society through curriculum development;[7] and two, the impact of racist name calling on black pupils.[8]

The purpose of this book is thus to analyze the method of implementation of two Education Support Grant projects with special reference to white children. The theory, policy and practice of multicultural education and antiracist education in all-white schools is also examined and discussed in detail.

My contention is that a multicultural education approach in all-white schools is more readily accepted by teachers and pupils; whereas an antiracist education approach is more difficult to implement. Further, a multicultural approach can lead to reinforcing racist views whereas an antiracist approach can challenge those views amongst pupils. It is suggested that teachers and pupils are willing to accept piecemeal changes to their every day practice so long as they can revert to their "normal" activities once multicultural education and antiracist education work has been completed. There is an overwhelming belief amongst teachers and educationalists that multicultural education and antiracist education issues are irrelevant to all-white schools and that bringing these issues to the fore only exacerbates the problem of racism in schools.[9]

The basis of the book is a series of models of multicultural education and antiracist education. The basic model is derived from a re-examination of the available literature on multicultural education and antiracist education in all-white schools. By juxtaposing the different models the book seeks to determine the nature and strength of each

3

model. Although the case studies are conducted in all-white schools, the framework of curriculum development, it is suggested, are applicable in all schools, whether multi-racial or all-white.

The research design centres around the belief that the most revealing knowledge about multicultural education and antiracist education in practice can be derived by the actual practitioner, in this case the researcher. The selection of various subject areas was difficult because of the wide range of activities in the two projects. It was felt necessary therefore to limit the discussion to three major subject areas, English, Home Economics and Mathematics; English and Mathematics are core subjects within the National Curriculum and have national priority. Home Economics, on the other hand has been relegated to the status of a "non-subject" in that it has been incorporated into the Technology guidelines within the National Curriculum. The findings of these subject areas are then transferable to other subject areas because the underlying philosophy remains the same.

The information was obtained by means of Action Research conducted over several years. It was felt best to adopt Action Research as a method for the investigation because, amongst other things, this approach enables a participant observer mode of research.[10]

I agree with Paul Gilroy's call for a "move beyond both multiculturalism and antiracism".[11] However, I do not think we can abandon the gains we have achieved through the fights that black parents, students and educationalists have fought during the past twenty years by moving beyond multicultural education and antiracist education. Also, we need to examine carefully what we are moving to? Further, in the rapidly changing face of education following the recommendations of the Dearing Report [12] and the publication by the School Curriculum and Assessment Authority in May 1994 of *Consultation on the National Curriculum*, [13] a series of draft proposals covering all the subjects of the National Curriculum and advocating a slimming down of the National Curriculum, it is becoming difficult to keep abreast of developments. Although a slimming down of the National Curriculum is to be welcomed, inevitably, with such a drastic measure, something has to go. And experience has shown that multicultural education and antiracist education as areas of focus within the school day may well be the first to fall by the wayside. Also to be cut back are support services such as educational psychologists and social workers.[14] Thus I would argue that it is imperative that we maintain a steadfast hold on the progress made through multicultural education and antiracist education initiatives as shown in the account of the two Education Support Grant projects under

4

discussion here.

I give below brief summaries of chapters which are the concern of the rest of this book.

The second chapter provides an introduction to the field of multicultural education and antiracist education, and discusses models for each thereby setting the context.

Chapter three sets the parameters of the book, giving reasons for the particular focus for the hypothesis that a multicultural approach is easier to implement than an antiracist one.

Chapter four is a literature review and examines three distinct areas of multicultural education and antiracist education. The first section looks at the main pre-occupations of educationalists and researchers in the field of "race" and education over the past thirty years, that is, the underachievement of black pupils. The second section studies all-white areas, focusing on the impact of the Swann Report. The last section examines specifically the literature concerning Education Support Grant Projects on multicultural education and antiracist education in all-white areas.

Chapter five examines the primary terms employed in the research, and offers detailed analysis of words such as black, culture, cultural, multicultural education and antiracist education. The chapter arrives at working definitions of the terms which are pertinent to this research and thus confines to particular meanings where there is such a diversity of interpretations. Indeed, it can be suggested that there are as many views of multicultural education and antiracist education as there are practitioners. Thus this chapter on terminology is vital to contextualise, and thereby focus, the whole debate into manageable components.

Chapter six gives the background to the Education Support Grant projects under consideration for this book, namely the project in East London and the project in the North East of England. Relevant demographic details of the two areas are detailed from the 1991 population census.

Chapter seven discusses the methodology used. The central focus of this research is Action Research, which includes field notes, lesson plans, pre-intervention negotiations, discussions, pre- and post-lesson evaluation by teachers and pupils, classroom observations (both as participant and passive observer), evaluation forms from pupils, head teachers and teachers, feedback from Governors and Parent Teacher Associations in terms of reports. There are also structured and unstructured interviews with teachers, head teachers, senior staff such as advisors and deputy directors.

Chapter eight looks at some case studies focusing on three subject areas - Home Economics, Mathematics and English. English and Mathematics are both core subjects in the National Curriculum; Home Economics has been relegated to the status of a "non-subject" since it became subsumed within Technology. Mathematics has been chosen because there is an inherent belief that Mathematics is a neutral subject - after all 2 plus 2 is 4, in whatever language or culture! Mathematics is far from value-free. Also, the public attack by no less a person as Mrs Thatcher, now Lady Thatcher, when Prime Minister ("Antiracist Maths, whatever that is!" as reported in several national papers on their front pages, including the *Guardian*) has caused the development of a multicultural and an antiracist perspective in this subject area to slow down particularly at classroom level.

English has been chosen because it is one area that has recently come under National scrutiny - the Kingman Report followed lately by the controversy about "standards". Also, English is important for all children - success, as measured by examination passes, and as used in schools, is through Standard English. It is often forgotten that standard English is merely one of a range of dialects. However, the sociological and political power of Standard English makes it a language that all children have a right to - whether working class or ethnic minority.

It will be interesting to compare the status of a non-subject with that of core curriculum subjects in terms of multicultural education and antiracist education - whether the status of a subject makes any difference to the class-room practice in terms of multicultural and/or antiracist approaches.

Chapter nine is concerned with a discussion of the pupil survey carried out to assess the level of racist attitudes amongst white pupils in a school in London. As well as providing graphs and tables as methods of analyzing the responses, some general conclusions are drawn from the data.

Chapter ten places into context the nature of institutional racism as it affects multicultural education and antiracist education in all-white schools. It is only by arriving at an understanding of racism that one can begin to be antiracist in approach. This chapter provides an historical perspective of how the system has become one where multicultural education and antiracist education as educational philosophies are made ineffective because of unequal structures established to favour one sector of the community more than another.

The last chapter, chapter eleven, returns to some of the findings discussed earlier, placing them in context and considering their implications for an antiracist approach to the National Curriculum.

In addition, I provide a black perspective to the whole debate about multicultural education and antiracist education in all-white schools, as well as drawing links between disability, gender and "race."

Notes

1   Bagley (1992) *Back to the future*

2   for example the Education Support Grant Project based in North Tyneside

3   Massey (1991) *More than Skin Deep*, pp 27-28

4   see chapter four (Review of Literature)

5   see chapter five (Terminology) for a discussion of the use of the terms antiracist education, multicultural education, black, etc.

6   see Chapter four (Review of Literature)

7   *Swann Report* (1985)

8   Troyna and Hatcher (1992) *Racism in Children's Lives*

9   *Swann Report* (1985); and Troyna and Hatcher (1992)

10   see chapter seven (Methodology)

11   Gilroy (1992) "The end of antiracism" in Donald and Rattansi (eds) *"Race", Culture and Difference*

12   Dearing (1994) *The National Curriculum and its Assessment*

13   SCAA (1994) *Consultation on the National Curriculum - an introduction* (plus draft proposals for the subjects)

14   Bridges (1994) "Tory education: exclusion and the black child", *Race and Class*, Vol 36, No 1, p 44

2 Setting the context

The purpose of this chapter is to place into context the two Education Support Grant Projects concerning multicultural education and antiracist education work in all-white schools, one in London and one in the North East of England, that I have been fortunate to have worked in. This is primarily done by looking briefly at the historical development of multicultural education and antiracist education in the United Kingdom and the relatively recent trend to address the issues of multicultural education and antiracist education in all-white schools. In line with Ali Rattansi, I would like to stress that I have not attempted to give a "detailed exposition or erect a comprehensive critique" of multicultural education and antiracist education. The discussion that follows is necessarily selective, highlighting some issues, but inevitably neglecting others. [1]

Multicultural education, as generally understood by teachers and educationalists, is the celebration of different aspects of the home cultures, such as religion and food, of black pupils whilst antiracist education, which grew out of a critique of multicultural education in the early 1980s, is an attempt to eliminate racism, sexism, other-isms, as well as class discrimination and prejudice from schools.[2] Multicultural education, as educational philosophy developed since the late 1960s as the chief alternative to the concept of "race" and education in British schools. Antiracist education revealed fundamental flaws in the policies and practices of multicultural education which were perceived to be essentially an approach to assimilate black pupils within British schools and society. Assimilation in practical terms meant that black people, whether newly arrived immigrants and settlers, or born in this country, had to conform to the norms and to take on the values of the majority white culture.[3]

9

During the 1960s the demographic composition of Britain changed rapidly as significant numbers of black and ethnic minority people were encouraged to come to the "mother country" to seek fortune and a better way of life. The new immigrants were promised a better standard of life, a greater prosperity for the future, and above all, a better quality of education for their children.[4] After the post World War Two labour shortage, Britain was in desperate need of workers to run the factories, London Transport and the newly formed National Health Service. And it turned to its former colonies to fill that gap. There had always been an unstated belief on both sides that after a number of years the immigrant workers would return to their country of origin, leaving Britain and the immigrants financially and materially better off as a result of the experience. This hope of the return has turned to a myth.[5]

The initial educational response to the presence of black pupils in any significant numbers in schools was two-fold. For African-Caribbean children, special services were developed which tried to meet the needs in terms of the children's self-esteem, in the mistaken belief that the African-Caribbean children lacked a culture because of the displacement experienced during slavery. The needs of Asian children, on the other hand, were clearly identified as language deficiency because their first language was not English - that is, they were given extra classes in English; it was hoped that once these children had acquired sufficient knowledge of English language they would be able to integrate into mainstream lessons.[6] As Cecile Wright has pointed out, "Asian pupils... were perceived as a problem to teachers because of their limited cognitive skills, poor English language,... poor social skills..." [7] African-Caribbean children, on the other hand, were "always amongst the most criticised and controlled groups in the classroom.... and teachers' images of Afro-Caribbean children tended to be negative." [8] Neither of the strategies concerning the educational needs of Asian and African-Caribbean pupils were long-term plans - they were short-term reactions to the presence of black and ethnic minority pupils in British schools. These were ad hoc initiatives, which were later developed into policies.

Because the black population resided by and large in the industrial cities, in some primary schools in urban areas their numbers made an enormous impact on resources and teachers' time. Pupils whose first language was not English were considered a burden to the school, using up valuable resources in terms of learning materials and teacher time. By the late 1960s, in some schools in parts of London, for example, Asian children made up around thirty per cent of the school population. A common curriculum could not be taught to children who did not understand English, or who found the English curriculum, which was Eurocentric and ethnocentric, alien. Some white parents in Southall, for instance, demanded that Asian children be bussed to out lying rural schools because they were perceived to be disadvantaging so-called indigenous (which is a euphemism for white) children.[9] The reverse of course did not happen: no-one suggested bussing in white children to multi-racial schools.

Multicultural education is given a name

During the 1970s, extreme right-wing political parties such as the National Front and the British Movement Party drew attention to the importance of "race" and education in an overt way by their activities in and around schools. They held public meetings in school halls, for instance. In addition they used schools as places for recruiting new members by leafleting inside and outside school premises. The issues of prejudice, discrimination and racism were given a new focus and this helped to cast doubt on the appropriateness of previously dominant educational policies and practices which had emphasised the particular cultures, languages and the specific needs of ethnic minority pupils. Racism, both overt and covert, experienced by black people in Britain has remained unabated throughout the past three decades as evidenced by numerous newspaper articles as well as several books on the daily racial harassment faced by black and ethnic minority people.[10]

An impetus for a complete re-evaluation of the then current practices also came about as a result of the growing awareness of black teachers, parents, educationalists, pupils as well as the main political parties that the educational response to ethnic minority children, far from alleviating the needs and concerns of these groups, was failing to secure any significant change.[11] The discussions and debates which centred around these issues led to the concept of multicultural education.

Theoretical models of multicultural education

Chris Mullard has identified three models of multicultural education - assimilationist, integrationist and cultural pluralism. These three models developed over time as a direct response to the presence of black pupils in British schools. Black pupils were seen as a problem - they were

11

perceived to be a problem because they were black; they were a problem because many, especially those from India and Pakistan, could neither speak nor write English well enough to take an effective part in, or benefit from, school education. Southall Local Education Authority, acting upon Circular 7/65 started a policy of bussing Asian children to outlying schools in the Borough because it was felt that about one-third of immigrant children is the maximum that is normally acceptable in a school if social strains are to be avoided and educational standards maintained.[12]

The three models can be seen to have a direct link between each other and are to some extent interconnected and interdependent. Mullard draws three periodical lines to distinguish each model - assimilationist phase from early 1950s to the 1965 white Paper; the integrationist phase and model from 1965 to the early 1970s; and finally the then current cultural pluralist phase and model which is essentially a revised version of the intergretionist model. The pluralist phase began in the late 1970s and extended to the late 1980s. These periodised phases are not intended to imply a neat and regular progression; there are cross-overs between and through the phases. Each model is discussed in turn.

Assimilationist model

At the base of this model rests the belief that a nation is a unitary whole, politically and culturally indivisible. Immigrant groups, black or white, should thus be absorbed into the indigenous homogeneous culture so that they can take an informed and equal part in the creation and maintenance of "society". While a certain respect should be encouraged for other cultures and social traditions, this should be only a secondary concern. In no way should it be encouraged to the point where it could possibly undermine the stability of what was seen as the "host" society.

One of the recommendations of the Swann Report was that the language of ethnic minority children should be the responsibility of the community and that schools cannot be expected to take an active part in teaching the so-called community languages. If their parents were brought up in another culture and another tradition, children should be encouraged to respect it, but a national system cannot be expected to perpetuate the different values of immigrant groups. Schools cannot be expected to foster this in any concerted or planned way; it is the responsibility of the immigrant groups to maintain their language in "society". It is unfortunate that Swann ignored the advice of the Bullock Report on the language issues when it stated that "No child should be

12

expected to cast off his [sic] home language when he crosses the school threshold." [13]

The assimilationist perspective was seen by many educationalists, politicians, and "race" professionals alike as one that embodied a set of beliefs about stability. The teaching of English along with a programme of cultural indoctrination and subordination would help in short to neutralize sub-cultural affinities and influences within the school. A command of the dominant group's language would not only mean black pupils could benefit from the education provided in school, but, more significantly, it would help counter the threat an alien group apparently poses to the stability of the school system and, on leaving, to society at large. [14]

> The presence of a high proportion of immigrant children in one class slows down the general routine of working and hampers the progress of the whole class, especially where the immigrants do not speak or write English fluently. This is clearly in itself undesirable and unfair to all children in the class. [15]

Underlying the assimilationist model is the belief in the cultural and racial superiority of the "host" metropolitan society. Hidden in the recesses of rationalized thought, and built into the very structure of policies ostensibly concerned with English tuition, dispersal, and educational testing is, as convincingly demonstrated by Coard, the imputation that black culture is inferior, that black values and beliefs are of secondary importance, even whimsical, when considered against those held by dominant white groups. [16] To assimilate, for black people, is to discard voluntarily or be forced to discard all that culturally defines their existence, their identity as West Indians, Asians, or Africans. To assimilate, for white people, means to stay the same.

> Continuous discussion of racial differences in culture and tradition serves only to perpetuate them. I do not consider it the responsibility of an English state school to cater for the development of cultures and customs of a foreign nature... I believe our duty is to prepare children for citizenship in a free, Christian, democratic society according to British standards and customs... [17]

13

Many politicians, including the former Home Secretary, Roy Jenkins, and possibly even more teachers by the mid 1960s, had already started to reject the inherently racist nature of the assumptions underpinning the assimilationist model. Jenkins urged that what was required was "not a flattening process of assimilation but equal opportunity, accompanied by cultural diversity, in an atmosphere of mutual tolerance."[18]

The assumptions of cultural superiority, social stability, and shared values and beliefs still figure prominently in this model. Though reformulated in terms of conditional cultural diversity, cultural superiority manifests itself in the emphasis placed on integration into *our* society, *our* way of life, which in turn undervalues, even negatively values, other cultural traditions and ways. In schools this meant that other cultures, other ways of life whether introduced as part of the formal or informal curriculum are seen and often openly evaluated against not their own value and belief patterns but, instead, those of the school and the wider British society.[19]

In fact, ultimate conformity and eventual cultural absorption become preconditions of a stable and racially harmonious society. While all that the integrationist model affords is immutable, these values and beliefs can in fact be reinforced through following a policy of mutual tolerance and reserved respect for other cultural values and beliefs. For what matters is not total but selective value orientation and acceptance; political and economic values and beliefs need to be separated from the rest - religious beliefs, cultural customs, and so on. By allowing limited diversity in respect of religious beliefs, customs, dress and even language, it is assumed within the framework of the model that black people will be more likely to accept than reject outright those values which shape our society.

The notion of equal opportunities in essence means social control. Equal opportunities for all can only exist in a society where there prevails a general acceptance of the dominant values and beliefs. Where this does not exist, equal opportunity is dependent upon the degree of mutual tolerance to be found. Given the racial dimension of the structural inequality that exists in our society, equal opportunity in practice means equal opportunity only for persons whose ideas and values conform to those of the dominant white middle-class culture. As Gus John has stated:

To wish to integrate with that which alienates and destroys you, rendering you less than a person, is madness. To accept the challenge to join it and change it from within, when it refuses to accept that you are there in your fullness and refuses to acknowledge the results of interaction between you and it, is double madness.[20]

Cultural pluralism model

Cultural pluralism is in effect a more refined version of the previous two; it expands the idea of cultural diversity and establishes the existence of this idea as a central observable feature of the social structure. The power assumption located at the base of the cultural pluralism model as interpreted by its mainly white British advocates - as a culturally defined form of integration and as the best of the other two models of assimilation and integration - is to all intents and purposes identical.

All models assume various degrees of cultural change on the part of black groups in school and society without any corresponding change on the part of white groups in school and society. Power is held by white groups in society; white groups and schools can insist that black groups and pupils assimilate or integrate. Real power in a capitalist society is indivisible. Although disguised and dressed up with platitudes or good intentions, the three models are in fact power models. These models are constructed by dominant white groups for the protection of the power of white groups, for the continuation of society as it is perceived by those groups.

Multicultural education has above all meant the assimilating or integrating of alien black groups, without disruption, into a society dedicated to the preservation of social inequality and a seemingly unchanging and cherished stock of central values, beliefs and institutions. As interpreted and practised by many teachers and educationalists, multicultural education has appeared to become an instrument of control and stability rather than one of change, of the subordination rather than the freedom of black pupils in schools and of black people in society as a whole. In the context of schools and against a wider societal background of institutionalized racism, multicultural education programmes, from the assimilationist's view on English teaching to the integrationist's stance on multicultural and black studies, have in fact integrally contributed to the increased alienation of black youth.[21] What multicultural education is teaching black pupils is that they will always remain second-class citizens; and ironically, that in order to survive or

15

exist as black people it is necessary to resist racist authority within and outside school.

Without a radical reappraisal of multicultural education theory and practice, our society's materialist and racist culture will continue to be transmitted by all schools: without a radical reconstruction of our society as a whole and of the meaning and practice of multicultural education in particular, we shall for some time to come continue to talk about black kids in white schools, rather than merely children in schools.[22]

Antiracist education

Early developments

In the early 1980s, there grew a general critique of multicultural education.[23] This particular discourse focused on the many layers of racial disadvantage faced by ethnic minority pupils in schools and in society generally. Antiracist education, as it came to be known, had many strands which were parallel with multicultural education, but developed along different lines because it raised questions about the nature of institutionalised racism and racial inequality, especially within those policies which subsumed "race" under other forms of inequality such as class and gender. The elements of antiracist education revealed the necessity for further change and prompted the desire to examine and analyze the then current multicultural practices, found almost exclusively in multi-racial schools in inner cities, the general assumptions and deficiencies, their political and educational role and function as educational philosophy.

It was during the 1980s too that a "polarization" of two fundamentally opposed educational movements, multicultural education and antiracist education, occurred. As Rattansi points out, these were based on different understandings of racism. Multicultural education has been represented as a broadly liberal programme, while antiracist education claimed the mantle of left radicalism. [24]

As we enter the 1990s, activities at classroom level in the field of multicultural education and antiracist education is somewhat abating. With the introduction of the National Curriculum, and the failure of the Council to set up a Committee/ working group to look at multicultural education in relation to the National Curriculum is an indication of the lack of interest in this field at least at national level. It should be acknowledged that there are pockets of multicultural education work

16

being undertaken in inner-city schools where there is a significant number of black and ethnic minority pupil intake. As the Education Support Grant funding is coming to an end, there is growing evidence that the local education authorities are not continuing to fund classroom work in multicultural education and antiracist education as had been the intention behind the Central Government funding. However, there is still a growing body of literature being produced in the UK and other Western Countries on multicultural education, even if this is mainly confined to the perceived needs of, and the problems caused by, the presence of black pupils in British schools. For example, at a Department of Education in a University in the South of England, a Post Graduate Certificate of Education student has recently completed a project/ assignment, as a major component (one-sixth of the total course) of the course looking at the self-esteem of black girls in two London single sex schools.[25]

Antiracist education - a model

We have seen above a range of models for which by and large address the issue of the presence of black pupils in schools in terms of deficiency - in terms of the dominant culture being "better" or "superior" than others. Multicultural education in this sense deals only with the content of what constitutes the school curriculum, whereas an antiracist approach would include the context of the school curriculum. Godfrey Brandt states that "the context of antiracist teaching starts at the global level and relates to the national, local and the institutional levels." [26]

Thus one begins to see clearly how antiracist education ranges from the global right down to the self, thereby placing antiracist education in a global context. As a well-known Oxfam poster puts it: THINK GLOBALLY, ACT LOCALLY. This seems to me to be the central tenet of antiracist education, because racism is so pervasive in British society and legacy of imperialism is still with us when people from the so-called Third World countries are facing discrimination in all spheres of life, including, and especially, education.

Brandt gives examples of Antiracist class-room practice in several primary and secondary schools. It should be mentioned here that all examples that Brandt uses are in multi-racial schools - he does not tackle the issue of "all-white" schools.

One of the lessons that Brandt observes in a primary school uses a very popular book by Judith Kerr. The book is entitled *The Tiger Who Came to Tea*. The teacher concerned identifies five aims of this lesson

17

and it will be useful to summarise these here:

1   Enrich pupils' vocabulary and encourage oral/aural abilities in English, Gujarati and Punjabi.
2   To show that this story could have taken place in any household, ie Indian, African-Caribbean, etc.
3   Show that different races, eat different foods, i.e. plantains, samosas, etc.
4   Gender roles, i.e. role of father and mother in the home.
5   Sequencing the story.

It is interesting to note that Brown, Barnfield and Stone (1990) in *Spanner in the works* too use *The Tiger Who Came to Tea* as a good example of antiracist teaching. However, my own contention is that both approaches are really multicultural in essence because rather than implying that the story could have taken in any household, an antiracist approach would have tackled this issue head-on by asserting that the story in fact takes place in a white household. This leads on to discussing notions about the author, publisher, and so on, and who ultimately holds the power to decide which books are read by the class.[27] As an article by Petronella Brienburg asks: "Who is writing what and for whom?" [28]

An interesting parallel is Roald Dahl's extremely popular *Charlie and the Chocolate Factory* in which a competition to win a free trip to Mr Wonka's chocolate factory is held world-wide; bars of the chocolate are sold in all parts of the world, yet the five winners are all white and come from either United States of America or England.

In cinematic terms, the film *ET*, which is one of the most successful films in the history of the cinema, the extraterrestrials land in North America, when there are thousands of places in the world to choose from. Further, no one seems to have questioned why ET should befriend a white boy in suburban America; why not an African girl in inner-city Lagos, Nigeria? These are questions which an antiracist approach would include in discussions about curriculum content.

Multicultural antiracist education

Some writers and practitioners have attempted to combine the two concepts, multicultural education and antiracist education into a single concept in the belief that by doing this they have the best of both sets of philosophies. Although I agree with McLean and Young that "the words "multicultural" and "antiracist" often provoke misunderstanding and confusion," this is mainly because there is no one agreed definition of these two words. I would further agree with them when they say that "multicultural" is usually seen to mean extra English classes for children whose first language is not English, and the inclusion in some way of cultures other than "British" (whatever that is). Also, some teachers may perceive "antiracist" as too provocative or negative. Other educationalists may confuse this for suggesting that they are racist, rather than that the education system is attempting to deal with racism. However, this stance of combining the two as Multicultural/Antiracist Education (MCARED) is rejected:

> Our use of the term MCARED acknowledges the importance of both. It incorporates a pluralist stance, while ensuring this is not seen as distinct from the structural dimensions of anti-racism.[29]

Although at one level this sounds acceptable and admirable, the two philosophies are in fact poles apart in terms of political positions, and more importantly, in terms of classroom practice. On the one hand it is quite possible to have a multicultural curriculum that is racist in that it reinforces stereotypes of black people, for instance; on the other hand an antiracist curriculum would challenge those stereotypes, while including elements of the multicultural nature of Britain.

Antiracist multicultural education

Mal Leicester has turned the term around and prefers the term "antiracist multicultural education".[30] This is marginally better in so far as it emphasises "antiracist" rather than "multicultural". However, I would argue that the overall effects of combining these two terms is, not as has been suggested, to take on the best of the two philosophies, but to become inactive and null so that teachers end up by practising a multicultural curriculum and sometimes claiming this is antiracist. Examples of this are to be found in the case studies. Leicester goes on to argue that "there need be no gulf between multicultural and antiracist education; that multicultural education ought to be antiracist and that antiracist education must be (in one sense of the term) "multicultural", to combat cultural racism".[31] This effort to combine the two sets of philosophies in order to make use of the most valuable features of each is unlikely to occur because multicultural education and antiracist education are unhappy bedfellows. I would argue that this is because the philosophical underpinning of the two perspectives are very different and one does not necessarily lead to the other.

My own contention is that there *is* a gulf between the two philosophies, and that to combine the two only leads to further confusion; as mentioned above, teachers and educationalists are unsure of the perspective they are adopting. I would argue that what results is a multicultural perspective which is sometimes defined by teachers as antiracist. I think what is missing from Leicester's perspective when she maintains that the two terms should be combined, is the fact that antiracist education grew out of a criticism of multicultural education, as *practised in the classroom*. At classroom level, multicultural education leads to tinkering of the curriculum - what Troyna has termed the three Ss, saris, steel bands and samosas - and does not change the institutional or structural aspects of the inherent inequalities in school and society. My view is that multicultural education and antiracist education are two very different educational approaches in a multi-racial Britain, as demonstrated by differing class-room practice. Multicultural education is sometimes seen as a "soft" option while antiracist education is seen to be more directly addressing the issue of racism in schools.[32]

The models can be represented in tabulated form:

ETHNIC/RACIAL POLICY	EDUCATIONAL PRACTICE
Assimilationist	Colour blind approach
Integrationist	Multicultural education
Pluralist	Multicultural education
Antiracist	Antiracist education
Separatist	Ethnically differentiated curriculum

Troyna has identified the first four phases, that is, assimilation, integration, pluralism and anti-racism.[33] However, I feel it is pertinent to include the fifth phase, separatism, because of recent developments following the Education Reform Act of 1988. The Act introduced the concept of opting out, whereby schools could get extra funding from central government if they chose to be independent of local education authority control. This has meant that Head Teachers and School Governors have the power to decide crucial factors such as pupil intake. In some parts of the country this has meant that schools are being chosen by parents on racial grounds. White parents are choosing to send their children to mainly white schools, whereas black parents are choosing to send their children to racially mixed schools.

Separatism

As we have seen above, the post-war response to the presence of black and ethnic minority pupils in significant numbers in British schools (cf. the long established Ethnic Minority populations in the slave ports of Bristol, Cardiff and Liverpool) gave rise to assimilationist policies, through to integration, pluralism and anti-racism. As we enter the 1990s a new phase has developed - that of separatism.

Recently, the demands which have long been made by the British Muslims for Islamic schools have been making headline news again; it would seem that on egalitarian grounds alone, the Government would be hard pressed to deny the provision of separate schools for Muslims in the same way that there are state-funded schools for the Jewish, Catholic and Protestant communities. As Yuval-Davis points out, Muslim fundamentalists, although very vocal, are not the only groups demanding separate schools. Ultra-orthodox Jews, Seventh-Day Adventists, Sikh and Hindu groups have all done the same.[34] However, I would like to concentrate on the Muslim demands here as an illustrative example because it is relatively well documented. The battle for voluntary aided status for the Islamia School in the London Borough Brent goes on. The Islamia School has been refused voluntary status for the second time in three years. Surplus places in other schools in the Borough was, once again, given as the reason for the decision - the Government pointed out that because there are 2,000 empty desks within two miles of Islamia School, expenditure on new places could not be justified. A visit to Islamia School by the Secretary of State Mr John Patten in the Summer of 1993, had raised the hopes of the trustees. The Government took four years to make a decision on their first application, made in 1986, turning it down in 1990. Iftikha Ahmed, director of the London School of Islamics, and a campaigner for Muslim eduction pointed out that they had already lost two generations of Muslim children. He claimed that the decision was influenced by a negative attitude to Muslims with world-wide repercussions, pointing to the examples of Bosnia, Kashmir,

Palestine in the same breath as the Islamia School.[35] In cities such as Birmingham, Leicester, Manchester and in certain parts of London, there are already schools where the pupils intake is over 90 per cent black or Asian. Baroness Cox has argued that black parents are motivated to demand their separate own schools not by dissatisfaction or frustration with the way that racism is institutionalised in state education, but because they want "a good old-fashioned education" for their children.[36] In contrast to this, of course, is the notion of "white flight" as exemplified in the multi-racial school in Dewsbury where a group of white parents insisted on their children attending a different school from the school allocated by the local education authority because the Church of England primary school had a majority Asian intake.[37]

As already noted, opting out, or Grant Maintained (GM) Schools is another factor which may be the way to segregated schools, particularly in inner-city local education authorities. Nazar Mustafa, chairman of the Muslim Education co-ordinating Council who has links with Conservative pressure groups felt that the way forward for Muslim education was now the Grant-maintained option, which would give Muslim parents greater control over education. It is possible that schools in Birmingham, Bolton, Bradford, Cardiff and London would be targeted for opt-out ballots.[38] Grant maintained schools was one of the articles in the 1988 Education Reform Act which stipulated that schools could opt out of local education authority control and be directly funded by Central Government. In grant maintained schools all the decisions about running the school are made by the school, and the school answers directly to parents. As grant maintained schools will decide their own priorities independently of any local education authority initiative, it is likely that multicultural education and antiracist education will be placed on the bottom of a school's priority - in fact it is likely that multicultural education and antiracist education may not feature at all on a school's agenda, particularly in the white highlands. White highlands can be described as ares where the black and ethnic minority population constitutes less than two per cent of the total population. On this premise, it has been estimated that around ninety-five per cent of the schools in the United Kingdom are in the white highlands.[39]

Recent evidence from the United States of America seem to indicate that schools there are becoming mote racially segregated. This is a turn around from the policy introduced in the 1950s to encourage the mixing of black and white children within the education system. The report by the National Schools Board Association showed that more black children attended schools where they are in the majority than at any time since the

1960s. In large cities such as Washington, Philadelphia, New York and Los Angeles where the black population averages over 37 per cent, the figures are even more startling. Fifteen out of every sixteen black pupils are attending schools where there is a black majority. The National Association for the Advancement of Coloured People (NAACP), which is America's oldest civil rights organisation, maintained that it would be futile to oppose the current trend. It cited studies which indicate that within three decades, half of all the Schools in the United States will be predominantly black or Hispanic.[40]

Multicultural education and antiracist education in all-white areas

Early developments

In the early 1970s, the debate about multicultural education shifted slightly with educationalists and teachers in all-white areas beginning to question and accept the relevance and importance of for all-white schools in a multi-racial Britain. Bodies such as the National Union of Teachers as well as the Department for Education were demanding a broader approach to multicultural education which suggested that multicultural education was just as important in all-white schools as in mixed-race schools. The Swann Report, published in 1985, clearly made the case for in all-white schools, stressing that perhaps multicultural education was more important in these areas than in mixed-race areas. It was felt that white pupils were being mis-educated if they were not made aware of the changed nature of British society - that is, the presence of black people in significant numbers. Those white children attending multi-racial schools were in a position to experience at first hand the fact of a multi-racial society. The white children in all-white areas acquired a picture of Britain that was "all-white", mainly middle class, and dominated my the male of the species. This is the picture they got from the media, the books they read in school and in their leisure time, from their parents and their peer group. They had no reason to believe that Britain was anything other than what their experience told them, which is that Britain is an all-white country.[41]

Although slow to take off, multicultural education in all-white schools had a spurt of rapid growth after the recommendations of the Swann Report were taken on board and money was available through Education Support Grants for specific curriculum development projects on multicultural education and antiracist education in the all-white sector.[42]

The present situation in all-white schools: Education Support Grant Projects

As Education Support Grant funded projects are coming to an end around the country, activities related to multicultural education and antiracist education at classroom level is almost non-existent. With Local Management of Schools (LMS) and the devolvement of power from local to central government, it is becoming apparent that local education authorities will cease to fund multicultural education and antiracist education initiatives within the mainstream curriculum. Further, whilst the 1988 Education Reform Act has instituted central direction over curriculum content, there has been devolution of management and finances to schools and increased parental choice. In this climate, it is unlikely that schools in the white highlands will be interested in taking up issues around multicultural education and antiracist education.[43] One of the intentions of the Education Support Grant funding was that the local education authority would take over the funding for the projects so that the work did not come to an end when the funding from Central Government ceased. However, this has not happened, and as Education Support Grant projects are coming to the end of their life-span, teachers are being re-deployed in other roles. This is certainly the case in the two projects which are under discussion here, as well as the Bedford Education Support Grant project which was brought to a close with the publication of curriculum development materials.

Theory, policy and practice

The issues around multicultural education and antiracist education have been articulated at three levels: theory, policy and practice. As far as multicultural education is concerned, it was classroom practice - as already mentioned, the ad hoc development of teaching materials to meet the needs of newly arrived African-Caribbean and Asian children in school - that led to theory which in turn fed policy development. Each of these, theory, policy and practice is discussed in turn below. The cycle of theory, policy and practice can be represented diagrammatically as below.

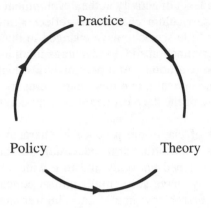

Practice

Policy   Theory

Diagram 1: The cycle of theory, policy and practice

Theory

The first element in the above diagram, theory, hinges on a philosophical understanding of the nature of institutional racism and the impact of this on educational policy and practice.[44] It is generally assumed by educationalists that theory will lead onto the development of policy and this in turn will lead to curricular developments at classroom level.

The second level, policy, has been a growing field over the past thirty years. Practices which were once ad hoc - meeting the needs of newly arrived immigrant children whose first language was not English, for example - led naturally to the development of policies as one response to the presence of black pupils in British schools. There is a plethora of policies on multicultural education and antiracist education particularly at local education authority level, and to a lesser extent at school level. After the civil disturbances of 1980 and 1981 in Brixton, Bristol, Birmingham and other major cities with sizable black settlement around Great Britain, there was a flurry of activity in policy development - almost a knee-jerk reaction to the perceived "problem" of black youth, who were unemployed and would remain unemployed, what Sivanandan has termed the "never employed".[45] Many local education authorities boast multicultural education and antiracist education policies which are sometimes backed by statements of intent, mission statements and of innovative approaches to curriculum development.

However, the relationship between policy and practice is often obscure and in some instances policy and practice contradict each other.

Moreover, despite the level of activity at the development of policies, and the development of curriculum changes to reflect a multicultural and antiracist perspective, little seems to have changed in the extent to which black people face discrimination and disadvantage in all aspects of British society, particularly in education. At a pragmatic level, racial attacks on black people are on the increase, and this trend seems likely to remain in the near future because of the deep economical recession that the country is in at the moment.

The development of classroom practice is characterised by similar problems and issues. Multicultural education as an approach to classroom practice developed unevenly and in a wide variety of forms. In its earlier days, as we have seen, multicultural education was an ad hoc reaction to the first black immigrant children attending British schools in any significant numbers. The practice was often tokenistic, more a method of controlling and containing black pupils than a development of innovative forms of educational practice which is appropriate to promoting equality of opportunity.[46] More often than not, multicultural education was an added extra, something bolted on as an acknowledgement of black presence in a particular school.

The main focus of this book is classroom practice, and particularly curriculum development. Theory, in terms of philosophical ideas, and policy are referred to where necessary, but as the ideology behind the setting up of the Education Support Grant projects on multicultural education and antiracist education in all-white schools relied on the development of curriculum innovations, it seems appropriate that this particular book deals with the later aspect of the three elements identified.[47]

The philosophical understanding of multicultural education and antiracist education are central to policy development at local education authority level, and have a direct impact on the practice at class-room level. Coupled with the commitment of individual teachers is the level of support and commitment from the local education authority in the form of local education authority statements on multicultural education and/or antiracist education - whether these are overtly multicultural or antiracist; whether these were developed at the grass-roots level as in one school in the ILEA where parents brought a race equality policy for consideration by the head teacher and staff; [48] whether directed from the top, without consultation with parents and pupils as in the case in a secondary school in Manchester where an Asian boy was stabbed to death by a white fellow pupil.[49]

Policy

It must be stated here that this is not a policy study - the book is primarily concerned with classroom practice and curriculum development. However, it should be acknowledged that both the Education Support Grant projects under consideration for this book, had policies on equal opportunities which included race equality, and these were the basis on which both projects acquired Education Support Grant funding from Central Government. Copies of the policy documents of the two local education authorities are found in the Appendix.

One of the underlying philosophies behind Education Support Grant projects on multicultural education and antiracist education in all-white schools is the notion that attitudes of pupils can be changed through curriculum intervention. It has long been accepted that the curriculum as taught in schools at the moment is ethnocentric and that a global perspective may go some way towards challenging racist attitudes of the majority white pupils.

As this book is concerned mainly with the issues and problems in implementing multicultural education and antiracist education approaches in all-white schools in two local education authorities, discussion of policy issues is not developed at any great length. Others, such as Troyna and Williams,[50] and Burt [51] have adequately developed this strand of multicultural education and antiracist education field and it would be spurious to develop this strand here. Suffice it to state that if educational policy on multicultural education and antiracist education had been developed first, then some of the problems faced when attempting to implementing multicultural education and antiracist education approaches at class-room level would have been avoided.

Practice

The development of classroom practice is characterised by similar problems and issues. Multicultural education as defined in chapter five, is an approach to classroom practice developed unevenly and in a wide variety of forms. As already noted, in its earlier days, multicultural education was an ad hoc reaction to the first black immigrant children in British schools in any significant numbers, even now it is often tokenistic, more a method of controlling and containing black pupils than a development of innovative forms of educational practice which is appropriate to promoting equality of opportunity. More often than not multicultural education is an added extra, something that has been bolted on as a reaction to the presence of black and ethnic minority pupils in the particular school. Multicultural education is really a facet of the "tolerance" aspect of the acceptance of black people in Britain, parts of "their" culture is tolerated on specific two or three days as a gesture of "good practice". The concept of "tolerance" is itself problematic in that it stems from a negative stance in which "the other" is tolerated, albeit with a grudge. It would be better if one did not have to "tolerate" the situation in the first place.

At each of these levels of activity, there has been general confusion which has been compounded by the language which has developed alongside the theory in an effort to describe the perceived issues and concerns and the prescribed solutions. The terms multicultural, multi-ethnic, multi-racial have been used interchangeably to refer to a wide range of approaches rather than a set of specific policies, practices and frameworks. Thus it has been virtually impossible to establish clarity about the meanings of these different terms. These concepts are clarified and defined in chapter five.

The main focus of this book is classroom practice, and particularly curriculum development. Theory and policy are touched on and referred to where appropriate, but as the ideology behind the setting up of Education Support Grant projects on multicultural education and antiracist education in all-white schools relied on the development of curriculum innovations, it seems appropriate that this particular book deals with this later aspect of the three elements identified.

Articulating the problem of "race" and education in all-white schools

Three general issues have dominated the debates around multicultural education and antiracist education: first, the relevance of established classroom practices to meet the needs of all pupils, whether black or white, in an increasingly multi-racial, multicultural, multi-lingual, multi-faith, indeed, multi-coloured Britain. Secondly, the relation of education philosophy and practice to racial inequality; and thirdly, the potential for education to reduce racial inequality through the curriculum.

The theoretical basis of antiracist education is located round two major issues. First, the fact of institutional racism, the relation between all forms of discrimination and oppression, especially that between race and class, and race and gender. Second, the response of the educational system to the presence of black and ethnic minority children in British schools following the post second world war settlement in the United

28

Kingdom of significant numbers of ethnic minority people. Rather than repeat some of the concerns of this, the discussion centres around the impact of the presence of black people in the United Kingdom on white pupils in all-white schools. Much of the work on multicultural education and antiracist education to date has focused on inner-city areas where there is a significant black population. The present book reverses the trend and draws attention to white children's attitudes and examine the effectiveness of educational innovation in the field of "race" and education in all-white areas and schools. This is done through a pupil survey on racism as well as curriculum innovation in several subject areas presented as case studies.

The process of antiracist education providing an adequate theoretical framework for an antiracist perspective for class-room practice is an on-going one, and has yet to be formalised. I hope to provide some synthesis in this sphere in the examination of the two Education Support Grant projects highlighted in this book.

There are two major strands in the antiracist critique of multicultural education. These are, first, the relation between the national, local education authority and classroom level as centres of activities where the development of multicultural education and antiracist education have taken place. The second strand is the relationship between the three levels on which institutionalised racism has been constituted, that is, the levels of theory, policy and classroom practice.

In general terms, many of the problems of the antiracist critique of multicultural education arise from an implicit notion that the three levels are homogenous and that there is necessarily a close correspondence between the three. As we shall see this is far from the truth - policy and class-room practice are often poles apart. There are complex and contradictory factors which relate to policy and practice which threaten to limit the effectiveness of antiracist education as educational policy.

One of the major focus of attention so far as multicultural education and antiracist education as educational philosophies is concerned has been the underachievement of black and ethnic minority pupils in British schools. Most of the books and articles published on multicultural education and antiracist education focus on black children. Even when a book purports to be about an all-white school, the focus is still focuses on racist name calling experienced by black pupils.[52] The focus is chiefly on black pupils in British schools - this raises the issue of black and ethnic minority pupils being seen as a "problem" and how they can best be fitted into the education system. I would suggest that the prevailing attitudes towards multicultural education and antiracist education of the

1970s and 1980s have remained with us in the 1990s.

Curriculum development: multicultural or antiracist education

It is generally accepted by educationalists, researchers and teachers that through curriculum development, it is possible to address issues of inequality - whether this inequality be gender, disability, class, or race, or indeed a combination of these and others. The underlying philosophy of Education Support Grant funding is based on this premise. For instance, in the 1970s there was a move to acknowledge class differences and point out how the white working class pupils were underachieving because their lack of proficiency in Standard English. It is a sad fact that only a minority of white working class pupils go on to further education at degree level.[53] Work undertaken in the 1970s and 1980s in the field of multicultural education and antiracist education also identified curriculum development as a crucial element in addressing issues of racism. In the United States of America particularly there developed a whole market of materials which dealt with black people in a positive way - "black studies" evolved as a result of curriculum intervention. The Education Support Grant projects too had their genesis in curriculum development, as exemplified in the bids which the two local education authorities put forward for Government grants. Indeed the philosophy of curriculum development underpins the funding of Education Support Grant projects on multicultural education and antiracist education in all-white schools.

A number of publications around the Education Support Grant projects have described curriculum development approaches used to tackle multicultural education and antiracist education at classroom level. Bedfordshire Local Education Authority have produced some teaching materials which were developed as part of their Education Support Grant project on multicultural education.[54]

Why this particular slant?

In the opening section of this chapter, the development of multicultural education and antiracist education from the 1960s, together with an examination of the preoccupation of educationalists and teachers over the past three decades was discussed. It was stressed that the underachievement of black and ethnic minority pupils formed the major concern within the practice of multicultural education and antiracist education at classroom level. Little or no work has been done in the all-white sector concerning multicultural education and antiracist education - thus this particular book can be seen to be overturning the tables with its focus on white pupils - albeit in response to the presence of black people in United Kingdom.

In this section I examine some of the grounds for this book before proposing the hypothesis posed for the book, namely that a multicultural approach is easier to implement than an antiracist approach in all-white schools. Further, a multicultural education approach can reinforce racist attitudes, whereas and antiracist education approach can positively act to challenge those racist attitudes. I finally define the parameters of the book, drawing out some of the limitations posed by time and nature of the research. In a book such as this, based heavily as it is on class room practice and curriculum development, it is not possible to discuss the full range of subject areas covered - from English to Technology, from Mathematics to Science. Hence I have confined my discussions and deliberations to a selected range of subject areas. Further, as I worked across the age range - from primary schools through to secondary schools, it is impossible to do justice to all the avenues explored during my time on the two Education Support Grant projects which are under consideration in this research. I shall thus confine the discussion to delving into the multicultural and antiracist aspects of curriculum development as it pertains to all-white schools, in three subject areas only. This is developed more fully in chapters six, seven and eight which deal with curriculum development at classroom level.

Salient features of multicultural education and antiracist education

There are a number of crucial factors which need to be drawn out from the preceding introductory sections of this chapter. Firstly, as already mentioned, the major focus of multicultural education and antiracist education has been on the (under)achievement of black and ethnic minority pupils in schools. Further, multicultural education and antiracist education work to date had been largely confined to inner-city areas where there is a significant presence of black pupils in inner-city schools. As demonstrated in the review of literature in chapter four, there is very little research that has been done in the all-white sector. Secondly, the educational developments over the past three decades have been confined to providing positive role models in terms of "black studies" in the belief that this would benefit black pupils and raise their self-esteem. Although there is some truth to this, the focus has been on black children. As we have noted, even when a book is deemed to deal with the all-white

31

sector, the major focus of the research falls into looking at the racism faced by black pupils.[55] In the course of this book this imbalance is addressed and the focus of the book is shifted to white pupils. It is argued that what is of disadvantage to the black pupils is of an advantage to the white pupils. For instance the negative pictures of black people is most books has the effect of giving black pupils a low self-esteem, while at the same time, white pupils are encouraged to feel "superior" because of this negative focus on black people. I would argue that this aspect has been largely ignored by teachers, practitioners and educationalists.

My contention is that while black pupils are being denied positive self-esteem because of racist name calling, the corollary is that the white pupils are receiving "positive" feedback from their experience as oppressors. This is graphically addressed in *The Eye of the Storm* where positive and negative input has been shown to have long-term effects on white children. In my opinion, this particular "experiment" has received insufficient coverage, but the issues raised deserve to be taken on board by all-white schools. It also highlights the fact that it is immaterial whether white pupils have had contact with black pupils at a personal level.[56] I would argue that white pupils already have negative images of black people and pupils and it is in this sphere that eduction can be seen to be fulfilling its role as perpetuating societal inequalities, rather than challenging long held (racist, inaccurate) views of the world. Through curriculum development it is possible to address this imbalance. Indeed the funding behind the two Education Support Grant projects on was acquired on this premise of attitudinal change in white pupils through curriculum development.[57]

It is generally accepted by educationalists and teachers that through curriculum development, it is possible to address issues of inequality - whether this inequality be gender, disability, class, or race, or indeed a combination of these and others. Thus in the 1970s there was a move to acknowledge class differences and point out how the white working class pupils were underachieving because their lack of proficiency in Standard English.[58] It is a sad fact that only a minority of working class pupils go on to further education at degree level.[59] Work undertaken in the 1970s and 1980s in the field of multicultural education and antiracist education also identified curriculum development as a crucial element in addressing issues of racism. In the United States of America particularly there developed a whole market of materials which dealt with black people in a positive way - "black studies" evolved as a result of curriculum intervention. The Education Support Grant projects too had their genesis in curriculum development, as discussed in chapter five dealing with the

32

original bids which the two local education authorities put forward for Central Government funding through the Education Support Grant. Indeed the philosophy of curriculum being seen as part of the stereotypical images that white pupils have of black and ethnic minority people underpins the funding of Education Support Grant projects on multicultural education and antiracist education in all-white schools.

There is not available a detailed analysis of any Education Support Grant projects from an action research point of view. Also, having worked on two Education Support Grant projects, I am in the fortunate position of being able to compare two such projects from a participant/researcher perspective. Further, as one of the few black advisory teachers who has worked on Education Support Grant projects, I am able to provide a black perspective. As far as I am aware, I am the only advisory teacher to have worked on two such Education Support Grant projects. In a research project such as this one, concerned as it is with "race" and education it is seemed crucial to provide a black perspective if possible.[60] In the same way that a woman researcher discussing issues around gender and education can justifiably put forward a feminist perspective, so it is fundamental to provide a black perspective here.

A reading of the literature around the field of multicultural education and antiracist education reveals some fundamental issues. Suffice it to summarise of the most salient points here. Most of the work undertaken in the past three decades on "race" and education has been either confined to the inner-city schools where there are significant numbers of black and ethnic minority pupils and have concentrated on the underachievement of black and ethnic minority pupils. As mentioned above, even when a book is purporting to be about the all-white sector, the main section of the research concentrates on the effects of racist name calling on black pupils.[61]

Educational response in a multi-racial Britain

Three main strands of educational response have emerged as a result of black and ethnic minority people in Britain. First, is the notion of self-esteem and the concept of positive image amongst ethnic minority pupils.[62] Second, if left well alone, the "problem" of ethnic minority education will go away - the doing good by doing little perspective.[63] The third response is the notion that multicultural issues are only relevant in inner-city areas where there is a significant ethnic minority population, and is not a concern in all-white areas.[64] Countless examples exist on studies which have focused on the home background of black and ethnic

33

minority pupils - lack of parental support amongst the African-Caribbean pupils and the need for English as a Second Language amongst the Asian population - to justify the poor performance of black and ethnic minority pupils at public examinations. The two most popular views which are expressed by teachers in all-white schools are: "we have no problem here" (because there are no black and ethnic minority children in the school) and "it's (multicultural education and antiracist education) is only relevant in inner-city schools".[65]

Teachers working in the field of multicultural education and antiracist education have by and large reacted to the presence of black and ethnic minority children in their classroom in an ad hoc manner. During the 1970s there was a move to undertake multicultural work in inner-city schools, along the lines of celebration of differences of the various cultures found in Britain. During the 1980s, with the advent of an antiracist stance, teachers adopted a more radical stance. However, as mentioned in chapter one above in the case of McLean and Young's attempt to marry the two concepts, all that has occurred is that the language has changed - the practice has remained the same.[66] Teachers are still doing multicultural work as opposed to antiracist work, as defined in chapter five.

As shown in chapter five on terminology, the two concepts, multicultural education and antiracist education are poles apart philosophically. This leads to different practices at class room level as demonstrated in the case studies in chapters six, seven and eight. It will be interesting, then, to find out whether an multicultural education approach is more readily accepted by teachers and pupils because of the tokenistic aspect. It is suggested that an antiracist education approach, as defined in terms of overall change at both content and pedagogy level, is more difficult to implement in all-white schools.

As already stated my contention is that in Education Support Grant Projects curriculum development involving a multicultural approach in all-white schools is more readily accepted than an antiracist approach to curriculum development, both by teachers and pupils. Further an multicultural education approach can lead to racist stereotypes, whereas an antiracist education approach can actively challenge those stereotypes.

Possible reasons for this include the longer history of multicultural education work, when compared to antiracist education, which is a relatively recent development, and therefore requires greater preparation, and is more likely to be avoided due to its perception as untried or untested. multicultural education is also regarded as less politically motivated, than antiracist education, which is sometimes conceived to be potentially divisive.[67] Recent argument by right-wing faction attacking antiracist education serves to highlight its potential for changing attitudes, in comparison with the relatively apolitical ambitions of multicultural education.[68] Thus, multicultural education is perceived to be less threatening, and is therefore tolerated, (as mentioned above, it is interesting to note in passing the negative connotations of the term "toleration") albeit, with certain reservations, such as its limited application and appreciation within the school programme.

By "accepted" I mean a willingness to be involved at curriculum development level in the class room with the advisory teacher/s in an effort to implement the projects in all-white schools. For head teachers, teachers, and heads of departments this means a willingness to be actively involved in action research leading to curriculum development which incorporates an multicultural education and antiracist education perspective, in partnership with the advisory teacher. For pupils "acceptance" means not merely being passive receivers of "knowledge" but becoming increasingly active in the learning process. A multicultural approach usually means a passive acknowledgement that the curriculum will become increasingly global in context, will include "other" cultures, the inclusion, for instance, of books by black authors concerning black "issues" or assemblies about other religions - the celebration of Diwali, or Chinese New Year. This approach I define as multicultural education and this, I would assert, is more readily accepted both by teachers and pupils.

Antiracist education on the other hand is an approach that directly challenges the status quo - an end to an ethnocentric curriculum, an end, in some measure, of the teacher as the font of all/ superior knowledge: this approach would rather lead to a partnership in the learning process.

My overall contention that in Education Support Grant Projects curriculum development involving a multicultural approach is more readily implemented that an antiracist approach, can be divided into macro and micro hypotheses. The macro hypothesis concerns the relationship between multicultural education and antiracist education with social and educational policy. The micro hypothesis is concerned with multicultural education and antiracist education as these operate in the class room.

Multicultural education, antiracist education and the National Curriculum

Antiracist education is not seen as replacing multicultural education as elements of the National Curriculum; it is not a matter of substituting one for the other. Rather multicultural education, it is hoped will feature in a proper context within antiracist education, which is to be favoured. The National Curriculum as developed by Central Government does not acknowledge an antiracist approach, only a multicultural one. My aim, as far as the National Curriculum is concerned, is to develop an antiracist National Curriculum, maybe even on a global scale, which will be constructed through the terms and philosophy of antiracist education. Otherwise, the multicultural education/antiracist education dichotomy and the constituent components of the debate may demand and generate further fragmentation; for instance, there may be demands, as we are already beginning to see, for separate Islamic/ African-Caribbean/ Asian/ Jewish/ Chinese/ Greek/ Turkish, etc schools. This would lead to a situation which should be avoided if at all possible, that of separatism.

A black perspective

It is generally accepted that women (black and white) will provide a feminist perspective in research and a feminist perspective has been validated by granting equal status as a male perspective. However, there is a growing debate that the black perspective, whether feminist or not, has to be accepted in the same vein.[70] One of the reasons that I have highlighted a black perspective for this book is the paucity of research conducted by black teachers. Almost all the literature published in the field of multicultural education and antiracist education has been by white educationalists, teachers and researchers. I am not aware of any studies that have been conducted by black researchers looking at white "subjects" in the same detail as the pupils survey carried out in an all-white school in London - there is a dearth of material by white researchers studying black people.

It is possible that there will be further studies looking at multicultural education and antiracist education in all-white schools in the future. One aspect that will perhaps not be touched on will be a black perspective, because there were only a handful of black advisory teachers employed on Education Support Grant projects working in the field of multicultural education and antiracist education in all-white areas. In this respect the present book would be able to develop a black perspective.

In the same way that female researchers have provided feminist perspectives in their work, I think it is crucial, in researching "race" and education that a black perspective be provided if at all possible.[71] It can be argued that a feminist perspective will provide an added dimension to

36

the research on, say, gender and education. In the same way a black perspective gives an added dimension to this book.

Summary

This chapter has attempted to contextualise multicultural education and antiracist education as educational philosophies as they relate to the all-white sector. A brief historical overview is provided of the development of multicultural education and antiracist education from the 1960s onwards. It is argued that as a result of the post World War Two labour shortage coupled with the immigration of black and ethnic minority people into Britain led to an ad hoc educational initiative which was geared to meet the specific needs of ethnic minority children. The initiatives were based on a deficiency model, that is, in the case of African-Caribbean pupils it was assumed that they lacked a culture and, therefore, needed to be provided with suitable material so that they could acquire a British culture. In the case of Asian children, it was obvious that their first language was not English and in order to make the most of British education they had first to learn English.

Through a discussion of three theoretical models of multicultural education taking into account the assimilationist model, the integrationist model, and the cultural pluralism model, we have seen how these three models have led to a fourth one, that of antiracist education.

The developing of antiracist education is then discussed with the fact that antiracist education provides a critique of multicultural education which began in the early 1980s. An antiracist model is discussed at some length which includes an examination of certain reading texts used in the primary and secondary sector. The terms multicultural, antiracist education and antiracist, multicultural education are then highlighted to show that, although terminology has changed, the practice at classroom level has remained the same, that is, a multicultural approach has been retained throughout the 1980s and the beginning of the 1990s.

The historical development of multicultural education and antiracist education in all-white areas is then discussed. The interest of multicultural education in all-white areas began as early as the late 1970s but it was only in the 1980s that multicultural education in all-white schools developed at a rapid rate. This was a result of the publication of the Swann Report in 1985 which highlighted that multicultural education and antiracist education is just as important in all-white areas as in multi-racial areas; the Swann Report was instrumental in providing funding for Education Support Grant projects from Central Government. This is followed by a brief look at the present situation in all-white schools regarding Education Support Grant projects concerning multicultural education and antiracist education initiatives.

It is then suggested that the issues surrounding multicultural education and antiracist education have been articulated at three levels: theory, policy and practice. So far as present book is concerned, most of the discussion will be centred around practice at classroom level.

The philosophical underpinning of Education Support Grant funding has been based on the premise of curriculum development in the belief that it is possible to address issues of inequality, whether that inequality be gender, disability, class or "race", or, indeed, a combination of these and others.

Notes

1   Rattansi (1992) "Changing the subject? Racism, culture and education" in Donald and Rattansi (Eds) *"Race", Culture and Difference*.
2   For a definition of black see chapter five.
3   The terms used here are discussed more fully in the chapter on terminology, chapter five.
4   There is an interesting parallel in English history when emigrants to South Africa were made similar promises of a better way of life, education, etc. see Sparks, Allister,*The Mind of South Africa*, 1990
5   see for instance, Anwar, *The Myth of Return*, 1979
6   For the purposes of this book I have not looked at the whole spectrum of ethnic minority pupils as this would make the debate over burdened with terminology. I have focused on the two biggest minority groups - the African-Caribbeans and the Asians (Bangladeshis, Indians and Pakistanis, whether from the Indian sub-continent or from Africa). I have deliberately not examined the specific needs of Chinese, Greek, Italian, Turkish or Vietnamese children, nor have I looked at the needs of East European children. Neither have I looked at the needs of refugee children or traveller children. Although the needs of these groups are in some ways similar to needs of African-Caribbean and Asian children, there are specific differences which could be highlighted. However, this is not attempted, because to do so would unnecessarily confuse the issue of "race" and education which is the main concern of this book.
7   Wright (1992) "Early education: multicultural primary school classrooms" in Gill, Mayor and Blair (Eds) *Racism and Education*, p 39
8   ibid
9   see the chapter on terminology, chapter five.
10 see for example, the CRE reports - *Living in Terror* and *Learning in Terror*; the *Burnage Report*, and Hesse, B et al (1992) *Beneath the Surface*
11 Coard (1971), *How the West Indian Child is made Educationally Subnormal in the British Education System*, reprinted 1991
12 Mullard in Teirney (1982), *Race, Immigration and Schooling*
13 The Bullock Report, *A Language for Life*
14 ibid, p 123
15 Second report by the Commonwealth Immigrants Advisory

Council, quoted in Mullard, op cit, p 124

16   Coard, op cit

17   Townsend and Brittan, 1973, p 13

18   The Rt. Hon. Roy Jenkins, 1966 - address given by the Home Secretary to a meeting of Voluntary Liaison Committee London, quoted in Mullard, op cit, p 125

19   An interesting case of institutionalised racism as it operates in the field of Architecture is proved by a black female architect in Haque, S (1988) "The Politics of Space" in Grewal, et al *Charting the Journey*

20   Gus John, the first and at present only, black Director of Education who heads the Education Department in the London Borough of Hackney quoted in Mullard, op cit, p 128

21   see Chapter ten for a discussion of Institutionalised Racism.

22   Mullard, op cit, p 131

23   ibid

24   Rattansi (1992) op cit, p 24

25   Student at Roehampton Institute a student teacher who undertook a project in two single sex girls' schools in the London area.

26   Godfrey Brandt (1986) *The Realization of Antiracist Teaching*, p 137

27   Brown, et al (1990) *Spanner in the Works*

28   quoted in Burgess-Macey (1992) "Tackling racism in the primary classroom" in Gill, Mayor, Blair, op cit, p 270

29   McLean and Young (1988) *Multicultural Antiracist Education*, p 76

30   Leicester (1991) *Equal Opportunities in School*

31   ibid, p 22

32   See for example, Sivanandan (1983)

33   Troyna (1990) "Reform or deform....", *New Community*

34   Yuval-Davis (1992) "Fundamentalism, multiculturalism and women in Britain", in Donald and Rattansi, op cit, p 286

35   *Education*, 27 August 1993, p 152

36   in Gilroy (1992), op cit, p 55

37   Hardy and Vieler-Porter (1992) "Race, schooling and the 1988 Education Reform Act" in Gill, Mayor and Blair, op cit, pp 103-105. See also Bridges (1994) "Tory education: exclusion and the black child" on the Dewsbury case, *Race and Class*, vol 36, no 1, July-September, pp 33-48

38   Hardy and Vikker-Porter, op cit

39   Wade and Souter (1992) *Continuing to think*, p 1

40   *The Voice* (21 and 28 December 1993) "Schools divided by race", p 14
41   *Swann Report*, especially chapter five
42   for example the original bids of the two Education Support Grant Projects.
43   Bagley (1992) *Back to the Future*
44   see chapter on Institutional Racism, chapter nine
45   Sivanandan (1982) *A Different Hunger*
46   Dhondy, et al (1981) *The black Explosion in British Schools*
47   see for example, original bids for Education Support Grant funding
48   Colverston JMI School, formerly in ILEA, now in the London Borough of Hackney
49   MacDonald, et al (1989) *Murder in the Playground*
50   Troyna and Williams (1986) *Racism, Education and the State* See also Tryona (1992) Can we see the join? An historical analysis of multicultural and antiracist education policies" in Gill, Mayor and Blair *Racism and Education*
51   Burt (1987) *Multicultural and Antiracist policies*, Unpublished PhD thesis, University of London
52   Troyna and Hatcher (1992) in their latest book, purporting to be about the all-white sector still persist in focusing on the racist name calling experienced by black pupils.
53   Even at present, very few working class white pupils go on to higher education at University level. (see note 49 below)
54   see chapter on Literature Review for further details, chapter four.
55   Troyna and Hatcher (1992) *Racism in Children's Lives*
56   Patel, K (1988) *Multicultural Teaching*, Summer
57   see chapter eight for a fuller discussion of this.
58   Barnes (1982) *From Communication to Curriculum*; and Rosen, "Language and class", in Douglas (1974) *Education or Domination?*
59   Professor Young of Cambridge University on the *Today* Programme on Radio 4, September 1992
60   Ahmed (1990) *Black Perspectives in Social Work*
61   Troyna and Hatcher, op cit
62   see Jeffcoate (1979) *Positive Image*
63   Kirp (1979) *Doing Good by Doing Little*
64   Patel, K (1992) "On the margins", *New Beacon*, Vol LXXVI, No 986, March
65   Gaine (1987) *No Problem Here*
66   McLean and Young (1988) *Multicultural Antiracist Education*

67   see for instance, Wellington (1986) *Controversial Issues in the Curriculum*

68   see for instance, Lewis (1988) *Anti-racism: a mania exposed*; and Palmer (1986) *Anti-racism, an Assault on Education and Value*

69   *Education*, 27 August 1993, p 153

70   see for instance Joseph, Reddy and Searle-Chatterjee (1990) "Eurocentrism in the social sciences"; and Mama, A (1990) *The Hidden Struggle*. Also, Ahmad, B (1990) *Black perspectives in Social Work*

71   see for instance, Fraser, A (1993) *The wives of Henry VIII*; and Knowles and Mercer "Feminism and antiracism"

3 Setting the parameters

Scope of book

In the previous chapter, the development of multicultural education and antiracist education from the 1960s, together with an examination of the preoccupation of educationalists and teachers over the past three decades was discussed. It was stressed that the underachievement of black and ethnic minority pupils formed the major concern within the practice of multicultural education and antiracist education at classroom level. Little research has been conducted in the all-white sector concerning multicultural education and antiracist education - thus this particular book can be seen to be overturning the tables with its focus on white pupils - albeit in response to the presence of black people in United Kingdom.

In this chapter I examine some of the grounds for this book before proposing the hypothesis for the book, namely that a multicultural approach is easier to implement than an antiracist approach in all-white schools. Further, an multicultural education approach can reinforce racist attitudes, whereas and antiracist education approach can positively act to challenge those racist attitudes. I finally define the parameters of the book, drawing out some of the limitations posed by time and nature of the research. Definitions of these terms are discussed in the chapter on terminology, chapter five.

In a book such as this, based heavily as it is on class room practice and curriculum development, it is not possible to discuss the full range of subject areas covered - from English to Technology, from Mathematics to Science. Hence I have confined my discussions and deliberations to a selected range of subject areas. Further, as I worked across the age range - from primary schools through to secondary schools, it is impossible to do justice to all the avenues explored during my time on the two Education Support Grant projects which are under consideration in this book. I shall thus confine the discussion to delving into the multicultural and antiracist aspects of curriculum development as it pertains to all-white schools, in three subject areas only. This is developed more fully in chapters six, seven and eight which deal with curriculum development at classroom level.

Justification for the book

There are a number of crucial factors which need to be drawn out from the preceding chapter. Firstly, as already mentioned, the major focus of multicultural education and antiracist education has been on the (under)achievement of black and ethnic minority pupils in schools. Further, multicultural education and antiracist education work to date had been largely confined to inner-city areas where there is a significant presence of black pupils in inner-city schools. As demonstrated in the review of literature in chapter four, there is very little research that has been done in the all-white sector. Secondly, the educational developments over the past three decades have been confined to providing positive role models in terms of "black studies" in the belief that this would benefit the black pupils and raise their self-esteem. Although there is some truth to this, the focus has been on black children. Even when a book is deemed to deal with the all-white sector, the major focus of the research falls into looking at the racism faced by black pupils.[1] In the course of the book this imbalance is addressed and the focus shifted to white pupils. It is argued that what is of disadvantage to the black pupils is of an advantage to the white pupils. For instance the negative pictures of black people is most books has the effect of giving black pupils a low self-esteem, while at the same time, white pupils are encouraged to feel "superior" because of this negative focus on black people. I would argue that this aspect has been largely ignored by teachers, practitioners and educationalists. This book is therefore an attempt to fill this gap in our knowledge of multicultural education and antiracist education initiatives in the all-white sector.

My contention is that while black pupils are being denied positive self-esteem because of racist name calling, the corollary is that the white pupils are receiving "positive" feedback from their experience as oppressors. This is graphically addressed in *The Eye of the Storm* where positive and negative input has been shown to have long-term effects on white children. This particular "experiment", in my opinion, has received insufficient coverage, but the issues raised deserve to be taken on board by all-white schools. It also highlights the fact that it is immaterial whether white pupils have had contact with black pupils at a personal level.[2] My contention is that white pupils already have negative images of black people and pupils and it is in this sphere that eduction can be seen to be fulfilling its role as perpetuating societal inequalities, rather than challenging long held (racist, inaccurate) views of the world. Through curriculum development it is possible to address this imbalance. Indeed the funding behind the two Education Support Grant projects on multicultural education was acquired on this premise of attitudinal change in white pupils through curriculum development.[3]

It is generally accepted that through curriculum development, it is possible to address issues of inequality - whether this inequality be gender, disability, class, or race, or indeed a combination of these and others. Thus in the 1970s there was a move to acknowledge class differences and point out how the white working class pupils were underachieving because their lack of proficiency in Standard English.[4] It is a sad fact that only a minority of working class pupils go on to further education at degree level.[5] Work undertaken in the 1970s and 1980s in the field of multicultural education and antiracist education also identified curriculum development as a crucial element in addressing issues of racism. In the United States of America particularly there developed a whole market of materials which dealt with black people in a positive way - "black studies" evolved as a result of curriculum intervention. The Education Support Grant projects too had their genesis in curriculum development, as discussed in chapter six dealing with the background to Education Support Grant funding which the two LEAs put forward for Central Government finance through the Education Support Grants scheme. Indeed the philosophy of curriculum being seen as part of the stereotypical images that white pupils have of black and ethnic minority people underpins the funding of Education Support Grant projects on multicultural education and antiracist education in all-white schools.

There is not available a detailed analysis of any Education Support Grant projects from an action research point of view. Also, having worked on two Education Support Grant projects, I am in the fortunate position of being able to compare two such projects from a participant/researcher perspective. Further, as one of the few black Advisory teachers who has worked on Education Support Grant projects, I am able to provide a black perspective. In a book concerning "race" and education it is deemed crucial to provide a black perspective if possible.[6] In the same way that a woman researcher discussing issues around gender and education can justifiably put forward a feminist perspective, so it is

45

fundamental to provide a black perspective here.

A reading of the literature around the field of multicultural education and antiracist education reveals some fundamental issues. This is discussed more fully in chapter four. Suffice it to summarise of the most salient points here. Most of the work undertaken in the past three decades on "race" and education has been either confined to the inner-city schools where there are significant numbers of black and ethnic minority pupils and have concentrated on the underachievement of black and ethnic minority pupils. As mentioned above, even when a book is purporting to be about the all-white sector, the main section of the research concentrates on the effects of racist name calling on black pupils.[7]

Three main strands of educational response have emerged as a result of black and ethnic minority people in Britain. First, is the notion of self-esteem and the concept of positive image amongst ethnic minority pupils.[8] Second, if left well alone, the "problem" of ethnic minority education will go away - the doing good by doing little perspective.[9] The third response is the notion that multicultural issues are only relevant in inner-city areas where there is a significant ethnic minority population, and is not a concern in all-white areas.[10] Countless examples exist on studies which have focused on the home background of black and ethnic minority pupils - lack of parental support amongst the African-Caribbean pupils and the need for English as a Second Language (E2L) amongst the Asian population - to justify the poor performance of black and ethnic minority pupils at public examinations. The two most popular views which are expressed by teachers in all-white schools are: "we have no problem here" (because there are no black and ethnic minority children in the school) and "it's (multicultural education and antiracist education) is only relevant in inner-city schools".[11]

Leading to the hypothesis

Teachers working in the field of multicultural education and antiracist education have by and large reacted to the presence of black and ethnic minority children in their classroom in an ad hoc manner. During the 1970s there was a move to undertake multicultural work in inner-city schools, along the lines of celebration of differences of the various cultures found in Britain. During the 1980s, with the advent of an antiracist stance, teachers adopted a more radical stance. However, as mentioned in chapter two above in the case of McLean and Young's attempt to marry the two concepts, all that has occurred is that the language has changed - the practice has remained the same.[12] Teachers are still doing multicultural work as opposed to antiracist work.

As shown in the chapter on terminology, the two concepts, multicultural education and antiracist education are poles apart philosophically. This leads to different practices at class room level as demonstrated in the case studies in chapters six, seven and eight. It will be interesting, then, to find out whether an multicultural education approach is more readily accepted by teachers and pupils because of the tokenistic aspect. It is suggested that an antiracist education approach, as defined in terms of overall change at both content and pedagogy level, is more difficult to implement in all-white schools.

Stating the hypothesis

My hypothesis is that in Education Support Grant Projects curriculum development involving a multicultural approach in all-white schools is more readily accepted than an antiracist approach to curriculum development, both by teachers and pupils. Further an multicultural education approach can lead to racist stereotypes, whereas an antiracist education approach can actively challenge those stereotypes. As Short and Carrington point out, in multi-racial schools, at classroom level, far more resistance has been shown to antiracist education than to multicultural education. Further, all-white schools have eschewed both types of intervention.[13]

Parameters of the book

Due to time constraints it has been impractical to conduct a longitudinal study. Both projects ran for a period of eight years, thus a longitudinal study would have taken over twelve years to complete, before any meaningful writing-up could begin.

As far as the case studies are concerned I have limited to detailed examination of three subject areas - these are, English, Mathematics and Home Economies. The first two are Core subjects of the National Curriculum with a high priority, while Home Economics has been denigrated to a "non-subject" in that it has been encompassed into Technology. Mention is made of other subject areas covered during the course of the researchers time with the two projects, but not in any detailed way.

It is interesting, in passing, to note that at secondary level, the following numbers of pupils took GCSE examinations in 1993. English -

630,087; Home Economics - 108,041; and Mathematics - 547,983. Thus we can see that a significant number of pupils studied these subjects in secondary schools.[16]

Summary

In this chapter I have looked at some of the reasons for the present book as well as putting forward arguments for the particular hypothesis which is, that an multicultural education approach is easier to implement than an antiracist education one in all- white schools. I then looked briefly at some of the problems and issues in implementing multicultural education and antiracist education approaches. Finally, a statement of the limitations of the particular book is provided.

Notes

1   Troyna and Hatcher (1992) *Racism in children's lives*
2   for a review of this see Patel, K (1988) *Multicultural Teaching*, Summer
3   see chapter five for a fuller discussion of this. See the appendix for the original bids for Education Support Grant funding
4   Barnes (1982) *From Communication to Curriculum*, and Rosen: "Language and class" in Douglas (1974) *Education or Domination?*
5   Professor Young of Cambridge University on the *Today* Programme on Radio 4, September 1992
6   Ahmed (1990) *Black Perspectives in Social Work*, p 3
7   op cit, Troyna and Hatcher (1992)
8   Jeffcoate (1979) *Positive Image*
9   Kirp (1979) *Doing Good by Doing Little*
10   see Patel, K (1992) "On the Margins", *New Beacon*, Vol LXXVI, No 986, March
11   Gaine (1987) *No Problem Here*
12   McLEan and Young (1988) *Multicultural Antiracist Education*
13   Carrington and Short (1992) "Towards an Antiracist initiative in the all-white primary school" in Gill, Mayor and Blair, *Racism and Education* p 253
14   see for instance, Wellington (1986) *Controversial Issues in the Curriculum*
15   see for instance Lewis (1988), *Anti-racism exposed and Palmer (1986) Anti-racism, an Assault on Education and Value*
16   *Education*, 27 August 1993, p 153

4 A review of literature

In the previous chapter some justifications for the present book were put forward. These ranged from providing a black perspective to suggesting that I was in a unique position for comparing two Education Support Grant projects as, as far as I am aware, I am the only advisory teacher to have worked on two such projects. I also suggested that this is on e of the few times that the attitudes of white pupils are taken into consideration when dealing with multicultural education and antiracist education - whether in all-white schools or in multi-racial schools.

In this chapter I look at three distinct areas in the field of multicultural education and antiracist education. The first section examines the limited relevant literature that is available concerning Education Support Grant projects on multicultural education and antiracist education in all-white schools. The next section looks at the available relevant literature in all-white areas generally. The final part looks at the major concern that has preoccupied educationalists and researchers in the field of "race" and education over the past thirty years, namely the underachievement of black pupils.

Education Support Grant Projects

All the relevant literature that I have come across on Education Support Grant projects concerning multicultural education and antiracist education initiatives in all-white schools is of a descriptive nature. Most of the material is in the form of short articles of "good practice", or anecdotal details about curriculum development, published largely in journals such as *Multicultural Teaching* [1] and *Perspectives* [2]. However, recently, a number of books and longer articles in the form of booklets have been published dealing with Education Support Grant initiatives. I discuss five of these publications below.

Debbie Epstein and Alison Sealey's record of their work in primary schools on the Education Support Grant project entitled "Promotion of Racial Equality and Justice" in Birmingham forms the basis of *Where it really matters*. The booklet is divided into four chapters and looks at "Racism", "Changing classroom experience", "The school as an institution" and "Looking to the future". Although in the second chapter, "Changing classroom experience", which provides examples of what they term "anti-racist" materials, the authors argue that "the imparting of "cultural" knowledge is not, in itself the key to preparation of all pupils for life in a multicultural society",[3] some of the examples they offer as good practice as antiracist education is concerned, falls into this trap. A prime example, interestingly also chosen by Godfrey Brandt in *The Realization of Antiracist Teaching* as an example of good antiracist practice and discussed in Chapter One, is the very popular children's book *The Tiger Who Came to Tea* by Judith Kerr.[4] Examples of multicultural elements are cooking and eating foods from various cultures, reading the story in different languages and listening to Indian music. I would argue that none of these elements are antiracist, they are in essence multicultural.[5] There is no attempt here, for example, to use Peters' Projection of the World map for route planning, or for the location of India. It could be argued that a mere inclusion of Peters' Projection of the World map which was developed over twenty years ago by Arnos Peters to represent actual land areas of the continents, is unlikely to change pupils' attitudes about superiority or inferiority.[6] However, I would argue that this needs to be seen in a broader context of education - all knowledge is inter-connected, and unless one is able to challenge fundamental beliefs such as the mistaken notion that one group of people is superior to another, then the inequality which exists in British society between white and black people will remain. Thus, on its own, Peters' Projection will have limited, or even marginal, effect on pupils' attitudes or beliefs. However, if the use of Peters' Projection leads to a re-examination of one's world view then we have the beginnings of an antiracist process. Mercator's Projection, on the other hand presents a favourable picture of the West by its pictorial depiction of the land areas which would lead to a reinforcing of the mistaken notion that one part of the world is superior to another. Furthermore, it can be argued that an antiracist approach would ask fundamental questions such as who wrote the book; why is it that the tiger came to a white family, and so on.

In *Spanner in the Works*, sub-titled "Education for racial equality and social justice in white schools", Clare Brown, Jacqui Barnfield and Mary Stone discuss various aspects of multicultural education. These are separated into eleven sections ranging in topis from "Working Towards Social Justice", "Whole School Approaches", to "Other people...Other countries" and "Celebrations and observations" and "Different and the same". All sections give details of various projects that the authors have carried out in all-white schools in Cumbria with discussions of lessons and pupils' work. Although the authors provide a range of activities labelled as antiracist, in essence the material is multicultural in nature, especially in Section IX, which deals with Chinese New Year, Diwali and Hanukkah, in a superficial way. There is no attempt to link these festivals to the multi-racial nature of present day British society. For instance, in learning about Chinese New Year, the children are thought to have formed "positive images of Chinese people".[7] However, the theme is not expanded to include the number of Chinese restaurants and take aways found in Cumbria, and how the Chinese people in the United Kingdom have been for a long time an "invisible" presence. It is only recently that research has been conducted into the Chinese community living in Britain.[8]

In *Education for a Multicultural Society*, Sally Tomlinson and Peter Coulson, give a descriptive analysis of a twenty-six Education Support Grant Projects in mainly white areas.[9] Although a few examples of class room material is included, there is no attempt here at examining the issues and problems of the actual implementation of the projects. The range of projects cover both primary and secondary sectors. This is the most comprehensive account on Education Support Grant Projects yet published. It is significant to note that this account was published privately by Tomlinson. At the time there was no interest in the field and she was unable to find any publishers for the book. This in a sense indicates that the whole area of multicultural education and antiracist education in all-white areas is not seen as a mainstream issue by educational publishers - nor is the issue seen as of importance by publishers who specialise in multicultural education issues generally.

Tomlinson has since published a book *Multicultural Education in schools*, which includes a chapter on the twenty-six Education Support Grant projects researched by Peter Coulson.[10] The book also provides a general background to the scheme while repeating the descriptive analysis of the earlier work. It is to this that I now turn.

In *Multicultural Education in white schools*, Sally Tomlinson repeats much of the descriptive analysis carried out by Peter Coulson, and provides a general background to the Education Support Grant scheme.

Again this is a purely descriptive analysis of the Education Support Grant projects. No attempt is made at looking at the issues, problems and concerns of the actual process of implementing multicultural education and antiracist education curriculum development in all-white schools. Tomlinson suggests that it is since the publication of the Swann Report that the focus of multicultural education has moved from issues concerned with the education of minority pupils to issues concerning the education of all pupils in an ethnically diverse society.[11] Although the Swann Report was instrumental in Central Government identifying multicultural education as worthy of funding through the Education Support Grant scheme, educationalists and teachers had been recognised the importance of multicultural education long before 1985, when the Swann Report was published.

Tomlinson goes on to state that the problem of how to offer an appropriate and relevant education to young white people, so that they will leave school able to accept that their non-white fellow-pupils are their equal fellow-citizens with equal rights and responsibilities, is becoming recognised as a serious question worthy of serious debate.[12] Although I agree with this sentiment, I find Tomlinson's use of the term "non-white" somewhat surprising. She continues to use this term throughout the book, when she refers to black and ethnic minority people.[13] There are countless examples of where Tomlinson is consciously avoiding using the word "black". I find this use unhelpful in the extreme. By the use of non-white, I feel that Tomlinson is denying the existence of black people - they become a non-entity, something only compared with the "norm", which in Tomlinson's usage is obviously white. The use of the work black is positive and should be encouraged. This, I would argue is the difference between multicultural education and antiracist education - even at terminological level. It would be interesting to see the reaction of women, particularly feminists, if one were to refer to women as "non-men"! Although it can be argued that "non-white" is an accepted form of usage and has currency in educational discourse, what I am attempting to do here is to go beyond this. As the sentiments of the Bob Marley and the Wailers song *Redemption Song* declare, we need to emancipate ourselves from mental slavery, and set our thoughts free of confining boundaries. We need to go beyond the boundaries set by "acceptable" language, by language that is loaded in favour of oppressors. I would argue that language is part and parcel of the oppression. I would further argue that language itself must change if multicultural education and antiracist education is to have any lasting effect on children's education. In the same way that "chair" or "chairperson" is now an accepted substitute for "chairman", I would hope that in the future the use of "non-white" would be replaced by "black." In addition, I find this persistence use of "non-white" to describe black people a rather negative way of doing things. Why describe people as negative of something else. We do not see the use of "non-black" to describe white people. Also, the use of non-white seems to me to be a way of implicitly stating that white is the norm to which other colours are compared; black people are the negative of white people. I would hope that black as a descriptive word gains greater currency so that eventually we stop using the negative non-white - black should be used as a positive word to describe black people.

The Education Support Grant project in Bedford was evaluated by an outside agency, namely Mal Leicester from Warwick University and provides detailed teaching materials developed during the life time of the Education Support Grant scheme. The material is confined to the secondary sector. They have published several documents bound in spiral ring binders, covering a wide range of subject areas, including English, Language Awareness, Prejudice and Power, Sikhism and Humanities, detailing some of the methods used and also providing some class-room material for use by all teachers in the local education authority. The materials were also published so that they could reach a wider sector of the LEAs teaching force - for dissemination purposes after the project had come to an end.

To summarise, then, as far as Education Support Grant projects on multicultural education and antiracist education are concerned there is a paucity of material available and there is very little commercially published material. Only three of the above publications were commercially published - Tomlinson and Coulson's work was privately published in ring binder format, as was the material from the Bedford project. The available literature on Education Support Grant projects dealing specifically with multicultural education and antiracist education initiatives in the all-white sector is limited to descriptive accounts of work carried out in all-white schools. In all the projects which are accounts by teachers either deal with the primary or secondary sectors. Only Tomlinson and Coulson deal with both sectors, but in this case they are secondary reports from the questionnaire survey which was carried out largely by Coulson on visits to twenty-six Education Support Grant projects around the country, including the project in London under discussion for this book.

None of the above accounts of the Education Support Grant projects outlined above deal in any detailed way with the problems and issues of implementation of multicultural education and antiracist education initiatives in all-white schools. Although there are examples of actual classroom materials, there is an unstated notion that readers and teachers understand the nature and implications of multicultural education and antiracist education. Also, apart from the last two mentioned, the discussions are confined to either the primary or the secondary sector, none of them deal with the whole age range, primary to secondary. As I have been fortunate to have worked across the age range, the present book aims to fill this gap.

Although all Education Support Grant projects are required by the Home Office to provide annual reports, these are not available for general consumption. Hence there is very little material available specifically on Education Support Grant projects. The present book goes some way to bridge this gap, with detailed analysis of two projects from a practitioner point of view.

Having examined the relevant available literature on Education Support Grant projects dealing with multicultural education and antiracist education approaches in the all-white sector, I would suggest that one can identify three main gaps in our knowledge of the Education Support Grant scheme and projects which deal specifically with multicultural education and antiracist education initiatives in the all-white sector that require addressing:

1   None of the above deal with the process of implementation.
2   None of the above cover both the primary and secondary sector.[14]
3   None of the above provide a black perspective.[15]

The present book goes some way to fill these gaps.

All-white areas

A general literature on multicultural education was relatively limited until well into the 1970s, but during the 1980s there has been a considerable increase in the range of writing which claims to be multicultural and antiracist. As Tomlinson points out, and as is demonstrated in the next section of this chapter, the expanding literature has been concerned mainly with issues and polemics related to the education of black pupils, focusing particularly on their perceived underachievement and the ethnocentric nature of the school curriculum.[16] Another focus has been the racism faced by black pupils in their daily lives outside and inside school. Little was published on the education of pupils in the all-white sector until the 1980s, although in as early as 1971 McNeal and Rogers proposed that their analysis of the educational needs of pupils in multi-racial schools should include white English children as that they were simply describing a rational approach for all schools.[17]

Tomlinson suggests that 1984 was a turning point in the shift of focus from black pupils to white pupils on the grounds that literature began to emerge relating multicultural education to the majority white society.[18] She quotes Davies' article "How pervasive is White Superiority?" in *Education* on the notions of white superiority and two reports published on behalf of the Church of England and the Catholic Church. The first one, entitled *Schools and Multicultural Education* was published in April 1984 by the Board of Education of the General Synod of the Church of England and the other one, entitled *Learning from Diversity - a challenge for Catholic Education* was published by a working party on Catholic Education for a Multiracial, Multicultural society in July the same year. A final example she uses is the article by Taylor, also published in 1984, entitled "Multicultural Education in a Monocultural Region" which appeared in *New Community*, as arguments for suggesting that 1984 was the turning point in the change of focus from black children to white children. However, I would argue that it was the publication of the Swann report the following year, in 1985, that can be seen to be the turning point in a real shift of focus from black to white pupils. None of the other reports and articles had the authority of the Swann Report - neither did they have the depth and breadth of research found in the Swann Report. Furthermore, the Swann Report had National importance and gave currency to educationalists and teachers who wanted to broaden their curriculum to include a multicultural dimension; they were now in a position to quote from a Government publication to justify a multicultural approach in their schools, whether black pupils were present in their schools or not. As Troyna and Hatcher point out, the Swann Report has been used by teachers in all-white areas as a peg on which to hang their justification for a multicultural approach.[19]

As early as 1973 the Select Committee on Race Relations and Immigration [Education] published the views of several bodies such as the National Union of Teachers and the Department of Education and Science calling for a broader approach to multicultural education in all schools, whether there were black pupils in them or not.[20]   In the same year, 1973, Townsend and Brittan published the findings of a survey which all types of schools were included - multiracial and white, primary and secondary.[21] They found that all-white schools in all-white rural areas were just as positive as the multiracial schools in urban areas in their aims and syllabuses as far as multicultural education was concerned. But significantly, it was the all-white schools in multiracial areas which were the least positive in their outlook to multicultural education. The all-white school can present widely differing views, as evidenced from the following two comments from head teachers:

1) Multicultural content of syllabi here would, because there is no immigrant problem, be purely academic and unreal.

2) We would welcome support in preparing children for life in a multicultural society, for clearly, living as they do on the edge of an industrial city, most of these children will find their livelihood within a highly multi-racial environment.[22]

Since 1977 Central Government policy has been one of broadening the view that multicultural education is not just the concern of schools with black pupils or restricted to areas of inner cities where there might be a substantial number of black residents.[23]

Between 1978 and 1980 Little and Willey undertook a Schools Council project at Goldsmith's College, University of London entitled "Multi-ethnic education in "all-white" areas".[24] They found that the schools in low concentration areas of ethnic minority population did not consider multicultural education to be an issue of concern, that enough was usually done through the World Studies module, that there were more urgent priorities, and hostility would arise if any action was taken. Very few schools said that the whole curriculum had been re-considered for education in a multicultural society. Little and Willey quote Baroness Young, the then Minister of State for Education and Science as saying:

...it is just as important in schools where there are no ethnic minority pupils for the teaching there to refer to the different cultures now present in Britain, as it is for the teaching in schools in the inner areas of cities like Birmingham and London. It is a question of developing a curriculum which draws positive advantage from the different cultures....[25]

Between 1982 and 1983 Arnold Matthews and Laurie Fallows conducted independent studies into the provision of the then contemporary situation vis a vis multicultural education in all-white areas.[26]

By the 1980s there was an open acknowledgement that multicultural education work was an important educational concern in all-white areas.

> All teachers have a professional responsibility to prepare their pupils for a multicultural society. Teachers in schools which appear to be mono-cultural and monolingual have possibly the greatest responsibility; their pupils are not likely to encounter the issues and implications of cultural diversity during their school lives, and yet the world outside the classroom is already interdependent and culturally diverse.[27]

It should be added that these pupils may one day be managers of a workforce that may include black people. This concept of multiracial, multicultural society is picked up by the Swann Report.[28]

Chris Gaine in *No Problem Here* provides a useful introduction and a practical approach to education and "race" in white schools.[29] This book grew out of a National Antiracist Movement in Education (NAME) Annual Conference for teacher held in Chichester, Sussex in 1987 on the theme of "antiracist education in white areas", which I attended. Gaine reiterates the most common refrain heard from teachers and educationalists in all-white areas with few or no black people that issues of multicultural education and antiracist education do not concern them. Gaine retells the story of how he set up a social studies course in which "race" was a major element which provided an honest and instructive example of the problems and pitfalls inherent in both the subject matter and teaching strategies. I was not surprised to note, for example that the white children were not interested in cultural attributes; they viewed all Asian people as "Pakis":

> They do not listen to the distinction between Sikhs, Muslims, Gujaratis and Bengalis, West Indians and Indians, because they are not interested, they do not want to know because the important thing to them is that these people are not white, and the students believe they are responsible for all the unemployment and bad housing.[30]

However, focusing on the attitudes of white children to black people does not help because it does not tackle the issue of institutional racism head on. The nature and issues concerning institutional racism are discussed more fully in chapter ten. I would argue that what Gaine passes off as antiracist education is really multicultural education and does not address the institutionalised forms of racist practices found in all schools. The concern is with white pupils' attitudes - and although these are adequately explored through a range of "games" - the kind usually found in Personal and Social Education (PSE) slots in secondary schools - they do not address the more important area of curriculum development regarding multicultural education and antiracist education as developed in this book.

From time to time in *Perspectives* - a journal which is a series of occasional publications on current educational topics and published by the School of Education, University of Exeter, there has been some coverage of multicultural education in the all-white context. In 1987, for instance, in *Perspectives 35* there were a series of articles written by teachers working in the all-white area in the South-West of England. Most of the teachers had previously worked in multi-racial schools in inner city areas. The education is a report of a conference during which a Standing Conference on multicultural education in the South-West was set up.[31]

More recently, the journal has covered some multicultural education work undertaken through the Education Support Grant projects in the Devon and Cornwall areas. These are thumb nail sketches of some innovative work in one or two schools. As Taylor points out there has been no co-ordinated approach in the field of multicultural education in the area: "Networks do exist - centred around the Education Support Grant projects in Cornwall and Somerset and around the four regional support groups in Devon. No regional network exists, because no finance has been forthcoming to facilitate its existence."[32] This highlights the lack of commitment from the local education authority in providing the necessary funding for such networks to function .

There have been a number of short articles dealing with the all-white sector and multicultural education and antiracist education. The Summer 1986 edition of *Multicultural Teaching* was devoted to looking at issues in the North East, a region deemed to be "a fertile breeding ground for crude racist activity and propaganda", covering as a result of the geographical area multicultural education and antiracist education issues in an all-white sector.[33] The periodical covered articles as diverse as white children's attitudes towards their black peers to a black perspective on current policy in the North East. Most other articles when dealing with multicultural education in an all-white context deal mainly with racist incidents in all-white schools - again the focus is chiefly on the impact of racism on black children. The white children's experiences are left untackled, and untouched.[34] This was reiterated by Swann : "...it might generally be felt that racist attitudes and behaviour would be less common in schools with few or no ethnic minority pupils...we believe this is regrettably far from the case."[35]

All five local education authorities in the north-east region have produced policy statements for education for a multicultural, multiracial society, and one of them, Newcastle-upon-Tyne, has produced guidelines for all its City Council Departments. This issue is particularly relevant here as one of the Education Support Grant projects is based in the north east of England.

In the Spring of the following year, 1987, five articles appeared in *Multicultural Teaching* dealing with issues of education in all-white areas. Trudi Levi, a victim of Nazi racism in the 1940s presented a moving memoir of his experiences in his contribution entitled "Hampshire Happening: Working Towards change". Another teacher in the same local education authority described the way in which a working party at his school used the recommendations of the Swann Report to make changes which permeated the whole school.[36] Roger Cartwright, in " "No Problem Here" - Multicultural Education in the All white School" the Head teacher of Temple Ewell C.E. (Controlled) Primary School in Dover, Kent offered positive suggestions for adding a multicultural dimension to the primary school curriculum in all-white areas.[37] Another teacher and educationalist described the development of a multicultural antiracist policy in a white working-class school, where although racist attacks against black people was commonplace in the area, the teachers at his school were initially reluctant to be involved in multicultural education and antiracist education initiatives.[38] The fifth, and final article to appear in this particular journal was by Cosway who offered an "institutional Racism" checklist for both multi-racial and all-white schools.[39]

Multicultural Teaching is one of the few journals which has consistently articulated the themes and concerns of multicultural education and antiracist education. Although confined in most cases to multi-racial areas, as we have seen above, there have been a few instances which have been devoted to multicultural education and antiracist education issues in all-white schools. However, the instances of this are not many.

Roberts, writing in the journal of the National Union of Teachers, criticized the attitude of the Department of Education and Science to work in all-white areas during the passing of the 1988 Act trough Parliament. Roberts' school, which was in Hampshire, was filmed for BBC TV schools programme on racism in 1987 and had developed a policy based on the recommendations found in the Swann Report together with the Hampshire Local Education Authority's response to the Swann Report. Roberts deplored the lack of consultation over multiracial issues in the National Curriculum, and the lack of leadership offered by senior ministers.

> People at the top should be publicly stating that racism is evil and ...those schools trying their best, in sensitive ways, to change racism should be commended. On the other hand, teachers must cease to give the impression that they are acting in a maverick way - they must consult at every level in a democratic way on any proposal for curriculum change in schools.[40]

Robin Richardson, formally an education advisor in the London Borough of Brent, and now Chief Executive of the Runnymede Trust, has been more overtly critical of the 1988 Education Act and what he identified as a retreat from racial equality policies by both central and local authorities. He argued that a major effect of the Act will be to shift influence away from teachers and advisors, who are the people most concerned with innovation in all-white schools.[41]

Sally Tomlinson is right to state that Teachers' Unions have so far been relatively muted in their support for a more appropriate multicultural and antiracist curriculum in all-white schools. The most progressive and forward looking statement has been produced by the Assistant Masters and Mistresses Association (AMMA). This statement concedes that understanding the nature and purpose of a multicultural curriculum is more widespread now, but notes that "Regrettably, some people still feel that a multicultural approach is irrelevant to their monocultural school...and more still reject the multicultural curriculum as irrelevant to the target of eradicating racism."[42]

As was stated above, *Spanner in the works* by Brown, Barnfield and Stone provides some useful teaching material of curriculum innovation which has been tried out in all-white schools. The major focus here is cultural diversity and racial attitudes amongst black and white pupils. The book provides a whole range of useable material that can be used in the classroom with slight modification to suit a particular group of children. As Gerry German points out in his Foreword, "Britain is multi-ethnic, and has always ben so. Cumbria is very much part of the richly diverse British tradition. But while British plurality is evident for those who want to see it, its pluralism has been stifled by the self-interested institution and perpetuation of class distinction, male superiority and white supremacy. If the quality of life is to improve for everybody, these myths must be challenged and exploitation and oppression resisted." *Spanner in the Works* goes some way to addressing these needs in all-white areas.[43]

Sally Tomlinson draws six main conclusions from her review of the relevant literature in all-white schools. I would be inclined to draw the same conclusions from my review of the relevant literature, which is more extensive than Tomlinson's, and in summary it will be useful paraphrase Tomlinson's findings here:

1   There is still present a whole range of negative views about the implementation of a more appropriate education for a multi-racial society. These views range from outright hostility and suspicion, through to apathy, indifference and a denial that the issues do affect the school and the area.

2   Strategies for curriculum change and intervention and implementation of multicultural education in all-white areas, by the small but growing number of committed teachers and educationalists must adopt a "softly softly" approach and include democratic consultation with colleagues and the wider community.

3   The antagonistic debates about multicultural education versus antiracist education adduction have little relevance for all-white areas, where cultural and global education, and education against racism are seen as necessary, but practitioners should still be wary of tokenistic curriculum changes which reflect cultural symbols only.

4   There are as yet no developed theoretical models of an appropriate education for all-white areas, although one possible model is that of a broad political education which takes account of class, gender and racial inequalities.

5   The literature that is predominantly emanating upwards from teachers and educationalists rather than being the production of academics or policy makers.

6   There is considerable uncertainty about how the requirements of the 1988 Education Act and in particular the National Curriculum, will affect multicultural education and antiracist education developments during the 1990s.[44]

All of these points are addressed in the course of this book to a lesser or greater degree. In particular, I try to fathom out some of the uncertainties of the National Curriculum with regard to antiracist education.

Multicultural education and antiracist education and the underachievement of black pupils

The term black is discussed more fully in the following chapter on terminology, but it will be useful here to reiterate that the term "black" is used to include pupils whose parents or grandparents originated from the New Commonwealth in the 1950s and 1960s to fill the labour shortage in Britain following the second world war. Most of these first settlers came to the UK at the invitation of the British Government who actively recruited for workers by placing advertisements in the press in the West Indies and India promising a brighter future in the "mother country". Moreover, the recruiting from the New Commonwealth was selective in that preference was given to those who had high educational standards. (This is true even today as the debate on Hong Kong has shown - only those very rich and/or with very high educational qualifications will be allowed British entry visas. Of the seven million plus British passport holders in Hong Kong, only a minority will be able to settle here in the UK.) As Bhikhu Parekh has pointed out, Asians provide nearly a quarter of the doctors in the National Health Service, and nearly a fifth of our General Practitioners. They also provide nearly six per cent of our accountants. When converted in crude financial terms, the Asian contribution is of staggering proportion. On a rough estimate it costs Britain nearly a hundred and twenty five thousand pounds to train a doctor, calculating the cost from the time a child is conceived until she qualifies to practise. Multiply this by 8,000, the number of Asian doctors who come here fully qualified and did not cost the British tax payer a penny, and we arrive at the figure of over a thousand million pounds the poor Asian countries have contributed to Britain.[45]

A large part of the literature on multicultural education and antiracist education is concerned with the achievement, or rather, underachievement, of black pupils. The focus is chiefly on black pupils in British schools - this raises the issue of black pupils being seen as a "problem" and how they can best be fitted into the Education System. The prevailing attitudes towards multicultural education and antiracist education of the 1970s and 1980s have remained with us in the 1990s. The plethora of books which has fed the multicultural education and antiracist education field took as their central theme the impact of the schooling system on black pupils. The field of multicultural education and "race" and education has grown into a veritable industry - hundreds of articles have been published in books, the educational press and specialist journals such as *Multicultural Teaching* and *New Community*, not only in this country but also in the United States of America, Europe and Australia.

Little would be gained by recounting all the works which deal with multicultural education: the bibliography indicates the extensive range of material available. Even so-called anti-antiracists such as Flew[46] and Lewis[47] have drawn attention to the underachievement of black pupils. There is no benefit to be achieved by repeating what others have already drawn attention to - there are several annotated bibliographies available on the subject.[48]

The Swann Report provides a useful summary of the historical aspect of multicultural education and antiracist education. As already highlighted, the Swan Report is particularly relevant to this book because it led directly to the funding of Education Support Grant projects on multicultural education in all-white areas, as is demonstrated later.

The Rampton Report,[49] the precursor of the Swann Report, was subtitled "West Indian children in our schools" - this immediately conjures up, for me, the image of "them" and "us", as well as the notion that "West Indians" are in some sense a "guest" community which must fit into our "host" (implying white) schools. This concept has not changed in the past twenty years - black people are still seen as outsiders. The chapter on "The Educational Needs of "Liverpool blacks" in Swann is indicative of the alienation of black people even when they have been a part of the British society for over four generations.[50] A reading of the literature makes clear that the majority of books, articles and specialist journals such as Multicultural Teaching take as the basic premise that multicultural education and antiracist education as ideologies which are tied up with black achievement and the progress of black pupils through the schooling system.

Chapter four of *Education for All* - the Swann Report - offers a historical perspective and it will be useful to briefly summarise the main points here. It is generally accepted that attitudes towards the educational needs of black pupils fall into a clearly defined chronological pattern, moving from "assimilation", through attempts to give at least some recognition in schools to the backgrounds of ethnic minority children, usually known as "integration", through to the more recent moves towards multicultural education.

Assimilation policies which were developed as a first as an initial reaction to the presence of black pupils entering the schooling system in the 1960s were ad hoc responses to the educational needs of black children designed on the one hand to "compensate" for their assumed deficiencies, and on the other hand to disrupt the education of white children as little as possible. So that assimilation policies included withdrawing children whose first language was other than English to teach them the basic skills as quickly as possible so that they could be subsumed within the overall school population. Some local education authorities also adopted policies of dispersal, so that large numbers of black children were bussed to outlying schools so that the majority white pupils' education, it was argued, would not be affected. To aid the local education authorities most affected by the presence of immigrants from the New Commonwealth, the Government introduced a special form of funding under Section 11 of the 1966 Local Government Act, whereby local education authorities could claim 75 per cent of staff wages while providing 25 per cent from its own budget. This meant that local education authorities could have four teachers for the price of one.

While the integration stance went some way towards acknowledging that the life-styles of black communities were valid in their own right, it failed to consider the broader implications for the traditional perception of the "British way of life" which the presence of communities with such diverse backgrounds might have in the longer term. In practice, of course, there was little real difference between the assimilationist and integrationist viewpoints in that both perspectives shared the common aim of absorbing ethnic minority communities within society with as little disruption to the life of the majority as possible.

Multicultural education, as educational philosophy, offered a move away from the previous two policies of assimilation and integration. Whereas the latter focused primarily on seeking to "remedy" the perceived "problems" of black children and to "compensate" for their perceived "disabilities", multicultural education has usually tended to have two distinct themes. First, meeting the particular needs of ethnic minority pupils and, second, the broader issue of preparing *all* pupils for life in a multicultural society. It is this last theme that led to the funding of Education Support Grant projects in all-white schools.

Only a very sketchy recounting of the response of the local education authorities to the presence of black pupils in their schools is provided above. As mentioned above there is a growing body of literature on multicultural education, and rather than offer a laborious recounting of all these books, I have chosen a cross section of four recently published books (Sarup[51], Troyna and Carrington[52], Verma and Pumfrey[53], and Todd[54]) which give the general flavour and illustrate the current state of play. The four chosen books also provide a cross-section of political perspectives, from Marxist (Sarup) through to liberal (Troyna and

66

Carrington; Verma and Pumfrey) and conservative (Todd). Although I would not recommend some of these books as good examples of writing on multicultural education and antiracist education, the four chosen titles give an indication of what is being published in the name of multicultural education and antiracist education by mainstream publishers. Todd in particular gives a very poor recounting of the multicultural education field - the book is moreover superficial and gives an inaccurate picture of the multicultural education field.

Sarup (1991) in *Education and the Ideologies of Racism*, though focusing on a whole range of issues in a n attempt to establish a link between "race", class and gender throws light upon various ideologies of racism as well as a discussion of multicultural education and antiracist education as educational ideologies within that framework. However, the major focus of the book os on black pupils in schools. A whole chapter is devoted to this.

In *Education, Racism and Reform* Troyna and Carrington (1990) the concern again is on black pupils. Apart form a spurious discussion of issues in "all-white" school the whole book is a focus on the problems faced by black pupils in school. There is a give away sentence which illustrates the general tone of this book :

> Time and again, journals such as Multicultural Teaching publish articles by exponents of multicultural education in all-white/non-contact areas who refer to the Swann report as the peg on which they have hung their argument.[55]

The rest of the book is concerned with the underachievement of black pupils with detailed analysis of "O" level and CSE grades between 1978 and 1982 with breakdown of "Asians", "West Indians" and "all other leavers". I find this breakdown into three separate categories rather unsatisfactory for two reasons. First, it lumps the "white" children in to one group, but splits the black group into Asian and West Indians. A breakdown of class differences amongst the white population would give a different picture. It also implies that the white group is a homogenous group whereas the Asian and West Indian do not constitute the "black" group. I would like to argue that if such breakdowns are used then both white and black groups should be treated as "homogenous" groups. However, this is clearly not possible as in actual fact non of the groups are homogenous. Second, this type of breakdown seems to imply that the "Asian" and "West Indian" groups are homogenous in their own" right. The reality is much more complex than this - if one breaks down the

Asian groups into say Indian, Pakistani, East African Indians, and Bangladeshi, one would get a different set of results. As is well known, the Bangladeshi community in Tower Hamlets is one of the most deprived community in Britain - and yet they are counted as being in the same bracket as "Asians" who are shown to do so well at school. The truth is that the Bangladeshi children are doing abysmally at school - one of the reasons because of the daily racial harassment faced by pupils in and out of school in the East End of London. Also, the West Indians are not a homogenous group - they have a variety of dialects and languages - from Patois and Creole to Brixton English and Jamaican English. Further, the issues of black middle class has yet to be explored by sociologists.[56]

Verma and Pumfrey (1988) in the collection of essays entitled *Educational Attainments - issues and outcomes in Multicultural Education* review recent thinking and research in the in the field of education, ethnicity and cross-cultural processes. Verma in his essay "Issues in Multicultural Education" sets the scene for what is to follow - the focus clearly is on the educational performance of Asian and African-Caribbean children. Kerr and Desforges draw attention to developing bilingual children's English in school; while Parekh concentrates on Ethnic Minority Attainment and the Swann Report. There are papers here using empirical research into, for instance, "West Indian and Asian Children's attainment" (Mackintosh, Mascie-Taylor and West); and a further two essays on the same theme. All this makes clear that the focus of multicultural education discourse is very much on black children. There is no mention here of the impact of black people's presence on the majority white children in schools. Reading this particular text (as well as scores of others) one gets the impression that multicultural education and antiracist education are merely to do with black underachievement and the "problems" posed to schools by black pupils presence in British classrooms. Although I would agree that this is an important issues in itself, I feel that not enough work has been down on the all-white sector of British schooling.

In *Education in a Multicultural Society* Roy Todd (1991) provides a useful overview of the development of cultural and ethnic diversity in Britain. He goes on to outline the development of educational responses, including educational ideologies, central and local government policy development, and some of the implications for the school curriculum. He also addresses the controversial issue of racism in society and schools, including discussion of teaching about "race" and race relations and ways in which schools have dealt with racist incidents. In all these major issues the focus, yet again, is very much on the black pupils in schools. Although Todd touches on the issues of the all-white sector, his perspective is very much in line with the recommendations and findings of the Swann Report and he offers no new angle on the subject. He quotes from the Swann Report to highlight the fact that:

> The development of hostile attitudes towards members of ethnic minority groups may thus occur in area as which are predominantly white. It does not depend upon immediate contact and there are clear differences between groups in the degrees of antagonism towards others.[57]

This is the only time that the issue of all-white schools is considered - and to reiterate the point made above, Todd does not offer any new material - he merely repeats Swann. In a sense the whole area of the influence of the racist nature of British society has been again problematised as being the preserve of black people.

It will be clear from the example of the four books discussed above that there is a diverse range of views on the current thinking in the multicultural education and antiracist education field. One can begin to appreciate that the concerns are still the same as they were in the 1970s and 1980s - namely the underachievement of black pupils in British schools.

Even when books are published purporting to be about all-white areas, the central concern is still the underachievement of black pupils. An example of this is the collection of essays found in T S Chivers in *Race and Culture in Education - issues arising from the Swann Committee Report.*[58] Chivers draws together papers which were presented at a conference on "Multicultural Education after Swann" organised by the British Sociological Association Race and Ethnic Relations Group and published in 1987. Apart from two papers which focus on the initiatives on multicultural education work in the North East, the book, as always, is concerned with the racism faced by black people in Britain, and the resultant underachievement. An example is Verma's paper entitled "The Swann Report and Ethnic Achievement: What Next?" Two-thirds of the book is taken up with the usual focus on black children's underachievement in schooling.

Troyna and Hatcher's recent publication, entitled *Racism in children's lives* is sub-titled "A study of mainly-white primary schools" - but even here the preoccupation is on black pupils. As they state in their concluding remarks:

The schools that we studied are similar to many hundreds of primary schools in urban areas, located in streets of Victorian terraces or new estates on the outskirts. They are similar, too, in containing a minority of black children, perhaps two or three, or half a dozen, in each class.[59]

The significant factor is that Troyna and Hatcher studied schools in urban areas - the present book includes not only urban, inner-city schools in the North East of England, but also focuses suburban areas in London, and on rural areas in the North East of England, where there are primary schools where there are no black pupils, or staff for that matter. Some of the village schools have never had a black person either as a pupil or as a member of staff. Of course, in a situation where there are a few black children, the impact of "race" and that of racist name-calling - the main focus for Troyna and Hatcher - will play an overt role. However, as this book aims to show, the factor of "race" is just as important in the, literally, all-white school.

Books and articles about multicultural education and antiracist education continue to be published. However, most of these are concerned with multi-racial schools. An example of this is *Education and the Social Construction of "race"* by Peter Figueroa.[60] Here the author asks whether the education system helps or hinders the fight against racism. Figueroa provides a critique of the Swann Report as well as other recent sociological research into racial and ethnic relations in the United Kingdom. We are offered a philosophical and sociological analysis of multicultural education and antiracist education. The author shows how the education system itself can reinforce racist assumptions and behaviour in society, but argues that through educational and social reconstructing it can promote constructive cross-cultural relations. There is no mention here of all-white schools.

Another example is *Education for cultural diversity: the challenge for a new era* by Fyfe and Figueroa.[61] This book grew out of a conference held in 1989 by Hampshire Local Education Authority and the University of Southampton where the impact and legacy of the Swann Report was discussed with a view to meeting the educational needs of all children in an increasingly culturally diverse society. Again, there is no reference here to the all-white sector in any great detail. The debate between multicultural education and antiracist education is addressed, as well as the underachievement of black pupils. multicultural education and antiracist education are put into context with the National Curriculum.

Two recent articles also deal with the multi-racial areas and focus on the underachievement of black pupils. The first one is by Sally Tomlinson entitled "Disadvantaging the disadvantaged: Bangladeshis and education in Tower Hamlets" which describes the way in which local education authority policies a section of the school population already suffering gross disadvantages. The article relates the saga in the 1980s when the now defunct Inner London Education Authority was unable to provide sufficient school places for children in Tower Hamlets - the majority of these children, ninety-five per cent, in fact, of these children were Bangladeshi. Sally Tomlinson suggests that this situation would not have happened had the children concerned been from a white middle-class background. Furthermore, she suggests that because Tower Hamlets is an inner-city deprived area, this too was a factor in the response (or lack of) from the ILEA - had this been white, middle-class area, the situation would not have been tolerated. She concludes that there is a tendency amongst policy makers to ignore the economic and social structures which create disadvantage while focusing on individual or family pathology as a major cause of disadvantage.[62]

The other recent article that merits mention is by Peter Foster entitled "Teacher attitudes and Afro-Caribbean educational attainment" which argues that there is very little empirical support for the theory that teachers' negative racial views and low expectations are a major factor in explaining the relatively low educational attainment of African-Caribbean students. Foster also questions the plausibility of this frequently advanced theory given other research evidence on teachers' perceptions of their students. He concludes that the failure of African-Caribbean students could rest n the fact that African-Caribbean students are perhaps more likely to attend less effective schools.[63] Although I would agree with Foster that inner-city, deprived schools are likely to produce poor academic results in their pupils, I would argue that to put so much emphasis on socio-economic factors denies the experience of black students even when they attend prestigious private schools. Furthermore, all pupils, whether African-Caribbean or white working class, will, and do, perform less well than their counterparts in middle class schools. This would seem to suggest that teacher attitudes, and expectations, do have a significant effect in the outcome of academic achievement of African-Caribbean, and other ethnic minority pupils in all schools.

71

Summary

This chapter has demonstrated the dearth of material that is available on multicultural education and antiracist education in all-white areas. This is sharply contrasted with the fact that multicultural education and antiracist education publications in inner-city, multi-racial areas is a veritable industry and there are publications on this subject by a whole cross section of writers. We have seen how there are opinions made by left wing writers as well as right wing educationalists who are hyper critical of multicultural education generally and antiracist education in particular. I would argue that this stems from a misconception of what multicultural education and antiracist education stand for.

In addition to this we have seen that there are very few black writers who have had their work published in this field. A few that are - for example, Godfrey Brandt, Hazel Carby and Chris Mullard - have confined themselves to multi-racial areas and schools.

Notes

1   for instance vol 4, No.3 of *Multicultural Teaching* (1986) was devoted to multicultural education and antiracist education issues in the North East of England

2   For instance, see *Perspectives* Nos 35 and 42. The journal is published by the University of Essex

3   Epstein and Sealey (1990) *Where it really matters*, p 26

4   Brandt (1986) *The Realization of Antiracist Teaching*, pp 151-154

5   see chapter three for a discussion how multicultural education is in essence the celebration of different cultures found in Britain today.

6   Mercator was the Latin nickname of Gerhard Kramer. Also, it is still common to see the widespread use of Mercator's Projection by commercial organisations. For instance, recently, the High Street Department store, British Home Stores, used to give away free carrier bags with Mercator's Projection on them in an effort to show how environmentally aware they were. And in 1988 Chase Manhattan, an insurance company introduced a Visa Credit card with Mercator's Projection on it. Charles Letts and Company Limited, the diary makers use Mercator's projection in their diary. They pointed out that they used Mercator's Projection in preference to Peter's "more accurate 1960s projection because of convenience rather than accuracy, as most people still recognise the Kramer projection." (Personal communication, dated 6 January 1993)

7   Brown, Barnfield and Stone (1990) *Spanner in the Works - Education for racial and social justice in white schools*, p 84

8   Au W K and Au K (1992) *Where to from here? A Handbook for Chinese Carers* Health Education Authority/ King's Fund Centre, London. This publication is also available in Chinese.

9   Tomlinson and Coulson (1988) *Education for a multi-ethnic society*

10   Tomlinson (1990) *Multicultural Education in white schools*

11   ibid, p 7

12   ibid

13   for instance she uses phrases such as "non-white fellow pupils" and "non-white minorities" (p 7); "people who are not white" to refer to black people (p 19); "non-white people" (p 16); "non-white minorities" (p 169); "non-white people" (p 171); "non-white world" (p 172).

14   except Tomlinson and Coulson (1988) *Education for a Multi-Ethnic Society*

15   Although the co-ordinator of the Bedford Education Support Grant Project was black, the project was evaluated by a white academic, Dr Mal Leicester

16   Tomlinson, op cit, pp 14-15

17   quoted in Tomlinson, op cit, p 15

18   ibid, p 15

19   Troyna and Hatcher (1992), *Racism in Children's Lives*

20   Select committee: vol III, House of Commons Report No 405, 1973

21   Townsend and Brittan (1973) *Schools Council Working Paper 50: Multicultural Education - Need and Innovation*

22   Quoted in Page and Thomas (1984) *Multicultural Education and the all-white school*

23   *Education in schools: A Consultative Document*, Cmnd 6869, HMSO, 1977, para 10.11

24   Little and Willey (1981) *Multicultural Education, the way forward*

25   ibid, p 28, in an address to the Commission for Racial Equality's Conference on Education for a Multicultural Society, given by Baroness Young, quoted in the DES Press Notice, 19 April 1980.

26   Their report is reproduced in Swann, pp 229-314, ibid note 5 above

27   Rampton (1981) *West Indian Children in our schools*

28   Swann Report, pp 229-314

29   Gaine (1987) *No Problem Here*

30   ibid, p 86

31   Perspectives 42, *The Struggle is my life*, July 1990, p 84

32   Taylor (1990) *Perspectives 42*

33   See for instance, the articles by Mould and Davey in *Multicultural Teaching*, Vol 4 No 5 Summer 1986

34   see for instance *Multicultural Teaching*, Vol 5, No 2, Spring 1987

35   Swann Report, p 36

36   Tomlinson, op cit, p 19

37   Roger I Cartwright, " "No problem here" - multicultural education in the all-white school", *Multicultural Teaching*, Vol 5, No 2, Spring 1987

38   Tomlinson, op cit, p 19

39   ibid

40   ibid, p 20

41   ibid

42   AMMA (1987), *Multi-cultural and Anti-racist Education Today*

43   Brown, et al,(1990) *Spanner in the Works*, op cit

44 Tomlinson, op cit, p 21
45 Foreword to *Charter 90 for Asians* Published by the Confederation of Indian Organisations, nd
46 Flew (1987) *Power to the Parents* - see particularly chapters 2 and 5.
47 Lewis (1988) *Anti-Racism: A Mania Exposed* : see particularly chapter 9.
48 see for example: Monica J Taylor (1988) *Worlds Apart* and Amin, Fernandes and Gordon (1988) *Racism and Discrimination in Britain - a select bibliography 1984-87*
49 Rampton (1981) *West Indian Children in our schools*
50 Swann (1985) *Education for All*, Chapter 15, pp 733-738
51 Sarup (1991) *Education and the Ideology of Racism*
52 Troyna and Carrington (1990) *Education, Racism and Reform*
53 Verma and Pumfrey (1988) *Educational Attainments*
54 Todd (1991) *Education in a Multicultural Society*
55 Troyna and Hatcher (1992) *Racism in Children's Lives*
56 see for example Landry (1987) *The Black Middle Class*
57 Todd, op cit, p 99
58 Chivers (1987) *Race and Culture in Education*
59 Troyna and Hatcher, op cit, p 195
60 Figueroa (1991) *Education and the Social Construction of "race"*
61 Fyfe and Figueroa (1993) *Education for cultural diversity: the challenge for a new era*
62 Tomlinson (1992) "Disadvantaging the disadvantaged: Bangladeshis and education in Tower Hamlets", *British Journal of Sociology of Education*, Vol 13, No 4 pp 437-446
63 Foster (1992) "Teacher attitudes and Afro-Caribbean educational attainment", *Oxford Review of Education*, Vol 18, No 3, pp 269-282

5 Terminology

The previous chapter gave an impression of the wide range of material that is published in the name of multicultural education and antiracist education. Details of the relevant literature in three sections - Education Support Grant Projects, the all-white sector and the underachievement of black pupils - showed that there is a paucity of material in the first section, while there is a relatively small amount on the all-white sector, but there is an abundance of writing on the underachievement of black pupils.

In this chapter some of the key words used in the course of the book are discussed and defined.

As we have seen, the debate about multicultural education and antiracist education is lively, diverse and on-going; it is surrounded with controversy where a wide range of differing views are strongly held and often vigorously expressed. A whole book of essays on multicultural eduction is sub-titled "the interminable debate". [1] Lewisham College in London recently employed the services of Bernie Grant, Labour MP for Tottenham to launch their anti-racist policy. [2] On the other hand, there is a school of thought that suggests that the debate between multicultural education and antiracist education "has become a sterile one." [3] However, as was shown in the previous chapter on the literature review, this is far from the truth. Although the National Curriculum in general, and the draft proposals in particular, published in May 1994 by the School Curriculum and Assessment Authority following the recommendations of Dearing Report for drastic streamlining of the National Curriculum, has been a negative effect on the impact of multicultural education and antiracist education as issues which are actively discussed, the debate in my view will be an important issue for many decades to come.[4]

"Race" as a concept is often a very emotive issue - educationalists find the topic rather difficult to discuss rationally or objectively. Thus

I think it is crucial that terms which are likely to cause confusion or are unclear and ambiguous are well defined. The terms defined here are clarified in the specific way that I wish to use them.

Black

As Avtar Brah points out, "over the past few years the usage of the term "black" to refer to people of African-Caribbean and South Asian descent in Britain has been the subject of considerable controversy." [5] She goes on to provide a discussion of the different uses of the term. However, I would like to confine myself to the following comments for the purposes of this book.

I should say at the beginning that the term "black" is used in preference to "ethnic minorities" because it serves to make multicultural education and antiracist education political issues and not marginal ones. However, some of the time both terms are used. My use of the term "black" includes all people living in Britain who suffer discrimination because they are readily identified by the colour of their skin. Thus people originating from the Indian subcontinent, China, Japan, Vietnam, Africa, Turkey and the West Indies are included in the term "black". Some writers have limited the term black to include only Asian and African-Caribbean peoples. [6]

Visible minorities

The Irish and the Jewish population who happen to be white are not included because they do not constitute the group that has been termed the "visible minorities". This term, visible minorities, is increasingly used by black people, especially by the minority press like the *Asian Times* and the *Caribbean Times* as well as bodies such as the Commission for Racial Equality. [7] "Visible minorities" as a term to define ethnic minorities who are not white is useful because it distinguishes black people from other groups such as the Jews and the Irish who too face discrimination because of their race. However, one cannot readily identify a Jewish person by their appearance only, unless of course they are dressed in traditional orthodox Jewish clothes. One can only identify an Irish person by their accent - and accents can be changed through elocution lessons and practice. Thus it is possible for these two ethnic minority groups to become "invisible": this luxury is not possible for black people. I have elsewhere stressed that there are black people who are Jewish and it must be remembered that there are black people in

Ireland. [8]

Culture

It has been pointed out that if one uses the term "culture" as an analytical concept, as is the case for the purpose of this book, then it is unlikely that "one will ever be able to fix on just one definition that will do for all occasions".[9] There are all sorts of "culture" - middle-class culture, working-class culture, gender culture, youth culture, street culture, school culture, intellectual culture, bacterial culture, agri-culture, and so on. Clearly the term is multi-discursive and that it can be used in any number of contexts. For instance, in the case of school culture, we have this definition from Bob Wild:

> It is possible to regard the school as a small society which manifests many of the features of a wider society outside. Such a perspective calls attention to the structure of the school, its formal and informal organization, hierarchies, as well as the values, norms, rules traditions, ceremonials and so forth, which constitute the school culture.[10]

In the context of multicultural education and antiracist education, culture has specific meanings. It is generally agreed that culture is something that black people have which is somehow different to the culture of the white majority. Not only is this ethnic minority culture different, it is also perceived to be inferior. Moreover, it is something that has been imported from abroad. Culture, in educational terms, usually refers to the religion, diet and language of black pupils. [11] Further, black pupils are somehow seen to be "disadvantaged" because of their "inferior" cultural heritage. Further, culture is "never fixed, finished or final. It is fluid, it is actively and continually made and re-made."[12] My use of the word "culture" is specific to the interpretation afforded by teachers and as used in the classroom. As I discuss below in the notes, others, notably Edward Said, use "culture" in a wider context but again defined to suit their own purposes.

Multicultural

"Multi" by definition is "many"; thus multicultural education encompasses the many cultures found in Britain today. Multicultural education first came to be expressed as an educational term as a reaction to the presence of black children in English schools. The accompanying demographic changes that occurred in Britain as a result of the post-war immigration which resulted as a result of labour shortage after the Second World War. Part of the British policy at this time was to recruit black workers from the West Indies to come to Britain, the Mother Country, on the busses and the National Health Service. Also, the post war expansion and full-employment stage resulted in the white working class masses no longer doing the menial jobs as they moved on to more white collar jobs.

Roy Jenkins in 1966 set the context of multicultural education which included notions not of assimilation but equal opportunity which was accompanied by cultural diversity in an atmosphere of mutual tolerance. Jenkins' speech was instrumental in placing multicultural education on the educational agenda and also give the notion political currency. No attempt had been made by Jenkins, or his critics, to define the terms which he used - there was no agreed definition of "assimilation", "integration", "equal opportunity", or indeed "cultural diversity". The word "integration" is much used nowadays to highlight the fact that the black community has yet to be "integrated" into British society (after 40 years of significant immigration into this country). It is still common to hear people refer to black British citizens as "fourth generation *immigrants* (emphasis added)".[13] Integration has in reality meant that the black people have had to take on the values of white British people. On a pragmatic level, this has meant, for instance, Sikh boys and men cutting off their hair and shaving off their beards in an effort to "integrate" into British society.

The term "multicultural" has been used by teachers and other practitioners often without any attempt at any definition: it has been the practice to assume that the reader will deduce the meaning implied through the context. However, it becomes clear that the agreed usage, in one sense, is that the term refers to black people, or to be more precise, "multicultural" refers to the presence of black children in British schools. In common parlance, or in common use, "multicultural" schools or "multicultural" curriculum has been taken to mean issues to do with black people - in the former, "multicultural school" is used to mean that there are black children at that school; in the latter example, "multicultural curriculum" the taken for granted meaning is that the curriculum in some way encompasses content which are not ethnocentric and there is reference to cultures other than British. For instance, in a multicultural English curriculum, texts by non-British and black writers would be studied - or there might be a separate course which would include books by black authors.

The terms "multicultural", "multiethnic", and "multiracial" are often used interchangeably. This is clear if one examines some journals which employ these in their titles. For example, *Multicultural Teaching*, *Multicultural Education Review* (Birmingham), *Multi-Ethnic Education Review* (ILEA), and the now defunct *Multi-racial Education* (National Union of Teachers). The contents of these journals makes clear that the focus of these publications is black pupils in British schools - or in rare cases the impact of black people in all-white schools.[14]

Attempts have been made to define multicultural education be various writers. Verma[15] suggests that multicultural education as a term has blind-alley implications which do not only take us away from moral and social realities, but directs us towards conceptual confusion. Parekh[16] maintains that multicultural education has gained considerable currency in Britain in the past decade, and has become a subject of acute controversy. He goes on to highlight the political aspects of multicultural education be suggesting that for the conservative critic, multicultural education "represents an attempt to politicize education in order to pander to minority demands, whereas fro some radicals it is the familiar ideological device of perspective the reality of racist exploitation of ethnic minorities by pampering to their cultural sensitivities".[17] One begins to appreciate that multicultural education can serve any view that one wishes.

Phillips-Bell[18] attempted to break down the phrase into two separate and discrete parts: "multicultural" and "education". He suggests that given the variety of possible definitions of "culture" the lack of simple or universally agreed definition of "multicultural education" is hardly surprising. He goes on to define multicultural education as education "through" many cultures, and both substantive and procedural elements of education are included.

For some, multicultural education is simply "good education".[19] This is now the stance taken for antiracist education. Other practitioners hold the view that multicultural education is only relevant for children in inner-city areas, that multicultural education was only applicable when black children were part of the school intake. As we have seen this view is still the dominant one in all-white schools.[20] Jeffcoate[21] maintains that multicultural education is important for ethnic minority children because it was good for their self-image, their self-esteem, multicultural education made the children feel good about their backgrounds and their cultural heritage. This "positive image" was directly related to the educational performance of black children. Multicultural education would give black children emotional security and self-respect and thus enable effective learning to take place. The argument goes something like this: if we are to educate black children properly we must incorporate the relevant cultures into the school syllabuses so that black children did not feel excluded. The role of racism in society is generally ignored in this model - effective learning cannot take place if the black child is preoccupied with the fear that s/he will be attacked on the way home.[22]

Yet another stance is that multicultural education is a moral obligation which must be used for the greater happiness and fullness of black children and had the notion that teachers were doing their bit for equal opportunities. Again, this approach was confined generally to inner-city schools where the presence of black children was greatest. It was felt that a moral stance was part and parcel of the effort that schools must undertake for the sake of better "race relations" in Britain. However, this perspective did not lead to any great curriculum innovation - in fact a moral stance was rejected by the MacDonald enquiry into the racist murder of 11 year old Ahmed Ullah in an inner-city school in Manchester.[23]

Cole [24] provides a useful summary of the historical context of multicultural education and draws out some important issues which it will be useful to examine here in some detail. Cole maintains that traditionally multicultural education has been seen as teaching about other cultures, thereby implying that white culture is the norm. This would in some way instill "respect for such cultures by white indigenous children and improving the self-image of non-white immigrant and indigenous children...generating tolerance and understanding *between* (original emphasis) minority groups." [25] Bad multicultural education has been described by Troyna as covering the three S's - steel band, saris and samosas - music, clothes and food, thereby taking on board the three most important aspects of a culture.

We have seen above that there is no one agreed meaning of multicultural education. What is clear is that multicultural education is concerned with black children. In educational terms it can be asserted that multicultural education is about the celebration of cultures other than "British" (whatever that is, but generally accepted to be white, Christian, middle-class values). Often these notions of "other" cultures are added on to the general school syllabus - for example, schools claim to be practising multicultural education when they include assemblies on Diwali or the Chinese New Year. Or if steel bands are developed and set up as an alternative to the school's orchestra. Or if the home economics department undertakes some lessons on cooking "exotic" foods such as curries, pitta bread, and so on. Indeed, it is often perceived that the ethnic minority groups enriched British culture by importing their own cultures with them. However, it is often forgotten that Britain has always been a pluralist country. As Fryer points out in this opening sentence: "There were Africans in Britain before the English came here." [26]

For the purposes of this book, multicultural education is taken to include issues such as celebration of world cultures, particularly those cultures found within the school population. Further, a multicultural education curriculum is one that includes mention of cultures other than "British". Parekh acknowledges that good education, which incorporates a multicultural perspective, is concerned with knowledge about different social groups, different religions, different values and different attitudes, in the context of the educational knowledge that makes up the whole curriculum.[27] However, it must be remembered that a multicultural curriculum can be delivered in a racist way and that the mere inclusion of a multicultural perspective does not mean that racist stereotypes are not reinforced. Indeed it is often the case that racist stereotypes are reinforced by a "bad" multicultural education. For curriculum that refers to equality of opportunity an antiracist education perspective is essential. It is to this that I now turn.

Antiracist education

Anti-racism grew out of a critique of multicultural education in the early 1980s mainly as a result of the dissatisfaction of the radical left practitioners who felt that multicultural education, far from challenging racist stereotypes and challenging racism was reinforcing racist stereotypes and widening the gap between black and white children in schools. Where there were no black pupils, as is the case in the majority of British schools, multicultural education was found to be reinforcing the mistaken notion that white people were/ are superior to black people. Visits to places of worship, such as mandirs, although enjoyed by the children as a day out and a break in routine, had the effect of reinforcing racist stereotypes. For instance, pupils often came away from these visits thinking that black people were somehow "odd" and not merely different in their own right. For example, the concept of many gods found in a mandir was a difficult concept for some white pupils to accept, particularly as Christianity is a monotheist religion. Following a visit to a mosque, children were overheard to say to each other that they could not understand the need to pray five times a day to God. Often these visits are not properly contextualised for the pupils. These visits are often "bolted on" to the regular curriculum, as a token gesture to multicultural education. When a visit to a mandir, for example, is not preceded and followed by discussions surrounding other issues such as the location of the mandir, the reasons for doors being heavily padlocked, the reasons for racist graffiti on the walls, or the historical context of the presence of black people in Britain, then the whole venture becomes meaningless as a learning exercise from an anti-racist point of view. This is not to deny the acknowledgement, acceptance and celebration of cultures other than "British" is not important, but when superficial visits lead to reinforcing entrenched racist views, then multicultural education as educational philosophy has to be questioned. As Ambalvaner Sivanandan, the Director of the Institute of Race Relations, so eloquently puts it:

> Now, there is nothing wrong with multiracial or multicultural education as such: it is good to learn about other races, about other people's cultures. It may even help to modify individual attitudes, correct personal biases. But that, as we stated in our evidence to the Rampton Committee on Education, is merely to tinker with educational methods and techniques and leave unaltered the whole racist structure of the educational system. And education itself comes to be seen as an adjustment process within a racist society and not as a force for changing the values that make that society racist. "Ethnic minorities" do not suffer "disabilities" because of "ethnic differences" - as the brief of the Rampton Committee suggests - but because such differences are given a differential weightage in a racist hierarchy. Our concern, we pointed out, was not with multi-cultural, multi-ethnic education but with anti-racist education, which by its very nature would include the study of other cultures. Just to learn about other people's cultures is not to learn about the racism of one's own. To learn about the racism of one's own culture, on the other hand, is to approach other cultures objectively.[28]

Increasingly, the discourse has shifted from multicultural education to antiracist education. As Cole has observed, "In the 1960s government rhetoric excluded anti-racism, the new offensive seems to include anti-racist education as part of the package." [29]

Antiracist education is inherently tied in with the notion of justice and equality. Antiracist education means the development of an education service from which racism, sexuality, gender, disability and class discrimination and prejudice have been eliminated so that schools can respond fully to the needs of our multi-racial society.

Indigenous

Often "indigenous" is used to describe white people in multicultural education and antiracist education discourse. However, this is misleading because black people in places such as Bristol, Cardiff and Liverpool have been living in Britain for more than four generations. I would question the notion of "indigenous" to refer to white people. How long must people have lived in this country before they become indigenous? I would argue that black people too are indigenous, not merely "British". This mental shift is necessary if "British" is to be inclusive, rather than exclusive as is sometimes the case, of black people. Rather than refer to black people as "immigrants" or "second generation immigrants", as black people born in this country are often perceived to be, as we saw above, they should be called indigenous.

One of the few people to use in "indegenous" in its proper and right meaning is Anita Roddick when she talks about the "indeginous tribes" of the rainforests of Brazil. She also refers to the indeginous population as "locals" and not "natives" as is usually the case.[30]

Summary

In this chapter, I have looked at some of the key words and phrases which I felt may cause confusion if not defined clearly and concisely. "Race" is an emotive and sensitive areas of research, particularly in all-white schools, where staff do not generally see the relevance of multicultural education and antiracist education because there aren't any black pupils on the school roll. Thus the following words are discussed and defined in a particular way to serve the deliberations in this book: black, visible minorities, culture, multicultural, anti-racist education, indigenous.

Notes

1. Modgill, S et al (1988), *Multicultural Education - The Interminable Debate*
2. *Education,* Volume 177, No 17, April 26 (Cover) 1993
3. Burt, S (1987) *Multicultural and anti-racist policies*, unpublished PhD dissertation, University of London
4. The Dearing Report, 1994
5. Avtar Brah (1992) "Difference, diversity and differentiation", in Donald and Rattansi, *"Race", Culture and Difference*
6. see for instance, Mac an Ghaill (1988), *Young, Gifted and black*, p 156, note 1.
7. Sheffield CRC (1988) (nd) *Because the Skin is black*, Sheffield City Council, see also unpublished essay by Tuku Mukerjee "Black - an evolving political colour"
8. *New Beacon*, April 1992
9. O'Sullivan, et al (1989) *Key Concepts in Communication*
10. in Stenhouse, et al, *Teaching about race relations*, p 21
11. J Gundara, et al, *Racism, Diversity and Education*
12. Paul Gilroy (1992) "The end of antiracism", in Donald and Rattansi (op cit). See also the specific definition of culture as used by Edward W. Said (1993) when he says that "cultures are humanly made structures of both authority and participation, benevolent in what they include, incorporate, and validate, less benevolent in what they exclude and demote", *Culture and Imperialism*, p 15. For Said "culture" means two things in particular - firstly, "all those practices, like the arts of description, communication, and representation, that have relative autonomy from the economic, social, and political realms..." and secondly, "a concept that includes a refining and elevating element, each society's reservoir of the best that has been known and thought..." (pp xii and xiii) My own use of the word is very much governed by the use made at classroom level and differs markedly from Said's definition. I raise these point here to illustrate the contemporary currency of the term "culture" and also to show the diverse meanings of the concept.
13. *Any Questions*, BBC Radio Four, 9 June 1991
14. *Multicultural Teaching*, Volume 4, No 3 Summer 1986 devoted to multicultural issues in the North East of England, mainly Tyne and Wear
15. Verma (1988) "Issues in Multicultural Education" in Verma and

Pumfrey (Eds), *Educational Attainments*

16   Parekh (1988) ,"The Concept of Multicultural Education" in Modgil (op cit)
17   Parekh op cit, p 19
18   Phillips-Bell (1981) "Multicultural Education: what is it?" in *Multicultural Education*, Volume 10, No 1, Autumn 1981
19   Parekh (1988) op cit
20   See chapter four on literature review on all-white schools. Also, Chris Gaine (1987) *No Problem Here*
21   Jeffcoate (1979): *Positive Image*
22   *Murder in the Playground* (1989); see also the CRE reports *Learning in Terror* and *Living in Terror*; and Troyna and Hatcher (1992)
23   *Murder in the Playground* (1989) op cit
24   Cole M (1988) "Teaching and learning about racism: a critique of multicultural education in Britain"; in Modgil, et al, op cit
25   Cole, op cit, p 124
26   Fryer P (1987) *Staying Power*, p 1
27   Parekh, op cit
28   *Race and Class* Vol XXV, No 2 Autumn 1983
29   Cole, op cit, p 127
30   Anita Roddick *Body and Soul*, for instance, p 197 and 293

6 Methodology

There is no agreed way of going about classroom research and the choice will rest on both practical and philosophical criteria.[1]

There is no single way of doing research in the classroom. The methods employed will depend to a large extent on the skills of the teacher, the nature of the research problem and the resources available.[2]

In the previous chapter the legislation leading to the funding for Education Support Grant projects dealing with multicultural education and antiracist education in all-white schools was provided. This was then followed by brief demographic details of the two projects with a description of the initial activities at classroom level.

This chapter is divided into two discrete sections - the first section deals with the theoretical aspects of action research, while the second section describes in brief the process which was carried out during the investigation for this book. Details of case studies and the pupil survey are found in chapters eight and nine.

Arguments are presented for choosing action research as the methodology for the case studies into curriculum development which form the basis of this book. Having established that action research is the best suited method for the investigation, I go on to define action research and the various elements, such as surveys, questionnaires and triangulation, which I employed during my time on the two Education Support Grant projects. I also examine some of the problems attendant with action research.

Educational research

As the methods of educational research are many and diverse, it was important to review some established methods of educational research before choosing one that suited this particular book. Educational research has been defined as a structured scientific inquiry about an educational question that provides an answer which contributes to increasing the body of generalizable knowledge about educational concerns.[3] As mentioned in the Introduction, a longitudinal study was felt to be impractical because of the time factor involved - a period of eight years for the two projects before any evaluation could meaningfully be conducted. It may have been possible to conduct evaluation on one project, along the lines of the Bedford Local Education Authority's Education Support Grant project in all-white schools which was evaluated by Mal Leicester, but this would mean that comparisons between the two projects would be lost.[4] As I am perhaps the only advisory teacher to have worked on two Education Support Grant projects dealing with multicultural education and antiracist education in all-white schools, it would have been a pity not to have utilised this experience. Hence another research method, besides a traditional and conventional evaluation one, had to be sought.

My background in the "race" field as co-ordinator and advisory teacher for multicultural and antiracist education in secondary and primary schools led me to look at Stenhouse's (et al) book *Teaching about race relations*.[5] This in turn led me to look at Stenhouse's earlier seminal work on action research, *An introduction to curriculum research and development*.[6] A reading of these two books led me to the conclusion that action research was perhaps ideally suited for this book as it contained many of the elements that were planned for the two projects. However, it was essential to conduct further research into the areas of action research methodology before I was fully convinced that this was the right method for the investigation proposed.

Why choose action research for this book?

Before I go on to discuss the various merits and reasons for choosing action research as methodology for this book, it will be useful to remind ourselves of the overall position regarding Education Support Grant projects dealing with multicultural education and antiracist education in all-white schools. To summarise what we gleaned in the review of relevant literature on Education Support Grant projects dealing with multicultural education and antiracist education in all-white areas, only a handful of studies have been devoted to Education Support Grant projects on multicultural education and antiracist education in all-white schools.[7] The few that are available are either devoted to the primary sector or the secondary sector, rarely both, with the exception of Tomlinson and Coulson who provide a descriptive analysis of twenty-six Education Support Grant projects located in primary and secondary schools.[8] As already noted, this report was privately published by Tomlinson, as she was unable to find any publisher interested in the research in 1989. Tomlinson has since published a book bringing together some of the relevant literature with the work done for the earlier report.[9] Saran Jeet Shan gives an account of the work she conducted in Birmingham secondary schools, focusing on Mathematics and Science.[10] Epstein and Sealey's[11] work is concerned with the primary sector, while the work in Bedford is a description of the project at secondary level.[12] None of these studies use action research as a method of investigation, most are descriptive and anecdotal. Furthermore, none of these projects examine the problems and issues of the *process of implementing* multicultural education and antiracist education in all-white schools across the age-range. This book is, therefore, an attempt to fill the gap by examining the problems and issues surrounding curriculum development at classroom level across the whole age-range, from primary through to secondary. I was fortunate in that I worked across the age-range - from nursery to primary to secondary.[13]

The present book focuses on three subject areas, English, Mathematics and Home Economics. The first two are Core Subjects within the National Curriculum, while the third has been relegated to a "non-subject" in so far as it has been incorporated into the Technology document of the National Curriculum. In fact the new National Curriculum draft proposals (published May 1994), what used to be called home economics has been allocated a single page. It is placed within the Design and Technology document and is called "Food Technology". So far as multicultural education is concerned, there is a mention of the word "culture" in the opening sentence of the Designing skills section. The sentence reads: " Pupils should be taught that food choice is affected by nutrition, culture, availability and cost." (p 23) There is also mention of "different population groups" and the needs of specific user groups". There is no hint here of an antiracist education approach to Home Economics.

In both Education Support Grant projects to be studied for this book, detailed case study materials have been collected, including notes on lessons taught, observations of class room interaction, content analysis of pupils written work, including evaluation notes made by the pupils after completion of lessons or schemes of work as relevant, as well notes on teacher discussions, which included teacher evaluation, both verbal and written. In the case of verbal evaluation, field notes were kept by the researcher. Some of this material is to be found in the appendix.

Part of the research method includes the following elements: field notes, lesson plans, pre-intervention negotiations, discussions with head teachers, heads of departments, both pre- and post-lesson evaluation, observations (both first and second hand), verbal and written evaluation from children, teachers and head teachers, and surveys in the form of questionnaires.

Before I go on to discuss how the various elements of action research will be used in this book, it is pertinent to define action research.

What is action research?

Action research is distinguished from other educational research by two factors: first, it is carried out by teachers themselves rather than being research carried out on teachers by outsiders; and second, its results are fed back directly into the classroom so that immediate action can be taken if the teacher/researcher feels that it is appropriate.[14] It becomes apparent, then, that action research is a practical method of research which can influence the direction of curriculum development in the light of any decisions reached through the investigation. As one of the main aims of the two Education Support Grant projects under consideration here is to provide an avenue for curriculum development, action research seems to be an appropriate mode of research for this book.

Action research as a model for educational investigation has been a key feature in number of major projects. For instance, the Ford Teaching project, the Teacher Pupil Interaction and the Quality of Learning Project, the Teaching, Handling Information and Learning Project, and Pupil Autonomy in Learning with Microcomputers which involves teachers in thirty schools in Cambridgeshire, Essex and Norfolk all use action research as a method for educational research. A considerable amount of action research has been carried out by teachers studying for Advanced Diplomas and Higher Degrees. Other studies have been carried out by teachers working either alone or in small groups, supported by organisations such as the Classroom Network or by higher education institutions.[15] Thus one can see that this method of educational research is an established one and ideally suited for the present book. However, as we have already noted, none of the Education Support Grant projects concerning multicultural education and antiracist education in all-white schools have used action research in their publications.

Hopkins and Antes have stated that "Action research is a tool of curriculum development used for the study of local problems to guide, correct, and evaluate educational decisions and actions."[16]

Cohen and Manion helpfully identify four tangible features of action research: situational, collaborative, participatory and self-evaluative. Drawing a distinction between applied research and action research, they go on to conclude that action research "interprets the scientific method much more loosely, chiefly because its focus is a specific problem in a specific setting. The emphasis is not so much on obtaining generalizable scientific knowledge as on precise knowledge for a particular situation and purpose."[17] Thus, it would appear that action research as a method of investigation lends itself naturally to the two Education Support Grant projects under consideration for this book.

The list of eight items below shows a range of possible kinds of action research:

1   spur to action
2   personal functioning, human relations and morale
3   job analysis
4   organisational change
5   planning and policy-making
6   innovation and change
7   problem-solving
8   theoretical knowledge.[18]

Action research is important because it enables teachers to participate directly in curriculum research and development. Stenhouse defines the central problem of curriculum study as "the gap between our ideas and aspirations and our attempts to operationalise them...The gap can be closed by adopting a research and development approach to one's own teaching, whether alone or in a group of co-operating teachers".[19]

Thus, in line with Stenhouse, I would argue that the curriculum received by children is wholly dependant on the teachers who deliver it; and involving teachers in action research is one of the most effective ways of closing the gap between aspiration and practice and ensuring that real curriculum development takes place. Within action research, curriculum development, professional development of teachers and research are combined in a single process.

Curriculum development

Curriculum development is central to the philosophy underpinning both Education Support Grant projects under consideration here.[20]   Both Education Support Grant projects were designed to be collaborative work with several teachers, working with the researcher in a team-teaching situation. All of the work described in the case studies was undertaken in someone else's classroom and thus it was important to build up a collaborative partnership with several teachers.   seems to enable collaborative partnerships to develop.

Since "the majority of action research projects in education are, or have been, concerned with the curriculum" it seems that the choice of action research for this book is an appropriate one. [21]

Action research as collaborative process

Action research is essentially a collaborative process and therefore of particular interest in combating the professional isolation of teachers; this is particularly important when so-called controversial issues such as "race" are involved. Although the researcher is the practitioner, it has been found that an outsider can be crucially important as an assistant, or facilitator, to the research process. At its simplest level this is because there is a problem in being a participant observer in social interaction if their role in the interaction is a central one.   Most of the famous participant observation studies have allowed the researcher to cast herself/himself in the role of a naive member of the group, able to spend a considerable part of the time collecting information.[22] This is not the case for this particular book as the researcher played a central role in curriculum development as well as class room delivery of the teaching material.

Action research presupposes that social interaction is highly complex and problematic. It recognizes that much human activity consists of ritualized patterns of behaviour in order to free the attention to grapple with what presents itself. Hence, while we are concentrating hard on something else, we may walk or drive home, without any real consciousness of where we are or what we are doing, indeed, we may have meant to go somewhere quite different! Action research identifies in these ritualised patterns the reason for the well-documented failure of many curriculum development projects to bring about real change in teaching style or teacher behaviour. It is predominantly concerned with re-examining the minutiae of social interaction and bringing about change. Teachers engaged in action research examine their practice to identify the actual (as opposed to intended) outcomes of behaviour; and then take action to minimize the inevitable mismatch they have identified.

Therefore, action research provides an ideal methodology for collaboration between the regular class teacher and a support/advisory teacher, in this case the researcher. An action research approach ensures the establishment of the right conditions for building the relationship essential for professional development to take place. At the same time, the presence of two teachers in the same classroom opens up obvious possibilities for collaborative action research and enquiry. There is a symbiotic link.[23]

The first phase of the action research is information or data gathering. This may range from the following range of possibilities:

(a)   A ten minute observation period, taking notes (during which time all responsibility for teaching will be taken by the other partner)

(b)   Interviews with students (either alone, in pairs, or in a group...probably lasting between ten minutes and half an hour);

(c)   Detailed analysis of a student's written work from photocopies;

(d)   A video recording of a lesson (to act as a focus for discussion later...between the two teachers...or involving the students...or with parents);

(e)   An audio tape recording (to be played back several times and then short extracts of particular interest transcribed to act as a focus of discussion);

(f)   A series of photographs (to be used in a similar way to the video film).

Clearly not all of the above have been used during the research for this book. As a beginning, classroom observation was utilised. Permission was obtained record a science lesson on video, but I have not had the time to analyze this. Photographs were taken in several subject areas to illustrate good practice for dissemination in the LEA concerned.

It was recognised early on that some heads and teachers were ambivalent about the contribution that enabling teams, in this case the researcher, might make to their schools. They recognised the value of extra help in developing aspects the practice to which they were committed but were concerned that selection to take part in the project singled them out as in some way failing or ineffectual. Thus they were somewhat apprehensive about the prospect of having the work of their pupils or their methods of teaching placed under scrutiny. This meant that the researcher sometimes had difficulty in establishing effective relationships in some schools, and thus some planned curriculum development did not take place. As exemplified in the next chapter in our discussion of case studies, a prime example of this is the Mathematics Department at school B in London.

However, it was recognised that the head teachers played a central role in the success or failure of the curriculum work undertaken. As Mary James and Dave Ebbutt to point out:

> The role of the Head was crucial. The Head was obviously concerned to have sight of all communication with the world outside the school, but having been consulted at an early stage and having cleared the questionnaire, he took no further part.[24]

It will be important here to remember that the head teachers in all the schools concerned will have to be kept informed at all stages of the project as it is likely that objections may be raised by parents particularly as controversial issues may be raised during the implementation of the projects.

I would argue that co-operative action research, where the researcher and class teacher work together as a team, is the most profitable, and the present book can be seen in this light in so far as the researcher works alongside the class teacher in implementing multicultural education and antiracist education curriculum development. Hill and Kerber define co-operative research in the following terms:

> Action research functions best when it is co-operative action research. This method incorporates the ideas and expectations of all persons involved in the situation. Co-operative action research has the concomitants of beneficial effects for workers, and the improvement of the services, conditions, and functions of the

situation. In education this activity translates into more practice in research and problem-solving by teachers, administrators, pupils, and certain community personnel, while the quality of teaching and learning is in the process of being improved.[25]

The principal justification for the use of action research in the context of the school is improvement of practice - that is curriculum development through the implementation of multicultural education and antiracist education initiatives.

Teacher-researcher and simultaneous integrated forms of action research also have attractions for feminist researchers because of the way that equality between researchers and practitioners is built into the project.[26] I would suggest that the same arguments can be put forward for a black perspective, in so far as there is mutual trust and co-operation between the teacher and the researcher. It is proposed, therefore, to extend this aspect of action research and provide a black perspective in the concluding chapter.

Case studies

As already mentioned, case studies formed the main component of looking at the process of implementing multicultural education and antiracist education curriculum development in all-white schools. These case studies included classroom observation, unstructured interviews and documentary evidence (e.g. bids, memos) were the main methods of social investigation used for this book.

Proformas were developed for both projects to record the work undertaken, especially for keeping detailed field notes of planning sessions with teachers. Examples of these are to be found in the appendix.

Participant observation

As long ago as 1958, Gold outlined four major roles for collecting data by participant observation: complete participant, complete observer, participant observer and observer as participant - the participant role fitted in with the researchers role.[27] To a greater or lesser degree I have utilised all of these roles during my time working on the Education Support Grant projects.

Surveys

The survey is one of the most commonly used descriptive method in educational research.[28] Some of the reasons for this may lie in the fact that the survey is an excellent way of obtaining data in a short period of time - surveys compare well with other methods of investigation such as qualitative methods which "are regarded as lacking "rigour" and presenting problems of reliability and validity"[29] Other researchers have preferred qualitative methods which include participant observation and unstructured interviews.[30] However, it is important to bear in mind what Trow pointed out: "it is not a question of the superiority of one method over another but the appropriateness of a method of investigation for a particular research problem."[31] Thus for this book several methods are used as part of the action research method to obtain as full a picture as possible as we attempt to show that a multicultural approach is easier to implement than an antiracist one.

Cohen and Manion highlight three stages to the design of a survey, and these stages were followed for the pupils survey - purpose of survey, population to be surveyed, and three, resources available.[32]

The second prerequisite to survey design, the specification of the population to be sampled was easier than in some instances. As Cohen and Manion point out: "Often the criteria by which populations are specified are difficult to operationalise".[33] However, in our case the survey was relatively easy and straightforward to conduct because the pupils were already identified as the cohort group. All that was required was to select which groups of pupils in terms of age range.

A lot of the problems associated with surveys were not relevant for this particular survey because of five factors which were identified. These are, firstly, there were to be no formal interviews - this meant that no formal training was in interview technique was needed; secondly, fieldwork was to be conducted in the school, thereby making the expense of travel negligible, thirdly, the questionnaire was drafted by the researcher and discussed at length at several meetings of the working party during which it was revised, modified and re-written; fourthly, the printing costs were paid for by the school; and lastly, as the questions were open ended, there was no need for computer programming and coding.

Ethical position vis a vis the pupil survey

I would like at this point to return to the problems of our ethical position as teacher-researchers. One may argue that giving control over the research process to participants will result in data loss, if not distortion. I would agree, but feel that in some circumstances ethical considerations must be allowed to override the desire to retain and publish all the data collected. It was thus decided, after lengthy discussions at the Antiracist Working Party meetings, that the pupil questionnaires would be destroyed once the data had been collected. This would also give the pupils a sense of security when filling out the questionnaire and they would not be inhibited about revealing their true feelings about their understanding of racism and racist behaviour. The pupils were assured that their anonymity would be maintained in any report subsequently circulated.

Questionnaires

It has been acknowledged that one of the best ways to collect data in a survey is through a questionnaire for subjects to respond to. Although there are several methods for conducting questionnaires, for example, by post or by telephone, for this book the method of operationalising this proved relatively easy as the questionnaire was to be given to pupils.[34] Also, the questionnaire provides a way to collect personal information from subjects that may not be readily obtainable using other methods. I was interested in ascertaining the level of understanding about "race" issues amongst pupils. Before the questionnaire was devised three important factors had to be taken into account:

1   The questions must be definite and clearly presented and generate responses that are definite and quantifiable.
2   The format of the questionnaire must be structured so that the respondent will not miss any item entirely and will have no difficulty in recording a response. It must be composed of a logical sequence of questions.
3   The instructions must be precisely stated so that all ambiguity is eliminated.[35]

Close-ended questions that ask the respondent to choose a response from a provided list will, in most cases, provide, more easily processed date than open-ended questions that permit the respondent to create a response. The response to an open-ended question must be interpreted, thus reducing the reliability of the data.[36]

The questionnaires were self-completion type thereby making

interviews unnecessary. Although some pupils were absent, all those present co-operated by filling in the questionnaire. This was a voluntary exercise and pupils were under no compulsion to fill in the questionnaires. (Some children handed in blanks, thereby effectively lowering the sampling.)

Cohen and Manion advice to avoid open-ended questions on self-completion questionnaires, because they maintain self-completion questionnaires cannot probe the respondent to find out just what s/he means by a particular response, the open-ended question is a less satisfactory way of eliciting information. Also, open-ended questions may be too demanding of most respondents' time.[37]

Having taken these factors into consideration, it was decided to use open-ended questions for two main reasons. One, because of the nature of the enquiry, and, secondly, because I wanted to elicit in as precise a way as possible what the pupils understood by racism, and related issues. Questions further in the questionnaire gave ample opportunity for respondents to give examples of what they perceived as racism.

The main objective of the pupil survey was to inform curriculum development. The Antiracist Working Party was fully involved in the design of the survey, as it was important to get their full co-operation prior to conducting the survey; it was assumed that the support of the head teacher would follow if the working party gave their support. This also had the advantage of removing the attention to a single person, in this case the researcher, and the attention could then be directed at a group of people. It was envisaged that there would be objections to the survey and the working party gave some protection to the researcher. This was fortunate because the local press got hold of the story and tried to discredit the work at the school.

In recent years there has been an increase in the popularity of qualitative methods in studying educational problems as reflected in studies of schools, classroom and curricula.[38] Burgess identifies 12 attributes of qualitative research. It will be useful to paraphrase the list here for three reasons. Firstly, they form the theoretical and methodological base of this book, secondly, the conflict between local and central government has been heightened as a result of the introduction of the National Curriculum, and thirdly, the research is based on the premise that there will be curriculum changes because of the intervention of the Education Support Grant projects at class room level. The twelve attributes are present to a greater or lesser degree in this book:

1   The focus is on the observed present, but the findings are contextualized within a social, cultural and historical framework.
2   The research is conducted within a theoretical framework.
3   The research involves close, detailed intensive work in the social situation under study.
4   The major research instrument is the researcher who attempts to obtain a participant's account of the social setting.
5   Unstructured or informal interviews in the form of extended conversations may complement the observational account.
6   Personal documents give depth and background to the contemporary account. It has not been possible to reproduce these here.
7   Different methods of investigation may be used to complement qualitative methods with the result that different methodologies may be integrated as needed.
8   The decisions regarding the collection and analysis of data take place in the field and are products of the enquiry.
9   The researcher attempts to disturb the process of social life as little as possible.
10 The researcher has to consider the audience for whom he or she is producing a report.
11 Research reports disseminate that knowledge which informants have provided without rendering harm to them, taking into account ethical problems that confront the researcher and the researched.
12 The researcher monitors the dissemination of materials and provides feedback to those who have been researched.[39]

Reasons for choosing action research for this book

The strategy chosen for this book was thus derived from a well established model of organizational development taken up by educationalists in this country as a means of promoting change and improving practice. And since the basic, overarching, philosophy of the two Education Support Grant projects was to implement curriculum change to reflect a pluralist society, this seems to fit in well. In line with Stenhouse it is important to restate that one of the aims of action research is to utilise information to collaborate in the process of implementing curriculum change; it is also important to note that teachers themselves will become researchers into their own practice and will thereby own and control their own professional development.[40]

In all cases it is important that the teacher-researcher is prepared to be very tactful with colleagues they will be working with, usually as a guest in the class room. However, it would be misleading to suggest that general support for the research activities was forthcoming in all quarters. Other researchers have faced the same problem. For example, Mary James circulated a questionnaire to sixty-eight staff in the school and received only ten responses. Further, both David Ebbutt and Mary James encountered apathy and scepticism from some of their colleagues, although never active resistance.[41]

Mary James's difficulty in introducing and gaining acceptance for what amounted to an innovation in her school created a need for support from a group such as that which already existed for Dave Ebbutt. Contacts made on the MA course that both Dave Ebbutt and Mary James attended formed the core of this group.[42] In a similar way, I had to seek the active support from colleagues in the Multicultural Development Service in London. In the North East of England, I was a founding member of a black support group which included teachers and other professionals as there were only three black teachers, including myself, in the Borough where the Education Support Grant project was located.

I would agree with Mary James and Dave Ebbutt when they state that they would hesitate to advocate only one methodological approach to insider research. The choice needs to take into consideration the nature of the research problem and the skills of the researcher.[43] However, my personal preference was for qualitative techniques. My reasons for this were various. Some were connected with the degree of statistical sophistication required to make valid and reliable quantitative comparisons. Others more directly concerned the economy of the research task. I was interested in examining the problems of implementing multicultural education and antiracist education approaches in all-white sectors. It was decided that rigorous comparative measures were unlikely to repay the amount of effort needed to develop them. Qualitative methods such as informal interviews, photographs, participant observation, open-ended questionnaires, diaries and original documents provided a rich yet manageable source of data.

Triangulation

Triangulation is defined as the use of two or more methods of data collection in the study of some aspect of human behaviour....Triangulation techniques in the social sciences attempt to map out human behaviour by studying it from more than one standpoint and, in so doing, by making use of both quantitative and qualitative data....If for example, the outcomes of a questionnaire survey correspond to those of an observation of the same phenomena, the researchers will be confident about the findings.[44]

Qualitative research

Qualitative research is distinguished from quantitative research in that quantitative research is concerned with frequency while qualitative research is concerned with abstract characteristics of events. Qualitative researchers maintain that many natural properties cannot be expressed in quantitative terms - indeed, they will lose their reality if expressed simply in terms of frequency.[45]

As Burgess states, "Qualitative research is based upon a fixed set of procedures."[46] The term "qualitative methods" has been used to cover approaches that are claimed to be "soft" and "non-rigorous" compared with the "hard", "objective", "rigorous" approaches that are referred to as qualitative methods.[47]

Having established that action research as a method of investigation is ideally suited as a methodology for this book I now turn to some of the issues and avenues which were explored in terms of curriculum development.

Curriculum development

One of the ways to investigate the proposal that a multicultural approach is easier to implement than an antiracist one is to offer the teachers the two different approaches and access how receptive the teachers are to each of the approaches. This can be done in a number of ways. One of the simplest ways is to see how much actual curriculum development is possible at class-room level. This can be demonstrated through lesson plans, pupil evaluation and so on. Theoretical models of multicultural education and antiracist education were discussed in chapter two, and through curriculum materials which were specifically developed for the two Education Support Grant projects, it is possible to find out whether a multicultural education or antiracist education approach is readily accepted by teachers and pupils.

It is possible to mention in general terms only some of the work here - details of the various curriculum development materials are found in the next chapter, and little would be served by repeating them here.

There are various ways by which the teachers can refuse to include either a multicultural or an antiracist perspective into their subject. For example, in the Mathematics Department at school B, the head of department offered the researcher an open invitation to come and observe his lessons. Observation of lessons went on for over six weeks as can be seen from the field notes. When it was suggested that the Mathematics material was in need of examination vis a vis to look at the multicultural and antiracist content of the syllabus, it was pointed out that the syllabus was dictated by outside bodies such as the public examination boards. When it was suggested that it is possible to change the curriculum to make it more appropriate to a multi-racial society, the head of department reluctantly acceded that this was the case. However, as the field notes and lesson plans undertaken at this school demonstrate, all the work carried out here was of a multicultural nature; no antiracist work was possible.

In the case of the London project, four secondary schools were to be involved in the curriculum development at a detailed level; the work at primary level was confined to the teaching of *The Heartstone Odyssey* by Arvan Kumar which included drama/dance work as well as creative writing and text analysis. Some of this work was carried out through secondary/primary joint collaboration where the top junior children joined with the first years of a secondary school for joint work. Even at the initial stage, when a meeting had been organised by a senior advisor of the borough, only three of the schools sent representatives to this initial meeting. One of the schools clearly indicated that it was not interested in developing antiracist or multicultural learning materials.

In the case of the project in the North East of England, potentially all schools and the college were to be part of the Education Support Grant scheme. In reality, this proved impractical in so far as two advisory teachers could not offer to carry out curriculum development work in all but a small proportion of schools. It was hoped that by producing teaching and learning materials all the schools in the borough would be able to adopt this to their own specific schools and needs.

How the research was conducted

Teachers

Only a brief overview is provided here; further details are to be found

104

in the following two chapters. Little would be served by repeating the discussion here.

By using an action research method of investigation, an analysis of field notes of discussions between the advisory teacher and head teachers, heads of department and classroom teachers concerned, it was possible to ascertain the level of support that multicultural education and antiracist education as educational approaches received at the hands of head teachers, heads of departments in secondary schools and teachers.

Pupils

The pupil survey on racism is one way to access the latent racist views of white pupils. Also, by asking pupils to fill in evaluation forms at the end of a unit of curriculum development, it was possible to see how receptive they have been to multicultural education and antiracist education. Although it has not been possible to provided these here, detailed lesson plans, coupled with post lesson discussions with the teachers concerned and the evaluation notes highlighted the level of acceptance by pupils. Also, as participant researcher, it was possible to engage pupils in discussions of multicultural education and antiracist education in formal and informal situations.

Summary

A detailed account of the theoretical basis of selecting action research as the method of investigation for this book was given to show how and why this particular method was selected, in favour of others. action research was then defined. The merits of various areas of action research - surveys, questionnaires, triangulation, case studies - was discussed and examples of the use of these by other researchers was demonstrated. The actual process used in the investigation was mentioned in brief as details are to be found in chapters eight and nine.

Notes

1   Carol Cummings (199) "Qualitative Research in the Infant Classroom: A personal account" in R G Burgess (Ed) *Issues in educational research : Qualitative Methods*, p 218

2   Nixon J (ed) (1981) *A teachers' guide to action research*

3   Stenhouse L (1977) *An introduction to curriculum research and development*, p 3

4   see chapter four on literature review for fuller details

5   Stenhouse L, G K Verma, R D Wild and J Nixon (1982) *Teaching about race relations*

6   Stenhouse (1977) op cit

7   see chapter four for further details of the relevant literature

8   Tomlinson and Coulson (1988) *Education for a multi-ethnic society*

9   Tomlinson S (1990) *Multicultural education in white schools*

10   Shan S J (1986) unpublished report of the first year of Education Support Grant project in Birmingham

11   Epstein, et al (1990) *Where it matters*

12   Bedford Education Support Grant Project (1989) - Evaluated by Mal Leicester

13   cf Barry Troyna and Libby Selman (1991) *Implementing multicultural and antiracist education in mainly white colleges*

14   Somekh, in Biott (1991) *Semi-Detached Teachers*, p 69

15   ibid

16   Hopkins and Antes (1990) *Educational Research*, p 453

17   Cohen and Manion, *Research Methods in Education*, p 217

18   ibid, pp 218/9

19   Stenhouse (1977) op cit, p 3

20   see chapter six for further details

21   Cohen and Manion (1980) op cit

22   see for instance, the Cambridge Research Project

23   Smoekh, in Biott, op cit, p 74

24   James and Ebutt in Nixon, op cit, p 83

25   Hill and Kerber, in Cohen and Manion, op cit, pp 221/3

26   Sue Scott, "Feminist Research and Qualitative Methods: A Discussion of Some of the Issues" in Burgess R G (Ed), op cit, pp 67-85

27   Gold, quoted in H Burgess,"Case Studies and Curriculum Research: Some Issues for Teacher Researchers" in Burgess, R G (Ed), ibid, note 29, p 180

28   Cohen and Manion, op cit, p 97

29 R G Burgess, *Issues in Education Research: Qualitative Methods*, p 3

30 ibid

31 ibid

32 Cohen and Manion, ibid, note 12, referring to figure on p 98

33 ibid, p 100

34 Hopkins and Antes, op cit, p 258

35 ibid

36 ibid

37 Cohen and Manion, op cit, p 109

38 Burgess, op cit, p 4

39 ibid, pp 4-5

40 Stenhouse (1977), also, McKenna, in Biott, op cit, p 100

41 Mary James and Dave Ebbutt, "Problems and potential", in Nixon, op cit, p 83

42 ibid, p 83

43 ibid, p 82

44 Cohen and Manion, op cit, pp 269/270

45 Kincheloe (1991) *Teachers as researchers*, p 143

46 Burgess, ibid, note 29, p 9

47 ibid, note 25, p 1

7 Demographic details

Background to the Education Support Grant projects

In the previous chapter, the terms which may cause confusion, or are not defined clearly by other researchers, were defined. The terms were defined so that they can be used in this book in a particular way with clarity and precision.

This present chapter is divided into three sections - the first section provides a background to the Education Support Grant Projects related to multicultural education and antiracist education in all-white schools. The second and third sections give brief demographic details of each of the two Education Support Grant projects under consideration for this book. Most of the material is taken from primary sources such as minutes, circulars, reports to the Department of Education and Science, now known as the Department for Education, original bids for funding, and so on. This chapter thus helps to place into context some of the philosophical underpinnings behind the Education Support Grant projects with regard to multicultural education and antiracist education in the all-white sector. It is important to focus on this aspect because the context of multicultural education and antiracist education in all-white schools is markedly different from multicultural education and antiracist education in multi-racial schools. Further, this chapter complements chapter four which is a review of the relevant literature pertaining to multicultural education and antiracist education in all-white schools.

Legislation

Circular 6/84 (issued on 18 July 1984 - a year before the Swann Report was published) first announced extra money available to local education authorities under the Education Support Grant scheme. This was a direct result of the 1984 (Grants and Awards) Act which empowered the Secretary of State to pay such grants to local education authorities. The money for Education Support Grant projects originated from the Department of Education and Science (DES) (now re-named the Department for Education). The aim of the grants was to encourage local education authorities to redeploy a limited amount of expenditure into activities which appeared to the then Secretary of State to be of particular national importance. The first of these grants would be available in the 1985/6 financial year and the Department of Science and Education had set aside the sum of £21 million for this purpose: the proposal stipulated that the local education authority would provide 30 per cent of any scheme approved by the DES while the Department would provide the remaining 70 per cent of costs. This effectively meant that local education authorities could get three teachers for the price of one - a most cost effective way to increase teacher numbers. The Department of Education and Science, with foresight anticipated an increase in spending during 1985/6 from the two combined sources, the DES and the local education authority at £30 million.

One of twelve

There were twelve broad categories under which local education authorities could apply for the Education Support Grant funding: these ranged from the management and appraisal of school teachers, the teaching of Mathematics and Science in the Primary School to Information Technology in non-advanced Further Education. Apart from Section 11 of the 1966 Local Government Act which was set up to assist local authorities with the "problem" of too many "immigrants" (i.e. black people from the New Commonwealth), this was the first time that Central Government had set aside money specifically for multicultural education initiatives in the all-white sector. Section 11 of course could not be used in the all-white schools as the pupils intake in these schools was less than 30 per cent, the figure laid down by the Home Office before funding under Section 11 would be made available. What is of concern to us here is the category entitled "Pilot projects related to educational needs in a Multi-Ethnic Society". Paragraph 32, on pilot projects related to the educational needs in a multi-ethnic society states:

> Grants will be available to support expenditure of up to £1m in 1985/6 on education projects designed to meet the needs of ethnic minority pupils and students, to promote racial harmony, or in

other ways to equip pupils and students for life in a multi-ethnic society. No limit is placed on the scope of the proposals to be put forward by authorities, except that they should neither be eligible for funding from the Home Office under Section 11 of the Local Government Act 1966 nor such as would be likely to attract Urban Programme support. The Secretary of State will give particular priority to well-conceived schemes:

-      which entail practical steps to counter racial harassment and promote greater racial harmony within educational institutions; or
-      which involve raising teacher expectations of ethnic minority pupils; or
-      which support minority groups who, mainly through self-help, wish to maintain their language and culture, and which foster closer links between voluntary agencies and maintained educational provision.

Financial implications

The next paragraph spells out the monetary commitment further:

It is envisaged that some of the projects supported through education support grants will begin in April 1985 and other in September 1985. The expenditure supported on each project is not likely to exceed £40,000 in a full year but authorities may submit more than one proposal. Projects are likely to be supported for a period of 3 years. When submitting bids authorities are asked to state how the projects fit in with their overall strategy for the education of ethnic minorities within their area.

Tomlinson and Coulson [1] give a breakdown of figures for the years 1985-87 and it is useful here to reproduce these:

1985/6   35 projects funded in 25 LEAs, approximate cost £700,000.
1986/7   35 projects funded in 32 LEAs, approximate cost £886,000.
70 projects: Total cost £1,586,000.

Thus one can begin to appreciate the great financial commitment to

Education Support Grant projects aimed at meeting the needs of all children for a life in multiethnic, multicultural, multiracial Britain.

Main objectives of the Education Support Grant scheme

The Education Support Grant scheme had three main objectives: first, which the Government deemed important enough to require national solutions were identified, for example Mathematics and Science teaching in the Primary sector; second, to set up networks of teachers to enable exchange of information on innovative ideas and co-operate in developing teaching materials; and finally, to allow space for pilot projects which would be experimental.

The decision to fund projects related to educational needs in a multiethnic society were prompted as a direct result of the Department of Education and Science receiving pre-publication documentation from the Swann Committee, the report which was published in March 1985.[2] As we saw above in chapter two, the Swann Report explicitly recommended that multicultural education is just as relevant, if not more so, in areas where there are few or no ethnic minority pupils in schools. As early as 1973 the Select Committee on Race Relations and Immigration [Education] published the views of several bodies such as the National Union of Teachers and the Department of Education and Science calling for a broader approach to multicultural education in all schools, whether there were black pupils in them or not.

As we saw in the chapter four on the literature review, as far as Education Support Grant projects on multicultural education and antiracist education are concerned there is very little published material available. The most comprehensive account is that provided by Tomlinson and Coulson.

"Tyneside"

Demographic details

"Tyneside" is a Metropolitan District with a population of over 200,000. It is one of the largest areas in Tyne and Wear, which gives rise to recognisable differences between localities and communities within the Borough. About half of the population is concentrated in the densely developed eastern part of the Borough. Here is found the majority of the older housing stock, local authority housing, industrial and commercial development. The western part of the Borough is less intensively developed; it contains suburban areas and villages separated by attractive countryside.

The ethnic minority population of "Tyneside"

Size and distribution

In 1990, the development officer of the local Race Equality Council (REC) conducted a survey of the 1989 electoral register for "Tyneside" revealed a *minimum* population size of 537 black and ethnic minority adults in the Borough. This figure represents a minimum since (i) it expressly excludes African and African-Caribbean people, their names not being readily identifiable as are Muslim, Hindu and Sikh names; and (ii) it is very difficult to estimate the non-registration factor among perhaps particularly Bangladeshi and Chinese people who might find it quite difficult to complete an electoral roll registration form in English language and who, because of a lack of sufficient English language skills, also might not be able to communicate the necessary information to an English-speaking electoral registration officer.

A second electoral roll survey, completed the following year, 1991, and based on the 1990 register revealed a rise of 13.4 per cent in the number of names identified to 609. This could be explained by an increase in registration, that is more people filling in their forms, but in the absence of a major publicity drive to increase registration among ethnic minorities or of a fundamental transformation of English for Speakers of Other Languages (ESOL) provision in the borough, registration by the black and ethnic minority population is unlikely to increase. The view of the local community leaders is that the increase is mainly in terms of Bangladeshi people moving into the area to escape racial harassment in a neighbouring borough. Bangladeshi people, so very often occupying underclass positions of multiple deprivation in British society, and who have particular difficulties in terms of English language, are therefore much more likely not to register as electors and therefore be missed in any electoral register survey. Thus the 13.4 per cent increase may itself be an under-estimation of population growth.

This is an even more likely since the figures show an increase of 18.1 per cent and 23.4 per cent of Hindu and Sikh names respectively. Bangladeshi people being Muslims would not come into these categories. Muslim names have only increased by 11.3 per cent.

However, even if a 13.4 per cent increase is taken as a correct

113

indication of population growth, despite the indications that it represents under-estimation, an increase of such a magnitude each year would lead to a doubling of black and ethnic minority population every six years in "Tyneside". This would have a significant effect on inner-city school populations, especially in the primary sector, in terms of percentages of black children as most of the black people are settled in urban areas.

The minority population of "Tyneside" is generally so small and scattered as to be insignificant. Recent statistics gathered from schools reveal under 300 bilingual or non-English speaking pupils, speaking 23 languages and attending 68 different schools. "Tyneside" is generally considered a monolingual, monoethnic, monocultural borough, with no Mosque, Mandir or Gurdwara, no Community language classes and no minority community centre. The long established Jewish group provides separate education for its members and is not therefore included in the numbers reported here.

Activities related to educational needs in a multi-ethnic society

In September 1986 there were 280 pupils listed on the "Tyneside" ethnic minority return and these were registered in 68 different schools in the borough. This is a very small proportion, about 2 per cent of the total school population, and is probably a smaller number than in many boroughs which consider themselves to have no minority residents at all. There is, however, also a long-standing Jewish Community centred around the internationally renowned Talmudic College. Children from the Jewish community are not shown on the return referred to above, since they attend separate schools; but their existence has possibly been a factor in the selection of "Tyneside" as the focus of attention for certain racialist groups and their activities.

In these circumstances, the Education Committee's statement of commitment to a pluralist society, and the inclusion of multi-cultural aims in the Committee's Curriculum Policy Statement have particular significance. (See Appendix for the local education authority's policy statement).

The main aims of the "Tyneside" Education Support Grant scheme

The three main aims of the Education Support Grant projects are as follows:

1) To enhance awareness and understanding of Britain's ethnic diversity among pupils, students and teachers from the majority community, by building upon advisory, in-service and curriculum development work, done to date in relation to Multi-Cultural Education, and extending it to reach a wider audience.

2) To enhance teachers' and lecturers' understanding of the background and experience of ethnic minority pupils and young people, and to raise expectations of their potential, through in-service, joint work and investigation, the sharing of information and production of teaching materials.

3) To promote mutual understanding and respect between pupils and students of different ethnic origins by building upon the Personal and Social Education course work already developed in schools, and through curriculum developments which have sprung from that. All three aims would be served through research into current practice, development of resources, approaches and in-service strategies for use in "Tyneside" schools in relation to the following:-

    a) Curriculum arrangements with regard to issues relating to awareness of the multi-racial nature of our society and the resultant social responsibilities shared by all.

    b) Curriculum arrangements as they affect the service to ethnic minorities in "Tyneside".

    c) The context in which the curriculum is delivered i.e. school ethos, hidden curriculum as it affects equality of access and the development of attitudes.

    d) Community relations as they are perceived and as they might be developed in relation to issues of social responsibility, in order to enable all members of the local community to contribute fully to its development.

    e) Investigating attitudes to community relations, identifying the skills and potential within the community which might be released - e.g. entrepreneurial skills, enterprise and energy so as to rejuvenate depressed areas of the inner city.

    f) Monitoring and evaluation models to be investigated, proposed and applied so as to ascertain progress in creating access and affecting attitudes.

    g) Concentrated investigation of specific areas of work, identifying appropriate approaches for classroom work and staff development in relation to these and piloting the materials, strategies and in-service devised. This work would be done chiefly in a selected group of schools, but made availabLe to others as the year proceeded, and on request.

h) Further joint work in classrooms.

i) Monitoring of curriculum developments and teachers confidence re affecting pupil attitudes.

j) Each school to have explored and drafted its own guidelines and policy for meeting educational needs in a multi-ethnic society.

To attract Education Support Grant funding, the original bid was couched in the following terms: "Tyneside" has demonstrated through the local education authority commitment and policy, the actions of its elected members, the response of its teachers and the initiatives taken by its residents and workers at a community level, that it is ready to support the project proposed. The needs of schools, college, children and students have been made clear in general terms by work done to date and we need the financial support to clarify and specify these further. "Tyneside" is a predominantly white area with a rich cultural environment, but has been targeted by groups seeking to ferment racist views and activities.

Other aims were to build upon advisory, inservice and curriculum development work prior to 1988 and extend it to a wider audience, and to work with students in all phases and sectors of education, and with teachers to enhance awareness in predominantly white schools of what it means to people to be part of our ethnically and culturally diverse society examine and address attitudes towards that diversity, including racism, and how they affect people's lives; pilot specially designed teaching materials and strategies across the curriculum to achieve the above raise in teacher/lecturer expectations of curriculum and student potential through support teaching, consultation, INSET, action research, the sharing of information and experience, and production of appropriate resources.

Context and background to the first year of the scheme

In order to describe and evaluate the progress of the project in its first year, it is first necessary to describe its context, the nature of "Tyneside" borough as a setting, and the background of work predating the establishment of the project. Since 1989 there has been an increase in the local the activities of racialist/fascist groups, and in the reported incidents of racial harassment in "Tyneside", particularly from black adults and children.

Racism had been identified as widespread among school-children in "Tyneside" and the region. Teacher observations and the research carried out by Alf Davey[3] and by Win Mould[4] have revealed disturbing attitudes among primary and secondary school students.

Given the climate of the borough as a whole, the prime aim of the Education Support Grant was to address attitudes among the majority white population, developing appropriate teaching and learning strategies, original materials and programmes for use in all phases and sectors, which enable teachers and students alike to examine and change those attitudes.

The local education authority's commitment to education in a multi-racial, multi-cultural society was demonstrated when in 1986 a Teacher Adviser for Personal and Social Education and Equal Opportunities was appointed and subsequently upgraded to Specialist Adviser in 1988. The Education Support Grant bid states that "The encompassing of Multi-cultural Education and Equal Opportunities within the ambit of personal and social development as a whole was considered an important policy decision, since it was designed to incorporate and integrate Multi-cultural Education and Equal Opportunities into all aspects pupil development, making them cross curricular issues."

The local education authority also showed its commitment by publishing in its 4-16 Curriculum Policy Statement as two of seven basic principles, a section on Education in a Multi-racial Society, and another on Equal Opportunities. These have since been updated and expanded. It has not been possible to provide these updated versions here.

As a result of the appointment of the Teacher Adviser, with the school based and centrally organised in-service that resulted from it, many secondary and some special and primary schools began to explore issues of diversity and inequality with students through a Personal and Social Education or World Studies framework. Particular strategies appropriate to local needs began to take shape and formed a valuable foundation upon which to build the approach and philosophy of the Education Support Grant scheme.

The first phase

The Primary sector was identified as a priority area due to the lesser involvement in education in a multi-racial, multi-cultural society and equal opportunities work of that Phase. In 1988 a teacher was seconded to research primary school perceptions of these aspects of education. This research revealed a general lack of understanding, a significant level of apprehension, and unwillingness to acknowledge issues of inequality as being of relevance to Primary education. Education in a Multi-racial, Multi-cultural Society and Equal Opportunities seemed to be defined in terms of second language provision, and tokenist events. The "no problem here" response was a common one.

However, the research revealed some committed staff who were keen to experiment in developing strategies-for raising issues of inequality and racism with primary school children. The results of the work in three primary schools and one special school which arose from this were extremely encouraging and in turn provided strong indications of the way forward for the Education Support Grant scheme.

The experiences of "Tyneside" teachers who tried to affect attitudes by using traditional approaches, also helped the Education Support Grant staff to make decisions about the way forward. For example, a primary school which had run an extension programme of visits and inputs focusing on cultural diversity, with the intention of building tolerance and respect for other races and cultures, found children making racist remarks when shown a video recording featuring a black presenter. A special school which had a series of exchanges and visits involving their students with the Jewish community, found them still using "Jew" as a term of abuse. A student teacher trailing anti-racist materials in a "Tyneside" Secondary school as part of a dissertation found students unable to relate to the experience of black people until they had explored their own experience of oppression and lack of rights as young people from an economically deprived inner city area.

Philosophy and approach of the Education Support Grant scheme

Through pilot projects in schools, which tested the practice agreed by the team, the following principles have been established.

The title of the project indicates its commitment to addressing the attitudes of the majority white population. The term "Multi-cultural Society" embraces gender culture, class culture, institutional culture, age culture, and so on, as well as black and ethnic minority cultures. These "cultures" need to be explored in depth and in terms of people's experience of living and working within groups alongside other groups and in the context of the macro society. This reflects the approach of the Education Support Grant scheme, since it interrelates issues of "race",

118

gender, class, age, disability, and all types of discrimination.

This approach to teaching about equality requires that students first explore their own experience of inequality, either personally as young people, girls, members of low income families etc. or less directly, because of their contact with others who experience it. The Education Support Grant scheme adopts a core process which begins by identifying key issues as students become aware of what they already know about inequality, and leads them to identify circumstances beyond their experience affecting people they do not know.

The experiences and feelings of students themselves are fully explored and valued so that from an understanding of the importance of the issues in their own lives, they can develop the ability to empathise with and relate to the experience of others.

This valuing of the students' experience empowers them. Being student centred it necessarily involves teaching staff in devolving control over the learning process, thus creating a situation of greater equality within the classroom. It is appropriate that learning for equality should take place in a situation of increased equality.

The schools involved were two Nurseries, five Primaries, a total eight projects, 20 to 50 students involved in each project); two Special Education Needs (SEN).

Entry points and aspects of the curriculum focused upon were different for each one. Entry points have included assessment, recording achievement, attitudes to Europe and Europeans, bullying, working together, enterprise, images, introduction to Shakespeare, the books we read, and the community. In Secondary schools, the subject contexts have included English, R.E., Personal and Social Education (PSE)/Tutorial, Modern Languages and Pre-Vocational Education and have included GCSE course work. All projects have involved cross curricular skills such as oracy, writing, analysis (e.g. literature, the media), problem-solving and collaborative group work. Some projects have involved parents and groups in the community.

Projects have lasted between three weeks and one term. Evaluation has been carried out by the Advisory Teacher, the teacher and the students who took part. External evaluations have also been carried out by a student teacher and an advisory colleague from a neighbouring authority. Each interviewed children involved in a pilot project and put questions to them to ascertain the understanding and skills developed. In both cases, the results were positive, inasmuch as the students were able to explain how inequality occurs, what should be done about it and to identify key equality issues in pertinent current affairs/events.

119

The pilots are in effect action research, and their findings have informed staff about attitudes and perceptions in schools and the most effective ways of addressing them. In addition, they also represent staff development through the close involvement of teachers and indicate their training needs.

All schools which were involved in the pilot projects have been visited by the Specialist Adviser for Personal and Social Education and Equal Opportunities, the Co-ordinator and Advisory Teacher for the Education Support Grant scheme in order to review the first year's work and also offer support. Most of the pilots were short-term without any follow-up for fixed objectives. It was encouraging to note that many schools and teachers had extended the work undertaken during the pilot project and were eager to maintain contact. A number of schools not directly involved in the original pilot projects have also been visited, in some cases because they had expressed an interest in curriculum development, in others to alert senior management to alarming reports of racial harassment faced by black residents and children in abuse experienced in their school's catchment area. Schools have been offered support in addressing the influence which such a climate will have upon their students and in dealing with racist incidents.

Teachers involved in pilot projects have commented that their expectations of students, their teaching style, their selection of literature and reference books, their programme planning, the issues they focus upon with their students, and their own attitudes have all changed. In network meetings they have been eager to talk with others about what has happened in different pilot projects and to compare approaches, starting points and outcomes. Their growing commitment and enthusiasm has been encouraging.

The pilot projects were essentially seen as experimental, and a means of identifying workable strategies, student and teacher needs, the types of teaching materials and curriculum intervention which would be most productive. They have achieved all those objectives and also affected practice in schools.

Problems with implementation

While so much both within and outside the local education authority is positive, it must be noted that the Education Support Grant scheme has encountered difficulty in convincing schools that everyone believes its work is integral and fundamental to the whole curriculum.

Even those schools which have volunteered to be involved in pilot projects and are committed to whole school development, see themselves as making a decision as a result of teacher interest and liaison with the Education Support Grant team and not because there has been any general message communicated to them by the local education authority as a whole or from the Department for Education (DFE).

Where there has been effective collaboration between Education Support Grant scheme staff and curriculum branch colleagues, or where there has been a coincidence of events between Education Support Grant staff contact and, for example National Curriculum Council publications, this problem has lessened. However, more coherent and obvious local education authority support for the scheme's work, and more encouragement to schools from the DFE is needed.

"London"

Demographic details

"London" is one of the Outer London boroughs which covers an area ranging from a continuation of the inner urban area of East London to a mainly residential area which functions largely as a commuter suburb. These are linked by an industrial area which developed in response to the building of the North Circular Road in the 1930s, but many of the industries have now declined or moved out of the area and the tendency is for redevelopment of the sites by service industries. The local authority has actively pursued a policy of encouraging these new industries to develop.

At the 1991 census, "London" had a total population of 215,000, a decline of 8 per cent since the 1971 census. Higher proportions of the population are under 16 or over retirement age than those for the total London region. The peak birth year was 1971, later than the national trend, and therefore the effect on school rolls occurred later.

There was a decline in the workforce resident in the borough by 12 per cent between 1971 and 1981, and between 1971 and 1978 there was a decline of 19 per cent in the numbers employed in manufacturing industry.

The major employment opportunities locally are in service and distribution industries, light engineering, electronics(which is expanding), customer outlets for banking and finance. The area is characterised by small businesses and workshops. Within the borough boundaries there are only 33 manufacturing establishments with 100 or more employees

121

and a further 20 in the 50-100 range. These are largely concerned with the manufacture of furniture, food and fabric, with some engineering. There is easy access to Central London and the larger industrial concerns situated outside the Borough in Essex and Hertfordshire.

The organisation of secondary education in "London"

Secondary Education in the Authority was reorganised in 1986. Prior to this pupils from primary schools transferred at age 11 to High Schools and then at age 14 to Senior High Schools. Pupils transferring from primary school in 1986 and subsequent years attend reorganised schools catering for 11-16 year olds. Seven of these schools are 4 form entry and the remaining eight have 6 forms of entry. Post 16 education is provided in two open access sixth form colleges and a college of further education. There is also a voluntary aided Roman Catholic school which will have been reorganised by 1988 to become a 5 form entry 11 to 18 school. A number of schools have or will be closed.

In order to maintain continuity for the pupils , the reorganisation is phased over a number of years. This results in the former High Schools having only 11 to 14 year pupils until 1989 when the 1896/87 first year cohort reaches their fourth year of secondary education. The one exception to this is School A which retained half of their 1983 intake into the fourth year in 1986 and is a complete 11 to 16 school from September 1987. Similarly, the former Senior High Schools continue to receive pupils into their fourth years until 1988, so that in 1987/88 they have pupils in their first, second, fourth and fifth years of secondary education together with a residual sixth form. The sixth form colleges officially open in 1988 and still retain fourth and fifth year pupils.

Four of the 11 to 16 year schools are single sex(two for boys and two for girls). All the other institutions are co-educational. Both boys' schools are former high schools whereas one of the girl's schools is a former Senior High School. Two former single sex schools are now co-educational. Both sixth form colleges were formerly boy's schools.

Education Support Grants

Background

"London" is a borough with approximately 17 per cent pupils of ethnic minority origin. The distribution of these pupils is however, very uneven, with the vast majority living in the central and southern parts of the borough. This is in strong contrast with the north of the borough, bordering Epping Forest, the North Circular forming a ready boundary.

In July 1982, the Council adopted a policy on "Education for Multicultural Society", the guiding principles of which are the education service "welcomes cultural and linguistic diversity, rejects and opposes racism, and is concerned to promote equality of opportunity, racial justice, and good relationships between all groups."

At the same time the council agreed to reformulation of the support services for ethnic minority pupils under section 11 funding. The English Language Service and the West Indian Supplementary Service had both existed since the 1960s and it was felt that the structures should be changed to reflect changing needs and roles. Hence the Multicultural Development Service was formed. Recently, however, I feel the borough has taken a backward step by splitting the Multicultural Development Service into three separate units. These are the African Caribbean Attainment Project, the bilingual service and the English as a second language support service. With the reduction, and I think the final demise of Section 11 funding, it is likely that these three services will eventually disappear from the borough. It is only a matter of time before this happens.

Since 1982 a number of steps have been taken to promote implementation of the policy document and it has been the case that teachers within both services, funded through Section 11, have often taken a leading role in developments within schools, in addition to giving direct language support to ethnic minority pupils. They have organised consciousness-raising courses, led staff working parties, worked with subject departments, helped formulate school policies and so on. But this support and expertise is not available in respect of the schools in the borough which do not have sufficient numbers of ethnic minority pupils, although the Council is determined that the policy document should be seen as equally applicable to all. Indeed it has been argued that the need for change is at least as great, if not greater, in these areas as in the multi-racial ones. Incidents of concern which have come to the attention of the Authority include the following: racist graffiti covering large areas of school walls, causing teaching to stop for a day during which it was removed; physical abuse of isolated pupils of ethnic minority origin (including Jewish children) within schools and harassment just off school premises; movements of youths from white areas to multi-racial areas with intent to harass; name calling and various expressions of racial hostility. Similar concerns are reported in the HMI report, "Race

Relations in Schools", together with an acknowledgement of the lack of evidence regarding successful practice required at tackling the problems. the situation in the Authority's schools needs to be seen in the context of an increasing number of racial attacks; evidence of which has been presented to the Council.

Proposal for Education Support Grant funding

This proposal is intended as a pilot project to help the Authority to assist those issues. it incorporates the concerns in Circular 6/84 for greater racial harmony in schools, for taking practical steps to counter racial harassment, and for challenging stereotypes and raising teacher expectations of ethnic minority pupils and wishes to explore these.

Support is requested for a proposal relating to two Advisory teachers to work in a linked group of such schools across the age range, one to cover the primary age group, and the other the secondary years. The authority is convinced of the need for a consistent approach from the earliest years to be effective in tackling such issues.

Aim   - to assist the schools to implement the policy statement in every aspect of school life in the community it serves.

Tasks - to examine, with staff, the range of attitudes towards cultural and linguistic diversity, the extent of racial harmony, and the range and extent of racialist attitudes and activities within the schools and the community as it pertains to the school.

- to appraise, with staff, the role of the school in promoting racial harmony, and good relationships and removing any bias, ethnocentrism, stereotyping, racism or discriminatory practice.

- to investigate and experiment with the forms of in-service training required to make the necessary changes, especially those which are school biased.

- to support necessary curricular developments.

- to investigate a range of responses to overt aspects of racism in order to establish the most appropriate forms of response.

Staff appointed would therefore need to be experienced and specially qualified teachers with knowledge and understanding of the needs and perspectives of ethnic minorities in general and of the local communities in particular. They would need to possess talents of diplomacy and persuasiveness as well as commitment and energy. The ability to relate well to teachers with a range of attitudes and values in a sensitive area would be crucial. Experience of in-school in-service training and also of research and development techniques would be helpful.

The advisory teachers would be responsible to the Assistant Education Officer (Curriculum) and work close in collaboration with the Adviser for Multicultural Education and the Multicultural Development Service. Expertise and some resource back-up would be available in this way, but the appointees would need additional funds to stimulate and support curriculum change. The work of the advisory teachers would be monitored and reported to the Steering Group for the Multicultural Development Service.

The first phase

The prime objective of the project was to implement the borough's multicultural policy in four secondary schools with relatively small numbers of black and ethnic minority pupils and this has remained unchanged. The following is a breakdown of the activities carried out to meet the aims of the project.

Curriculum intervention

The work revolved around curriculum intervention in several subject areas including English, Home Economics, Humanities and Science.

English

After discussions with the Adviser for English, I developed a Language Awareness Module for use in the lower forms of the schools. The content included looking at the great linguistic diversity found in Britain today; attention was drawn to the linguistic diversity within the local education authority; non-verbal communication, writing in code, standard and non-standard English and an examination of the power of language in terms of "race" and gender. The Language Awareness Module was taught in one school last year over three terms and the Module was adopted as part of the English syllabus in that school, and taught by the members of the English Department. The Module was taught in a team teaching situation at another two schools for possible adoption by the respective English Departments.

The work in this subject area was extended to include 2nd, 3rd, 4th and 5th forms (Years 7, 8, 9 and 10 respectively). Texts by black writers were purchased for three of the schools and schemes of work were developed with the close collaboration of members of the English Departments concerned. Some audio and video materials as well as posters and Peters Projection of the World Map were purchased to supplement the texts. Most of the work was trialled by the end of second term of the Education Support Grant scheme.

Home Economics

I extended and developed a 2nd year (Year 8) Home Economics syllabus in one of the schools. The new material was trialled in the four all-white schools; it was also in a multi-racial school in the south of the borough. Materials by way of cooking utensils-were purchased and allocated to the schools as the need arose.

I also set up a working party of interested Home Economics teachers in collaboration with two specialist Home Economics advisory teachers on producing an antiracist multicultural policy for the subject for the borough. This has involved a series of meetings over the four terms and a draft document for consultation was produced and distributed to all secondary schools in the local education authority. Details of this are to be found in the appendix.

Humanities

I was involved in the planning and teaching of a scheme of work on South Africa in one of the schools; the whole exercise took two terms and the material was adapted and extended in the light of the teaching experience. The local authority's Schools Lending Service developed a box of materials on South Africa and these were reserved for sharing with the Humanities Department. A set of books entitled *Journey to Jo'Burg* by Beverley Naidoo were purchased for classroom reading as part of the work on South Africa; also purchased were some audio and video materials.

Mathematics

The advisory teacher held Mathematics Departmental Meetings in three of the schools, although the work was undertaken in just one school. This involved teaching a scheme of work which has been developed on

126

different counting methods across cultures in an effort to broaden the Mathematics curriculum. I successfully taught Gujarati numbers to several first year forms at the school. Also developed were some lessons on area work involving comparisons between the Mercator's and Peters' projections of the World Map.

Science

I attended several Science Departmental meetings in three schools and began work on evaluating a first year syllabus in one of the schools with the department. Assistance was obtained from the advisory teacher for Science at the Multicultural Development Service who attended several of the Departmental meetings. A set of pupils' work books were bought for one of the schools and these have been incorporated within the first year syllabus.

At another school I assisted the Science Department to write their fourth and fifth year syllabus focusing on Equal Opportunities aspects of the course. Some of the material was included by Access to Information on Multicultural Education Resources (AIMER) in their index of resource material on multicultural education.

Other areas of involvement

Antiracist working party

I was actively involved in setting up a Working Party to develop a school policy on antiracist education in one of the schools. A draft document was produced and approved by the whole school staff so that the equal opportunities policy could be implemented in the school. It has not been possible to provide the documentation here.

Language across the curriculum

I was also actively involved in the drawing up of the schools Language Across the Curriculum Policy and one of my suggestions of including black and ethnic minority pupils in the illustrations was taken up in all documents produced by the school, for instance, the "homework" document which was used by the pupils to record all the homework set during the week.

My presence in this school led to there being a review being set up where all Departments were asked to produce statements on Equal Opportunities for staff briefing meetings and I was consulted by Heads of Department for some of these. This was an on-going exercise and a rolling programme was set up giving all departments to present their equal opportunity statements at these gatherings.

Expenditure and resources

Around £7,800 has been spent on resources. Materials bought have ranged from reference books for the Staff Library to pupils' sets of books; audio and video material has also been purchased as have posters and maps. For Home Economics around £350 has been spent purchasing utensils. The total expenditure includes the additional £5,500 which the DES agreed could be vired from the underspending resulting from the difficulties encountered in recruiting a teacher for the Primary phase.

Monitoring and evaluation

This occurred through fortnightly meetings held between the advisory teacher, the Head of the Multicultural Development Service and the adviser for multicultural education. Annual meetings were held with the Head Teachers and the link person identified in each of the four schools to review the work of the project and plan for the future. On-going evaluation of the teaching and learning material produced was an integral part of the project since its inception in April 1980.

Governors' and parent teacher meetings

I also attended several Governors meetings in several schools, as well as a Parent Teachers Association meetings at some schools. I wrote to the Chair of Governors of all schools to ask if a verbal report of his work could be presented to the governors. In addition, I also helped in a number of training sessions held for governors at the Multicultural Development Service.

The primary phase

After a third advertisement, an appointment was made to the Primary post. An experienced primary teacher, previously on secondment as an Induction Co-ordinator in ILEA took up post on 1 September 1988. In collaboration with the adviser for multicultural education, and the Advisory teacher for the primary sector have been working to identify the needs of the primary schools in the East of the borough, and to establish personal contact. She has visited all the schools, some in company with Elaine. They have attempted to identify issues as perceived by the Schools and assess the best starting including exploring ways of networking points, schools to ensure effective coverage.

This has built upon previous work undertaken under LEATGS. A residential weekend conference was organised for Heads and Deputies of Primary Schools in the area, at which the majority were represented. There was a follow-up day conference, held on a Saturday, which also drew a good response. These activities reflected in a significant element in school bids under LEATGS. Other sources of information are bids for support made to the Multicultural Development Service, and the policy statements previously developed in some schools.

Some activities have been generated on an ad-hoc basis as a result of the Primary teacher's visits to schools, such as the provision of some support materials for existing developments and her involvement in previously planned school INSET activities.

Summary

In this chapter, we have looked at the development of Education Support Grant projects as a result of the recommendations of the Swann Report highlighting the need for multicultural education work in all-white schools. Brief demographic details of the location of the two projects was described.

The second and third sections above give some idea of the range of activities in each of the Education Support Grant projects. Both projects have now come to an end and it is interesting to note that virtually all the initiatives that were started in the various schools have also come to an end. Apart from a handful of books being used for English lessons, none of the curriculum developments have survived the demise of the projects. Reasons given are many and varied; the most frequent being the lack of time due to concentration on the National Curriculum. Other reasons articulated have been to do with lack of support at Senior teacher level, change of staff has generally meant that the work has gone with the teacher/s concerned. The work started by one teacher has not been followed on by the new teacher. Although in principal the work had become part of a department's plans, in practice this has gone by the wayside as soon as the project came to an end.

Notes

1   Tomlinson and Coulson (1988) *Education for a Multi-Ethnic Society*
2   Swann Report, 1985, HMSO
3   Davey (1986) "Learning to be prejudiced", *Multicultural Teaching*, Vol 4, No 3, Summer
4   Mould (1986) "No Rainbow Coalition on Tyneside", *Multicultural Teaching*, Vol 4, No 3, Summer

8 Case studies

And it ought to be remembered that there is nothing more difficult
to take in hand, more perilous to conduct, or more uncertain in its
success, than to take the lead in the introduction of a new order of
things. Because the innovator has for enemies all those who have
done well under the old conditions....[1]

In the previous chapter, an account of the demographic details of the two
Education Grant Support projects was provided by way of background
information. It was felt necessary to do this in order to locate the two
projects in their different geographical areas - and also to see the
similarities of approach within the two projects.

The present chapter is divided into two sections. The first section
gives brief details of four of the schools where curriculum development
was undertaken during the course of the research. The second section
provides examples of aspects of curriculum development undertaken
during the two Education Support Grant projects in London and the
North East of England. This second section is further sub-divided into
the separate subject areas covered. The subject range covered during
my time on the two Education Support Grant projects was great and it is
impossible to detail all the subjects here. Further details of the range of
activities is to be found in chapter seven, which gives the background to
the two Education Support Grant projects under consideration for this
book. It is worth noting in passing that I recognise that one cannot
replace one set of teaching materials in a geographically different place
without modification. However, it was found that the material developed
for the English Department at school A was applicable in all schools in
"London"; it was also found to be applicable in one school in
"Tyneside", without modification. Most of the other curriculum
development work was geared to each individual school, be it in London

131

or "Tyneside".

Section one

The first three schools are in the London borough, while school D is in "Tyneside". The London schools are all secondary schools, while the "Tyneside" school is a primary school.

School A

This is a predominantly white, mono-lingual school (about 96 per cent of the pupils are white). The catchment area of the school consists mainly of owner-occupied housing and, although it is very close to the school, it has avoided the major council estate in the area. On appeal, however, parents can get their pupils into the school in just under a quarter of the next year's first year intake will come from the estate. The general picture, therefore, is a fairly wealthy one with house prices varying from, say £70,00 to £200,00.

Pupils arrive at the school by car, train, or in the case of those who live near enough, walk. A number of the older pupils (18 year olds) also appear to have their own cars, or certainly have unlimited to access to a car. Though no data is available, by talking to pupils, teachers and parents, generally one also gets the impression that a substantial number of parents are employed in professional or skilled jobs either in the city or locally. Many of the pupils, particularly at least two fifth years, appear to be in a position where qualifications are not so important to them since they will be able to get work with, or through, their parents, a number of whom appear to have their own businesses of one sort or another.

Amongst lower school pupils, issues which may give rise to a discussion of parental occupations do not attend to arise so frequently; therefore it is not possible to make any further comment at this juncture. However, it would appear that a larger number of the younger pupils come from homes which are not "stable".

The Parents Teachers Association (PTA) is particularly active, primarily being involved in raising money for the school fund. Events in which they are involved are barn dances, discos, barbecues and quiz nights. Other than this, there is little informative school affairs. The Board of Governors meets regularly and, at present, I believe tends to go along with the school, though this may change in future.

132

As mentioned earlier, this is a predominantly white, mono-lingual, mixed secondary school in the North East of London. Having undergone reorganisation in 1986, along with the other secondary schools in the borough, it can be regarded as a new school. That is, almost the entire staff is new, as is introduction of the lower school pupils aged eleven to thirteen. In its first year a new ethos was also found regarding the school's aims and general running as developed by senior management.

One major development that was included in the reorganisation was an examination of how the school was undertaking the implementation of abolishing multicultural education which was drawn up in line with the borough policy statement.

This policy statement of the school and the borough was one of the levers I was able to use in conducting Curriculum development work through the Education Support Grant project at this school. This is true for the other three secondary schools as well as the two primary schools which were involved in Education Support Grant project in "London."

School B

During the reorganisation in 1986, this was one of the few schools which remained an eleven to fourteen middle school. This again, like School A, is a predominantly white, mixed secondary school. The catchment area is 50 per cent working class in council housing and 50 per cent owner-occupied housing. The house prices arrange from £50,000 to £100,00 within a mile radius of the school. The school's intake is 98 per cent white.

Again, as in the case of School A, the school, after reorganisation, went through a phase of in service work and set up an antiracist working party to look at the implementation of the multicultural policy document of the Borough. The active support of the antiracist working party as can be seen in the case studies was vital for the Education Support Grant Curriculum development that was undertaken at the school.

School C

This, again, is a predominantly white, mixed secondary school. Eleven to eighteen year olds attend the school. About three-quarters of the school population is of working class background while 25 per cent of them come from a middle class background. There is a large council estate and other council housing which the school serves. It was at this school that the pupils' survey was conducted. As with School B, this school had an antiracist working party and support of the party was crucial in carrying out the pupil survey.

School D

This is an inner city school in "Tyneside" serving a predominantly white working class catchment area. A majority of the pupils come from a large council estate and the others from owner-occupied property comprised of mainly terraced houses with the front doors leading straight onto the pavement.

Section two

Curriculum development

As already pointed out both Education Support Grant projects were based on the premise that curriculum development would form the major focus of the school based work. Hence, as advisory teacher, I was involved in a range of subject areas with a view to developing the material along multicultural and antiracist lines to see if there was any difference in acceptance between the two approaches.

Three subject areas are discussed here, beginning with English, which is followed by Home Economics and finally the discussion centres around Mathematics.

English

To begin with a discussion of a scheme of work developed especially for the Education Support Grant pilot project in London; this scheme was also used in one of the schools in "Tyneside". It has not been possible to include lesson plans and teaching materials here.

Antiracist English in all white schools: an approach

The aim of the language Awareness Module is to explore several aspects of language per se; it is necessarily selective.

Most eleven-year-olds are familiar with hieroglyphics, codes and fables, for instance, and this can be used to foster a deeper understanding of other aspects of language; for example dialects and Standard English.

134

By exploring and writing in a variety of scripts the pupils are made aware that people around the world communicate in languages other than English. Another dimension of this is the reading of a story in another language.

It should be emphasised that this module is only the beginning of a long process. When one is involved in attitude change, every little helps when trying to break down pre-conceived barriers. If at the end of the half-term's work the pupils have begun to accept other languages as being just as valid as their own mother tongue, English, then this can be used to good effect in their overall perception of school life in particular and society in general. A deeper understanding of the complexity of Chinese script may make the pupils less disparaging when they next visit a Chinese restaurant.

An understanding of how language can be racist and sexist may be the first step to realising the power of language.

This is a short 6-week (double lesson/week) module which has been utilised in an all-white school in London and in "Tyneside" with 1st year (Year 7) pupils. I feel it is important to begin with the 1st years in this approach to awareness of language issues which can be built upon during their subsequent years in school.

The Language Awareness Module became an integral part of the 1st year English syllabus in the London school, so it was seen by pupils as an essential aspect of their English work. It is undertaken by all 1st year pupils.

The introductory lesson is an examination of non-verbal communication and a comparison between human and non-human "language" - e.g. communication in dolphins and bees. This is contrasted with, for instance, human facial gestures. From this the pupils are led to look at signs and signals including traffic signs and international symbols (e.g. "left luggage"). This is to show that signs and symbols operate across cultures and languages - especially traffic signals which can be understood by illiterate people. Also included are some religious symbols.

The second lesson looks at one of the earliest forms of writing - hieroglyphics. Mention is made of the elaborate systems of picture-writing deployed by the Akan people on the West coast of Africa, prior to the more famous Egyptian system. The next part looks at writing in code - yet another form of communication. Pupils really enjoy breaking the codes and inventing their own codes which are used to send messages to other 1st year pupils for deciphering. An example of codes was taken from Peter Wright's *Spycatcher* (1987), which gave the lessons a contemporary feel at the time of the great controversy surrounding the suppression of the book.[2] The book was at the time banned in England - I had purchased a copy of the book in India while on holiday the previous Christmas. The children were fascinated by the actual book as none of them had previously seen the banned book. The level of interest in this section of the language module shot up by at least four hundred per cent!

This is followed by an examination of non-written communication:

- sending a messenger as in ancient times
- using drums as some people did in Africa
- this is expanded upon and mention is made of how some drummers are able to imitate the human voice. Also how early white "explorers" were surprised by the efficient system of communication developed by African peoples who did not use the written form. (For instance, the use of water to reflect voices from one bank of a 2-mile river to the other without raising the voice).
- smoke signals as used by native Americans. This was also used in 1977 to commemorate the Queen's Jubilee. Smoke signals are also used by the Roman Catholic Church when announcing the election of a new Pope.

The third lesson gives information about the different languages found around the world. The pupils are always surprised when it is pointed out that 131 different languages are spoken in London alone - when asked, they had imagined maybe 5 or 7. This is followed by a quick survey of the languages found in the classroom - English, French, German, Hebrew, Italian, Gujarati (myself). Even in an all-white school some of the children's parents will know one or two European languages. (The work on dialects is left to the following lesson).

A language quiz is undertaken consisting of 10 different languages using a variety of scripts - some relatively easy to recognise - such as Chinese, as seen on the street on restaurant signs. It came as a surprise that some pupils not only recognised Hebrew but could read it. This was a good way to give space to pupils to share their knowledge of languages with others.

The language quiz is followed by a reading of a story in Gujarati - in this case *Mithu the Parrot* by Susheila Stone. It is possible to use taped stories if the teacher is not bilingual - just to give the pupils an opportunity experience another language. The discussion centred around familiar/English words - e.g. "master" and "jungle".

This is followed by a language quiz on a tape to see if the children have any aural recognition of the various languages - from Turkish to Hindi. In practice it is possible, due to the limited concentration span of the pupils, to use only 4 or 5 of the languages. Use is made of the "Fire" poster produced by the Home Office in six different languages besides English, to reinforce the fact that people use these languages in their daily lives. This lesson is concluded by writing out numerals 1-10 in 6 different languages and similarities/ differences with English numerals discussed. The children are taught a Gujarati number-counting nursery rhyme.

The penultimate lesson expands on the theme of written language by getting the children to write one or two sentences in Chinese. Mention is made of the fact that Chinese children have to learn 3,500 characters by the time they are in their teens, whereas the alphabet in English has only 26 letters; Gujarati has 36, with pronunciation indicators, which makes it a phonetic language.

This is followed by a discussion on the necessity of the Chinese standardising their language for effective communication in their vast country. This leads to looking at Standard English - what is it? Children are given 20 examples using a variety of dialects to explore the notion of "correct" English.

The final lesson is used to reiterate dialects and their use in written form. This is followed up by a reading of *Ndidi's Story* to explore the use of language - specifically focusing on the word "black". A quick discussion on the use of fable as a teaching tool. Mention is made of Aesop - familiar to all children and found in most cultures - who was a slave of African descent in a Greek household.

The story is followed by a brainstorming session where words with "black" in them are written on the board - eg.blackbird. In a matter of 10-15 minutes the pupils usually come up with 30 words. The pupils are then asked to place the words in three different columns - words which they think have a **positive** meaning, words which have a **negative** meaning, and the rest which have a **neutral** meaning. In this way the pupils begin to examine, and hopefully have a deeper understanding of, the nature of language, and how it is loaded against black people. There is usually time to do a similar exercise on the word "white", and comparison is made between the number of times black is used with negative meaning and the number of times white is used with positive meaning.

This is a broad outline of how language can be used to raise awareness of racism in an all-white school. This work leads nicely to a discussion of sexist language: I have successfully included "The Story of Baby X". This children's story was first published in America as far back as 1978 under the title *X: a fabulous child's story*. It is written by Lois Gold. It found its way to London as a short story in the feminist magazine *Ms*, from which the story has been adopted for use in schools.

At the particular school in London (school C) the 1st years all have done the Language Awareness Module and in their 2nd year read as a class *The Peacock Garden* by Anita Desai, which discusses issues of loyalty etc., at the time of partition in India from a young girl's point of view. Although this book is out of print, the Head of Department had borrowed a copy from the public library and thought the story worthwhile enough to get the school secretary to type it on to a computer disk. With illustrations taken from two different editions, the Head of English duplicated thirty copies for use by the pupils. The pupils also read *Journey to Jo'Burg* by Beverley Naidoo in their second year.

A number of possible avenues for diversifying the work was found to be possible, and grew naturally out of the English Language Module. One teacher did a series of lessons in mime which grew out of the lesson on non-verbal communication, while another teacher did follow up work on famous people and language, e.g. Biro; yet another one explored the notion of borrowing words from other languages, for example "bungalow".

Initially, at school C when I was first introduced to the school staff, one member of the English Department was keen for some development work along multicultural and antiracist lines. He was one of the first teachers to take up the offer of collaborative work at this school. It transpired later that this particular teacher was in his probationary year at the school and that he was getting a lot of help from the Local Education Authority Advisor for English. It is significant that the Head of English did not attend this first meeting; also of note is the fact that none of the other longer established members of the English Department did not feel that multicultural and antiracist work had any relevance for them. It is interesting to note that it was a probationary teacher, one fresh out of teacher training college and not yet moulded by the ethos of the school who chose to attend the first meeting and ask to be included in the curriculum development work. However, there were no objections for me to work with the probationary teacher.

I now turn to other subject areas where curriculum development has been possible.

138

Home Economics

This work was again undertaken at school C where the Head of Department, in search of a more lucrative job in a bigger school, felt that the Education Support Grant project would benefit her in terms of interviews and innovative work addressed. Although it appeared at first glance that the Home Economics Department was willing to undertake multicultural and antiracist work with the active help of the advisory teacher, it transpired that the Head of Department had other personal motives, besides those of curriculum innovation.

It is possible here to limit the discussion to a single module of the Home Economics syllabus. This particular module is specifically interesting in that it tackles the aspect of "culture" through food. I had agreed to look at the second year syllabus with a view to developing appropriate multicultural and antiracist approaches to the material taught. The topic began with a section on "What is Culture?" with a Mercator projection of the Indian sub-continent which led to a description of the three major religious groups - Hindus, Muslims and Sikhs - found in the sub-continent. This led to a section on "Culture through food", with the preparation of a *thali*. The section was supplemented with four recipes to enable the children to cook the thali.

The cooking of the thali was then followed up with an examination of food eaten around the world, entitled "Daily menus around the World". This last section was handwritten and photocopied.

This module was approached along antiracist lines, bearing in mind that the children had to be involved from the start. This was achieved by beginning with a simple poem "I am", which the children found easy to identify with. Appropriate multi-racial illustrations were introduced to back up the text. In addition to this, Peters' projection was used instead of the Mercator's one that the children (and the staff) were so familiar with. This led to a lengthy discussion about map-makers and the people who control our view of the world.

Science

Preliminary discussions had taken place at school B for work with the Science Department. However, it soon transpired that the Head of Department and the other teachers concerned were not very keen for any curriculum development to happen within the department. The field notes for two of the meetings illustrate rather well how the multicultural

139

and antiracist work can be ignored and negated by the actions (or rather the inaction) of staff members. Further, because of the nature of the Education Support Grant project - that is, only being able to work at the invitation of staff members, I was unable to make any headway with the particular department at school B.

After preliminary discussions on the telephone with the Head of Department, it was agreed that I could come in to the school to discuss the work he had been carrying out at school C with the Home Economics Department, as discussed above, as the Science Department were planning to do work on nutrition shortly. It was felt by both parties that this work might fit into the scheme of work planned. Two meetings were subsequently held - at the first meeting, after the Head of Science Department had perused the material developed at School C, she stated that the nutrition topic would be deferred until the final term of the academic year. The meeting took place in November, the first term of the academic year. Thus I was left with the situation where I would have to wait two terms before embarking on the nutrition topic. Also, it was pointed out to me by the Head of Department that this would suit the Head of Science Department better as the "Science Department staff were very busy". As there was some collaboration between the Science and Home Economics, it was suggested that I try and negotiate some work with the Head of Home Economics Department. A date was agreed for the meeting.

When the I turned up for the meeting, I was told that the Head of Home Economics was away on a course and discussions would not be possible. However, the possibility of working in the Science Department was pursued, only to be informed that the Head of Science may be leaving at the end of the year, that is in December. This clearly had implications for the work of the Education Support Grant Project within the Science Department - I would have to re-negotiate with the new Head of Science Department in January.

Although a meeting had been arranged with the Head of the Home Economics Department, the Head of Science was going to confirm the meeting nearer the date. In fact this never happened; I had to abandon any hope of working within the Science or Home Economics Department at this school.

The above scenario illustrates some of the difficulties of carrying out multicultural and antiracist work in all-white secondary schools. The above shows how easy it is to ignore multicultural and antiracist work, even when there is pressure from the outside, in this case through the Education Support Grant Project.

Mathematics

This work was undertaken at school B in "London". The Head of Department at this school gave me an open invitation to come to his lessons. In fact six lessons were spent "observing" the mathematics lessons, before the Head of Department felt he could let the advisory teacher do some multicultural work. In fact the way the time scale was controlled by the Head of Department meant that only one lesson was possible during the life-span of the project at this school. However, the Head of Department was keen for all the three first year classes to experience this one lesson. This lesson was on Gujarati counting rhymes, and totally unrelated to any of the other work being undertaken by the pupils. I reluctantly agreed to do this piece of work in the hope that this would be a way into the Mathematics Department. However, this was not to be, as by the time the lessons were agreed upon, the project had come to the end of its life in the London Local Education Authority.

"Unity"

I mention this as a case study here because I find it ironic that in a project which was funded for curriculum development in all-white schools, one of the few avenues of work open to me in "Tyneside" was to produce a black edition of *Unity*. This was the first, and as far as I am aware, the only black edition of the Tyne and Wear Anti-Fascist Association (TWAFA) youth magazine. This also puts into context some of the difficulties encountered by black teachers working in the field of "race" and education. [3] As Bonnett points out *Unity* is a publication of TWAFA and has been published since 1987.[4]

TWAFA is funded by the Race Equality Council (REC) and all the Tyne and Wear local authorities, with "Tyneside" being the lead authority due to the level of its contribution and its support. TWAFA has existed for about nine years now, and has a national reputation for its anti-fascist work. *Searchlight* magazine, the leading investigative journal which focuses upon fascist organisations' activities in Britain and Europe, both recognises and supports TWAFA.

The responsibility for producing *Unity* is usually delegated to a different school or youth group in one of the Tyne and Wear authorities for each edition, under the general supervision of TWAFA executive, its full time organiser and members of its education sub-committee.

Unity was endorsed by the Council's Education Committee in 1986.

The members agreed that *Unity* should be distributed in all LEA schools and that the LEA should offer advice and support on ways of using it with students.

The aim of the *Unity* newspaper is to involve young people, in the investigation and exposure of fascist and racist activities, in constructing arguments which counter fascist and racist propaganda, and in building positive attitudes which will help to unite young people against fascism and racism.

To that end, adults work with the group which is producing *Unity* as consultants, facilitators and supporters only. The newspaper is written, edited and designed by the young people.

At a public meeting in 1989 to discuss *Unity*, concern was expressed that most editions had been produced by mainly or all white groups. A future black edition was suggested by a member of TWAFA executive.

"Tyneside" LEA was invited to produce an edition of *Unity* the previous year. An attempt was made to integrate this into a joint English Humanities and Education in a Multiracial, Multicultural Society (EMMS) initiative which led to a study of the history of fascism in Europe, with a writing project.

However, pressure of work and other difficulties prevented this initiative. At a meeting between senior advisers, it was agreed that the Education Support Grant/EMMS scheme would undertake to lead a different initiative, i.e. a black edition of *Unity*, as a pilot project, with the advisors offering support as appropriate and involving the Local Education Authority Newspaper Unit. Possible pilot schools were mentioned.

The Education Support Grant/EMMS Co-ordinator has been investigated such a pilot project as one of his short term targets. It has been agreed with TWAFA's full time organiser, that a final proof copy for *Unity* will be prepared in the Local Education Authority for the end of the Summer term.

Two days of writing workshops were organised, plus follow-up for black students from the borough's schools and colleges. Some bilingual workers from the Local Education Authority, members of *Saheli*, a black women's group and staff from the Black Youth Movement in a neighbouring authority offered support on the two days.

The initial work was done with a small number black students after letters had been sent to around twenty primary and secondary schools. In the end three primary pupils and four secondary pupils took part in the writing workshop. At the end of the two days, poems, short accounts and drawings were produced which were incorporated into the black education. I wanted to incorporate a disabled outlook too, so that one of the short accounts was provided by a partially sighted young woman living in a neighbouring borough. Her article was converted into Braille and "printed" *Unity*. Following the print edition, I wanted partially sighted people to have access to the magazine. A taped version was produced by a local Talking Newspaper group - as far as I am aware this is the first and only time that a black edition as well as a taped edition of *Unity* has been produced. A double first, as it were!

The educational development to be encouraged by this project includes the following:

- Language skills
- Writing skills
- Planning, decision-making, negotiation and communication skills
- Technological and IT skills
- Enterprise skills
- Graphic design skills
- Raising self esteem
- Recognising the experience of black students
- Raising the status of ethnic minority students in the LEA.

Summary

Brief details of four of the schools where some of the curriculum development was undertaken was given at the beginning of this chapter. Details of subject areas was given. It has not been possible to provide an analysis of the material discussed here. Neither has it been possible to include detailed lesson plans or field notes concerning these developments. I have restricted my comments here to just four subject areas - English, Home Economics, Mathematics and Science. However, the above curriculum initiatives illustrate in more detail than the description provided in the previous chapter, the range of work undertaken in several schools during the life-time of the two Education Support Grant projects. Also highlighted are some of the problem that I faced as advisory teacher trying to undertake multicultural and antiracist work in all-white schools.

Notes

1   Nicolo Machiavelli, *The Prince*, first writeen in 1513. The quote is from the 1993 Wordsworth Edition, p 43

2   The coded message in chapter 13 (p 183) was photocopied and used with the children. The mixture of words and numbers proved to be of great interest to the children. The mixture of words and numbers proved crack the code, it was interesting to see an actual real-life example of the use of coded message by real-life spies. Part of the message reads: ".... 68971 71129 EXTREME CAUTION AT PRESENT TIME 56690 12748 92640...." One begins to understand why the pupils were so interested in this aspect of the language module.

3   See also Sharan Jeet Shan's account of her first year on the Education Support Grant project in Birmingham where she faced racism both from teachers and pupils on the grounds of "race" as a black woman.

4   Bonnet, A (1993) *Radicalism, Anti-racism and Representation*, p 140

9 Pupil survey

Pupil survey

Questionnaire

The questionnaire was conducted during one week at a mixed comprehensive school (school C) in London. Lengthy discussions, stretching over two terms, had taken place at the meetings of the Working Party on Equal Opportunities. This group had the brief of looking at gender and race as separate issues - its brief was to bring forward items on policy matters to the whole staff for discussion and ratification. The support of the Head Teacher had been secured by the working party so that the survey could be carried out with the full support of the staff.

Parallel surveys amongst the pupils and staff had been planned, but because of industrial action, the staff survey did not come to fruition. However, a questionnaire was developed for the staff survey and is found in the Appendix.

At a meeting of the Working Party on Equal Opportunities, it was decided to target two year groups for the questionnaire. I felt it was important that the first years [Year 7] be one of the survey groups as the issue of multicultural and antiracist education has to begin with young children. With this in mind, what better place to start than the first years? I suggested the fifth years [Year 11] as the other group because this would give us a good gap in the two groups in terms of ages. The first year group were eleven years old while the fifth year group would be fifteen years old. However, it was pointed out that at the time of the survey, some of the fifth years would have left following Easter, and their fifteenth birthday; the remaining pupils would be heavily involved in preparing for external examinations. The fourth year [Year 10] group was eventually chosen as the next best age group so that meaningful comparisons could be made between the two age groups. It would also give us a range of views on racism across the different age range (11 and 14 year old respectively).

Once this had been agreed, at a meeting of the Working Party on Antiracist Education, Year Leaders and teachers of the first and fourth years were invited for comments on the proposed plan of the questionnaire survey. At this meeting I suggested that the survey be conducted during a double English lesson to give the survey the status of importance. The Working Party had the co-operation of the Head of English Department, and as there were two members of the English Department in the Working Party, this was a relatively easy solution. However, it was argued by the members of the Working Party that the survey be conducted during Personal and Education Lessons, that is, during Tutor times. It was pointed out the Personal and Social Education had a very high profile at the school where important issues were discussed. I was assured that in no way would the status of the survey be diminished by being conducted during Personal and Social Education lessons. I would have preferred the survey to have been conducted during English lessons to give them a higher status, but all the staff members on the Antiracist Working Party were unanimous in carrying out the survey during Personal and Social Education lessons. This is understandable as there would be minimum disruption of "proper" lesson time. Notwithstanding this reservation, comments on each of the questions in the pupil survey are offered in order to tease out some generalisations.

One of the concerns that the pupils expressed when the survey had been mentioned to them was the factor of anonymity - the pupils were assured that they would not be expected to put their names on the questionnaire. However, some pupils, particularly in the fourth year, were quite vehement about this aspect of the survey and suggested that the questionnaires be destroyed after the results had been analyzed. Some were afraid that their handwriting would be recognised by their teachers. As we wanted truthful answers, it was important that the pupils felt completely at ease when answering the questions. This was discussed at the next Working Party meeting and it was agreed that the questionnaires would be destroyed once the reports had been written. This was passed on to the pupils, who seemed happier at the outcome. On reflection, this was a wise move, as some first year pupils included their names on the questionnaires.

In the first year there were a total of 110 questionnaires; in the forth year there were 83 questionnaires. A blank pupil survey, five first year reports together with a summary of the first year report, and the report of the fourth year are included as an Appendix.

The figures have been converted into percentages and graphs drawn for the ones where figures are available. The tables of the percentages are to be found in the Appendix.

Once the figures had been translated into percentages it was deemed necessary to illustrate this information by graphs so that comparisons could be made between the first and fourth year pupils. Although the number is not very large (110 in the first year and 83 in the fourth year, giving a total of 193) it is possible to use the percentages to raise particular issues about the attitudes of white children to the nature of racism found in British society. This was not a quantitative survey, more a qualitative one.

Where appropriate, Chi-square analysis has been applied to the figures of the pupil survey for probability purposes. Where figures are available, each question is followed by a graph to make comparisons easier. The graph is followed by the relevant tabulations of the actual numbers and Chi-square values. This is then followed by a short comment on the significance of the results of the pupil survey. Full tabulations are to be found in the Appendix. The chapter is concluded with an overview of the pupil survey together with a discussion of the wider implications of the survey.

Question 1 - What is racism?

It has not been possible to collect figures for this question because this was a descriptive question. The responses were subjective and aimed at eliciting whether the cohort group had an understanding of the concept of racism and whether there were differences between the two age groups. However, it is noteworthy to note that most of the pupils, in both groups, have linked the issue of racism with colour, culture, race and religion. Religion has been mentioned by some respondents to include the few Jewish pupils at the school, as well as the handful of Asian pupils. Comments such as the following are typical of the responses: "when a person from one culture makes another culture feel inferior" or "when something is said or done against a person without reason". Further details are found in the Appendix.

Question 2 - *Have you suffered racism in this school?*

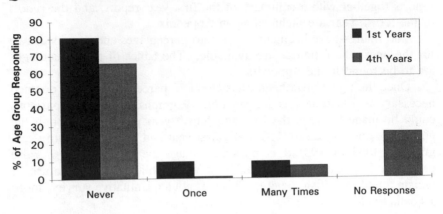

Numbers responding:

	Never	Once	Many Times	No Response	Total
1st Years	88	11	11	0	110
4th Years	54	1	6	22	83
Total	142	12	17	22	193

Chi-square = 35.379 with 3 degrees of freedom, significant at 0.0000001 level, with Yates' Correction.

Excluding non-response:
Numbers responding:

	Never	Once	Many Times	Total
1st Years	88	11	11	110
4th Years	54	1	6	61
Total	142	12	17	171

Chi-square is *not* significant.

Discussion

The real difference here arises from the non-responses in the 1st year. Everyone responds in the 4th year. This is what is significant.

The figures for the fourth year pupils who had not suffered racism is slightly lower than the first years. (1st years 88%; 4th years 66%). It was expected that this figure would be very similar; however, they proved to be significantly different. However, given that there are 94% white pupils in first year group and 92% in the fourth year group this may explain the difference. (see Question 22 below) Another possible reason could be that even by the time the pupils are in the fourth year, and fifteen years old, they have not yet learned to recognise racism when they meet it. It may be that the children have learned not to react or be seen to be over sensitive to racist incidents. It is hardly surprising that the children have not suffered racism as they form the majority population in the school, particularly as racism is defined by the pupils in terms of colour, culture and race. (see Question 1 above)

149

Question 3 - If yes, was this because of colour or race?

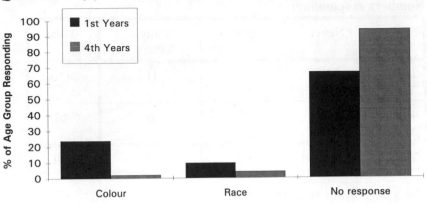

Numbers responding:

	Colour	Race	No Response	Total
1st Years	26	11	73	110
4th Years	2	3	78	83
Total	28	14	151	193

Chi-square = 20.687 significant at 0.000032 level with 2 degrees of freedom. (With Yates' Correction)

Excluding non-responses:
Numbers responding:

	Colour	Race	Total
1st Years	26	11	37
4th Years	2	3	5
Total	28	14	42

Chi-square is *not* significant.

Discussion

As with the previous question, the real differences between the year groups lie in rates of non-response.

It has not been possible to differentiate between religion and language as offered by the pupils because of the small numbers of the cohort group. However, the religion/race, colour/race/country, and colour/race/religion/language/country categories are combined and included in the race column. The results of this question are rather surprising - having defined racism in terms of colour (see question 1 above), the respondents did not choose to divulge this information here. Just over 2% of the fourth years linked this to colour. Again, it would appear that if one is white then one is not likely to suffer racism because of the colour of one's skin. Thus we should not be surprised at the results of this question.

Question 4 - Describe one incident

As this was a descriptive question, numbers of respondents were not collected. However, a vast majority of the incidents involved racist name-calling. For instance, one fourth year Asian pupil wrote: "I was sitting in my car when a group of boys shouted "Paki go home". They threw a half-eaten Mars bar through the open window". It has not been possible to convert the responses into meaningful percentages. However, bearing the limitations on numbers, it has been possible to categorise the responses into two broad bands - physical abuse and verbal abuse. The responses described by the fourth year pupils are equally divided into physical and verbal abuses whereas in the first year group nearly twice as many respondents described a verbal abuse rather than a physical abuse. This is to be expected as physical abuse is the easiest abuse to carry out, and it can be done at a distance and in relative safety. Further examples of comments made by pupils are found in the Appendix.

Question 5 - Did you tell anyone about it?

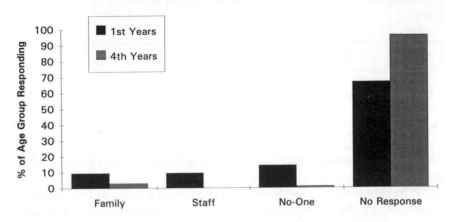

Numbers responding:

	Family	Staff	No-One	No Response	Total
1st Years	11	11	15	73	110
4th Years	3	0	1	79	83
Total	14	11	16	152	193

Chi-square = 24.343 significant 0.00002 level with 3 degrees of freedom. (With Yates' Correction)

Excluding non responses:
Numbers responding:

	Family	Staff	No-one	Total
1st Years	11	11	15	37
4th Years	3	0	1	4
Total	14	11	16	41

Chi-square is *not* significant. Differences are due to non-response.

Discussion

It is interesting to note that none of the fourth years felt able to tell their teachers about the racist incident; on the other hand only 10% of the first years were able to confide in their teachers. A possible reason for this low reporting of racist incidents may include the fact that the pupils know that no action will be taken even if they were to tell any member of staff. (see question 6 below). Another reason may be that the children saw little value in raising the subject with their teachers as this facet of schooling, prior to conducting this survey at the school, had no importance attached to it, particularly at curriculum level. This was one of the reasons why I would have preferred to have conducted the survey during English lessons, rather than during Personal and Social Education lessons. The same reason as for non-reporting to school staff could apply to family members in that their parents would be powerless in trying to do anything about the racist incident. The fact that 14% of the younger group of children could not tell anyone at all is rather worrying - talking about the racist incident is one way to come to terms with the experience, both for the victim and the perpetrator.

Question 6 - Was anything done about this?

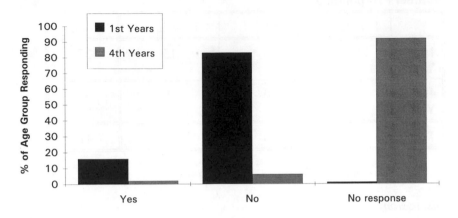

Numbers responding:

	Yes	No	No Response	Total
1st Years	91	18	1	110
4th Years	5	2	76	83
Total	96	20	77	193

Chi-square = 159.681 significant at 0.00000000022 level with 2 degrees of freedom. (With Yates' Correction)

A very highly significant difference in response between the two year groups - but not when counting non respondents.

Excluding Non-respondents:
Numbers responding:

	Yes	No	Total
1st Years	91	18	109
4th Years	5	2	7
Total	96	20	116

Chi-square converted is *not* significant.

Discussion

In the 4th year, instead of saying "No", most children made no response. The findings from this question seem to confirm that confiding in staff members is pointless - 66% of the first years claimed that no action was taken when they reported the racist incident. Yet only 6% of the older group said that nothing was done. This difference may indicate the different levels of development between the two groups of children: the younger pupils may have wanted a more dramatic outcome, such as suspension, exclusion and such like action being undertaken by the teachers. The fourth years on the other hand may have been satisfied with less obvious actions, such as a verbal reprimand.

Question 7 - Were you satisfied with the result?

Although percentage figures are not available for this question because the responses were of a descriptive nature, most pupils claimed they were not satisfied with the outcome. As noted in the summary of the first year results (see Appendix) some of the incidents referred to by the pupils are not described in sufficient detail, and in some instances answers are omitted altogether. Thus is has been impossible to quantify this answer. Reasons given for not reporting racist incidents varied from comments such as : "It didn't change anything", to "I was just told not to worry about it". It may be that by the time the pupils reached the fourth year, they had come to the conclusion that the teachers were either powerless, or were unwilling for other reasons, to do anything about the racism they experienced.

Question 8 - Do you know anyone who has suffered racism in school?

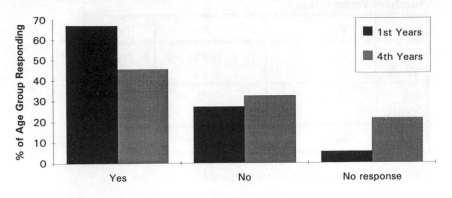

Numbers responding:

	Yes	No	No Response	Total
1st Years	74	30	6	110
4th Years	38	27	18	83
Total	112	57	24	193

Chi-square = 23.777 significant at 0.0000068 level with 2 degrees of freedom. (With Yates' Correction)

When omitting non-respondents Chi-square is *not* significant.

Excluding non-respondents
Numbers responding:

	Yes	No	Total
1st Years	74	30	104
4th Years	38	27	65
Total	112	57	169

Discussion

Taking the difference in pattern of non-respondents into account, there is a very significant difference between the year group samples. The difference in the first and fourth years would suggest that the older pupils had become more sophisticated in their perception of racism - or that they did not necessarily view some incidents which were clearly racist as such. They may have thought them to be bullying, rather than racist. The first years are much more clear cut about seeing someone being a victim of racism. It is not surprising that 27% of the first years and 32% of the fourth years did *not* know anyone who had suffered racism (as defined by the pupils in terms of colour and race and exemplified in question one above) given the low number of black and ethnic minority children in the school. (see question 22 on Ethnicity below).

Question 9 - If yes, explain what happened.

As this question tried to illicit subjective views of the pupils, it has not been possible to quantify the responses. The responses are descriptive in nature. However, comments such as the following are indicative of the range of racist incidents found at this school: "A boy called someone a Paki and kicked them over", "A child said something to a teacher (Asian)". Although percentage figures are not available, it has been possible to categorise the responses into two broad categories - physical abuse and verbal abuse. It has been estimated that in the 4th year there were 30 respondents describing verbal abuse and 6 describing physical abuse. In the 1st year 52 respondents described verbal abuse, while 4 described physical abuse. This is represented diagrammatically below. Further comments from respondents are to be found in the Appendix.

157

Question 10 - If you did not report these incidents, please explain why.

Again this was a descriptive question, asking pupils to be subjective in their responses. Consequently, figures were not tabulated for this question, so comparisons are not possible in terms of percentages. However, the following comments indicate why some children were unwilling to report racist incidents: "Self-preservation", in the case of a victim who felt that they would be in bigger trouble if they reported the racist incident; "Nothing to do with me"; "Because I was being racialist" (from a perpetrator); "Fear", in the case of a victim who felt hurt but did not like telling other people that he had been called a name. Further comments are to be found in the Appendix.

Question 11 - Have you witnessed racist attacks outside school?

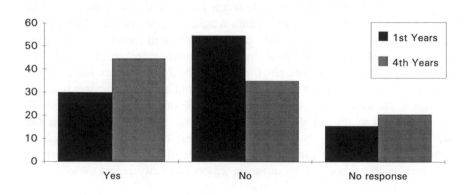

Numbers responding:

	Yes	No	No Response	Total
1st Years	33	60	17	110
4th Years	33	32	18	83
Total	66	92	35	193

Chi-square = 12.276. Significant at 0.002 level with 2 degrees of freedom. (With Yates' Correction)

Discussion:

In the 1st year 30% of respondents claim to have seen a racist incident outside school. In the 4th year 43% said they had seen a racist incident outside school. This could indicate that as children get older they see more of life, and are more observant and aware of racism.

Perhaps the fourth years felt more comfortable in reporting racist incidents outside of the school situation when compared to the first years: 30% of the first years and 44% of the fourth years, respectively. One reason could be that the first years did not necessarily perceive incidents as racist when they may have been - the older pupils would be more likely to identify racist incidents when they saw them. Another reason for the higher reporting amongst the fourth years may be because the incidents happened outside of the school situation and consequently they would not be directly affected by the outcome.

Question 12 - If you were to witness a racist incident in school, what would you do?

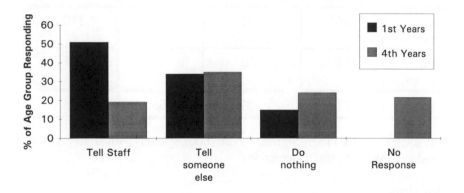

Numbers responding:

	Tell Staff	Tell Someone-else	Do Nothing	No Response	Total
1st Years	56	17	37	0	110
4th Years	16	20	29	18	83
Total	72	37	66	18	193

Chi-square = 103.722. Significant at 0.00000000014 level with 3 degrees of freedom. (With Yates' Correction)

Excluding non-respondents:
Numbers responding:

	Tell Staff	Tell Someone-else	Do Nothing	Total
1st Years	56	17	37	110
4th Years	16	20	29	65
Total	72	37	66	175

Chi-square = 13.115. Significant at 0.0014 level with 2 degrees of freedom. (With Yates' Correction)

Discussion:

It is interesting to note that less than 2% of the fourth years would tell a member of staff about the racist incident, whereas over 50% of the first years would feel comfortable in telling their teachers. This may indicate that the first years still have some faith in the staff being able to do something about the racist incident. The fourth year pupils, on the other hand, would have learned that telling their teacher would have little impact. This is collaborated by the findings to question 6 above, where we saw that an overwhelming 83% of this cohort said that nothing was done about the racist incident they had reported to their teacher.

Question 13 - Should children learn the language of their parents?

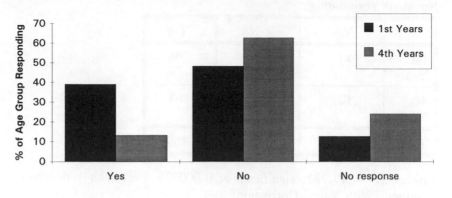

Numbers responding:

	Yes	No	No Response	Total
1st Years	43	53	14	110
4th Years	12	51	20	83
Total	55	104	34	193

Chi-square = 15.924. Significant at 0.00034 level with 2 degrees of freedom.

In the 1st year sample, 39% agree; in the 4th year sample, only 15%. This is quite a significant difference. Also, in the 1st year 12% don't respond on this question, in the 4th year the number doubles to 24%.

Excluding non-respondents:
Numbers responding:

	Yes	No	Total
1st Years	43	53	96
4th Years	12	51	63
Total	55	104	159

Chi-square = 17.781, significant at 0.000025 level with 1 degree of freedom. (With Yates' Correction)

Discussion:

There is a marked difference in the percentage of pupils who felt that children should be taught to read and write in their mother tongue: 39% of the first years and 13% of the fourth years. This would seem to suggest that as the children got older, their negative attitudes towards "differences" gets more entrenched. Another factor may be that the pupils see little or no value in learning a language other than English: this factor is inevitable tied in with the status accorded non-European languages generally, and in the National Curriculum in particular. Further details of this aspect are found in my MA thesis on the teaching of community languages in one London Borough which I undertook as teacher fellow at the University of East London. It would be interesting to see the response to this question in an all-black (Asian) school. It is significant that almost 50% of the first years and over 60% of the fourth years thought teaching someone's mother tongue was not valid in school time. The majority of the fourth years went on to offer racist reasons for this conclusion. For example, "they are in England so they should speak English"; "It is up to the parents....I would refuse to speak an Asian language in school".

Question 14 - Should pupils learn a non-European language?

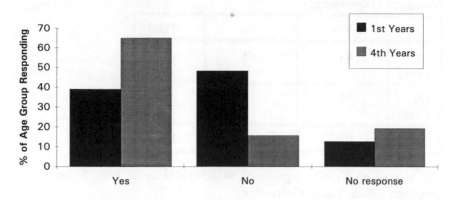

Numbers responding:

	Yes	No	No Response	Total
1st Years	43	53	14	110
4th Years	54	13	16	83
Total	97	66	30	193

Chi-square = 22.272, significant at 0.000015 level with 2 degrees of freedom. (With Yates' Correction)

Excluding non-respondents:
Numbers responding:

	Yes	No	Total
1st Years	43	53	96
4th Years	54	13	67
Total	97	66	163

Chi-square = 20.995, significant at 0.000028 level with 1 degree of freedom. (With Yates' Correction)

Discussion:

In both year groups over 60% of the pupils felt that learning a non-European language was a good thing. This is surprising as the majority of the cohort felt that black children should not be taught their mother tongue (see question 13 above). Some of the reasons given in favour of this had sound educational basis, for example, "so you could understand more about other people". However, once again, those who thought that learning a non-European language was not a good idea gave racist reasons to back up their arguments: for instance, one fourth year pupil wrote: "We live in England - they should learn English like the rest of us."

Question 15 - Should letters be sent home in the language of the parents?

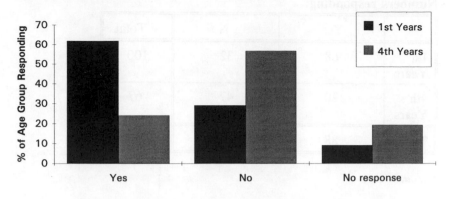

Numbers responding:

	Yes	No	No Response	Total
1st Years	68	32	10	110
4th Years	20	47	16	83
Total	88	79	26	193

Chi-square is *not* significant.

Excluding non-respondents:
Numbers responding:

	Yes	No	Total
1st Years	68	32	100
4th Years	20	47	67
Total	88	79	167

Discussion:

It is interesting to note that almost half of the first year pupils were in favour of sending letters home in a language other than English. This figure drops dramatically to just under a quarter in the case of the older pupils. Once again, the reasons could be that the pupils see little value in sending letters to parents in their home language. However, the reasons given would seem to suggest an entrenched racist position adopted by the older pupils. Also, nearly 60% of the fourth years and 42% of the first years felt that letters should *not* be send home in the child's home language.

Question 16 - Should we celebrate all religious festivals?

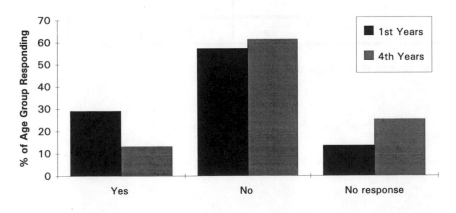

Numbers responding:

	Yes	No	No Response	Total
1st Years	32	63	15	110
4th Years	11	51	21	83
Total	43	114	36	193

Chi-square = 8.916, significant at 0.012 level with 2 degrees of freedom. (With Yates Correction)

Excluding non-respondents:
Numbers responding:

	Yes	No	Total
1st Years	32	63	95
4th Years	11	51	62
Total	43	114	157

Chi-square = 4.921, significant at 0.026 level with 1 degree of freedom. (With Yates Correction)

Discussion:

Again, the is a marked difference between the two year groups in their answer to this question. Only 13% of the fourth years were in favour of celebrating non-Christian religious festivals, whereas almost 30% of the first years favoured celebrating all religious festivals. Significantly, more than half of the respondents in both groups said that they would *not* like to celebrate all religious festivals. This would seem to suggest that by the time the children are in the fourth year, their attitudes to anything other than what they perceive as the "norm" (i.e. white Anglo Saxon Protestant) is seen to have no relevance in their school lives. It would

167

be illuminating to conduct this question in a mainly Asian school and see if there were any differences in the responses to this question.

Question 17 - Should teachers use examples of other countries and cultures?

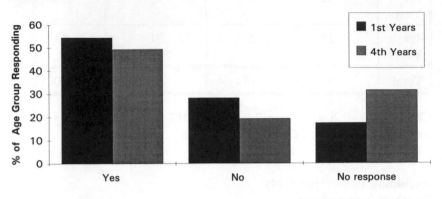

Numbers responding:

	Yes	No	No Response	Total
1st Years	60	31	19	110
4th Years	41	16	26	83
Total	101	47	45	193

Chi-square is *not* significant.

Excluding non-respondents:
Numbers responding:

	Yes	No	Total
1st Years	60	31	91
4th Years	41	16	57
Total	101	47	148

Chi-square is *not* significant.

Discussion:

The fourth year group is less positive about the study of other countries, as compared to the first years. This may stem from two sources. The first reason could be related to the children's experience throughout their years at secondary school. In the case of the fourth years, their three and a half years at the school had not been one of acceptance of a "multicultural" approach. If this aspect is not valued by their teachers, the pupils are unlikely to value this area of the curriculum. Although some sound educational reasoning was postulated in relation to question 14 above, this does not translate into any sort of reasoning here. Again, racist views are expressed, particularly by the older pupils. One such example is: "they do it too much now, it gets on my nerves. This is England, not India they are guests or immigrants to the country so they should fit into our way of living as best they can." (This has been quoted verbatim from the pupil's response, and grammar has not been corrected).

Question 18 - Do people make enough effort to pronounce your name correctly?

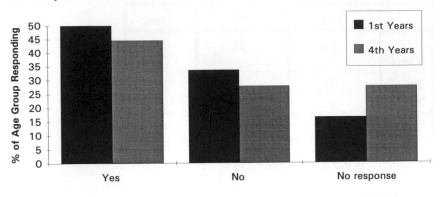

Numbers responding:

	Yes	No	No Response	Total
1st Years	55	37	18	110
4th Years	37	23	23	83
Total	92	60	41	193

Chi-square = 7.840, significant at 0.0051 level with 2 degrees of freedom. (With Yates' Correction)

Excluding non-respondents:
Numbers responding:

	Yes	No	Total
1st Years	55	37	92
4th Years	37	23	60
Total	92	60	152

Chi-square is *not* significant.

Discussion:

Again, the differences between non-response rates are the really significant differences here. The results of this question are rather surprising as one would have thought that with only 6% of the pupils from an ethnic minority background in the first year and 8% of the pupils from an ethnic minority background in the fourth year, there would be no problem in teachers (and other staff members and pupils) pronouncing the pupils names correctly. However, nearly a third of the respondents in both year groups said that teachers did not pronounce their names correctly. If this question was asked specifically to Asian pupils, it is possible that the outcome would have a different response.

Question 19 (a) - Have you ever discussed your cultural or religious beliefs with your teacher?

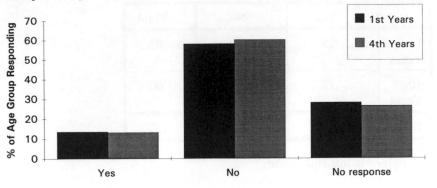

Numbers responding:

	Yes	No	No Response	Total
1st Years	15	64	31	110
4th Years	11	50	22	83
Total	26	114	53	193

Chi-square is *not* significant. The differences are negligible.

Question 19 (b) - Have you ever discussed your cultural or religious beliefs with your class?

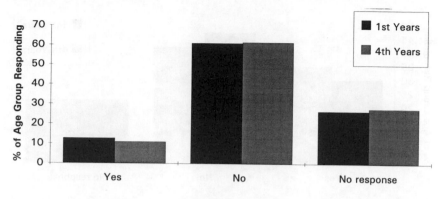

Numbers responding:

	Yes	No	No Response	Total
1st Years	14	67	29	110
4th Years	9	51	23	83
Total	23	118	52	193

Chi-square is *not* significant.

Question 19 (c) - Have you ever discussed your cultural or religious beliefs with your friends?

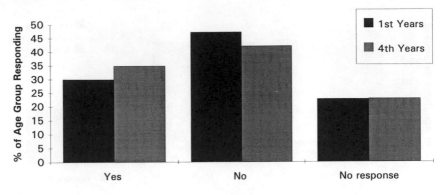

Numbers responding:

	Yes	No	No Response	Total
1st Years	33	52	25	110
4th Years	29	35	19	83
Total	62	87	44	193

Chi-square is *not* significant.

Discussion:

Clearly, most pupils did not feel confident enough to discuss this issue with their teachers; neither could they discuss this with their peers in their class. Both groups were only able to raise this subject with their friends. This may be indicative of the curriculum, or culture, of the school in that issues about one's personal cultural or religious beliefs are not deemed proper school topics for discussion. The similarity of responses between the first years and the fourth years is striking.

Question 20 - Do teachers expect you to do well?

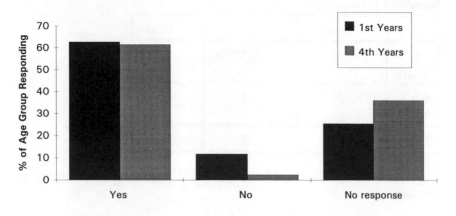

Numbers responding:

	Yes	No	No Response	Total
1st Years	69	13	28	110
4th Years	51	2	30	83
Total	120	15	58	193

Chi-square = 6.549, significant at 0.038 level with 2 degrees of freedom. (With Yates' Correction)

Excluding non-respondents:
Numbers responding:

	Yes	No	Total
1st Years	69	13	82
4th Years	51	15	66
Total	120	28	148

Chi-square = 4.139, significant at 0.042 level with 2 degrees of freedom.

Discussion:

As expected, most pupils felt that their teachers expected them to do well at school. This would hardly be otherwise given the all-white pupil intake and staff membership. One would have expected to get different results were the school one in which the majority of pupils were black and the staff were all-white. However, it is significant to point out that one fourth year pupil said that "Many teachers think black people are more stupid".

Question 21 - Should there be more black and Asian teachers in school?

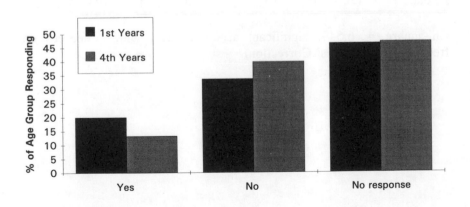

Numbers responding:

	Yes	No	No Response	Total
1st Years	22	37	51	110
4th Years	11	33	39	83
Total	33	70	90	193

Chi-square = 6.857, significant at 0.032 level with 2 degrees of freedom. (With Yates' Correction)

Excluding non-respondents:
Numbers responding:

	Yes	No	Total
1st Years	22	37	59
4th Years	11	33	44
Total	33	70	103

Chi-square is *not* significant. The real differences again lie in the rates of non response.

Discussion:

Again, as expected, when pupils do *not* have a wide experience of being taught by black teachers, then the response to this question is not surprising. Significantly, there were more negative comments offered than positive ones. Some of the negative comments are clearly racist in tone: "I'm sick and tired of Pakis that can't teach", "Most Asian teachers that we have cannot speak good English and don't earn respect for themselves", "white people should be offered jobs before immigrants".

Question 22 - What is your ethnic origin: defined in terms of black or white?

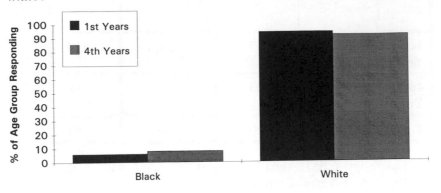

Numbers responding:

	Black	White	Total
1st years	7	103	110
4th years	7	76	83
Total	14	179	193

Chi square is *not* significant. The proportion of black pupils are not significantly different in the two samples.

Discussion:

This is really more a statement of fact. The figures for home languages and religion has not been broken down into separate categories as the number is too small to be meaningful. However, the ethnic origin section of this question reveals that there are only 8% of the two year groups who come from an Ethnic Minority background - 92 % of the pupil make up is white in the total 1st and 4th year cohort. Although this school is classed as an "all-white" institution, an overwhelming 95% of schools in the United Kingdom do not have *any* or at most 1 per cent or

2 per cent of pupils who are black. It would be interesting to conduct this survey in a range of school, from all-black, to 80% black : 20% white; and vice versa, 20% black and 80% white; a fifty-fifty black/white school, and so on.

Q 23 Anything else to say about racism?

Figures for this question are not available as this was a descriptive question. The comments that are available in the responses can be categorised into two broad bands - racist and neutral. These are represented diagrammatically below. There were 16 neutral comments from both year groups, and 15 racist comments from the 4th years and 6 racist comments from the 1st years.

Summary

The pupil survey conducted at school C in London raised some important issues concerning the attitudes that white children have about black people living in the United Kingdom. Most of the views of white children in all-white schools have been developed from their reading, the images seen in the media, and their experience at school, both in terms of other pupils and staff at the school, as well as the curriculum they are taught.

The survey revealed quite conclusively that racist attitudes, largely based on colour, is rife amongst white pupils: the survey enabled some pupils to write freely about their views of racism. For example a number of questions asked the pupils for their subjective views. For instance they were asked to describe a racist incident they had experienced or witnessed, or to write about racism in general and specific terms. The full range of experiences ranging from racist name calling to physical abuse were described and details are to be found in the Appendix.

Several factors emerge from this pupil survey. The first one is the time scale involved in carrying out the survey, and analyzing the results before action is undertaken. Discussions at the Equal Opportunity Working Party took over two terms with the questionnaire being revised several times. Analysis took about two weeks after the responses had been collected. This means that it took almost three terms to undertake the pupil survey. In terms of my time at the school, the survey was quite time consuming, even though I was not involved in the actual process of pupils filling out the questionnaire. In the context of time spend at the school, the survey took up a large section of allocated time. What this

179

means is that while the survey was being discussed and undertaken, the time available for curriculum development was restricted. Also, teachers at the school were unwilling to carry out curriculum development work before the results of the survey has been analyzed. In a sense teachers felt quite "safe" with the survey - they did not have to think about what they were teaching while the survey was being undertaken. So long as the survey was being discussed, curriculum development could wait. And because the time scale of the Education Support Grant project was a finite one of three years, any time taken up with work other than curriculum development would suit the teachers very well. The survey filled that gap admirably.

A parallel to this scenario is the monitoring that goes on in the name of equal opportunities. Monitoring is often used as a delaying tactic for direct action - in equal opportunity initiatives a lot of time and energy is spent in collecting data which sometimes becomes the product itself, rather than a means to an end. It is a way of avoiding the real issues of oppression - while people are very busy collecting statistics, those in power continue to operate in an unequal and prejudiced way, in the knowledge that they will be unhindered in this because of the smoke screen of monitoring. In the same way, the pupil survey can be seen as a delaying tactic which the teachers at the school were very happy to undertake because it left them free to continue teaching their subjects without interference or fear of curriculum development and intervention.

However, once the results had been analyzed, the teachers realised the extent of racist attitudes amongst their pupils and were motivated to undertake curriculum development as quickly as possible. The survey had the effect of mobilising the teachers into action concerning curriculum development work. Some of the teachers on the Equal Opportunities Working Party had early access to the responses and they "felt disgusted and disturbed by the responses". Further, they realised that a more direct approach is needed to tackle pupils' racist views. Some of the work carried out in the English Department is described in the following chapter.

Over seven months later, the pupil survey was reported in a local newspaper when the subject was raised at a meeting of the local education authority's Community and Curriculum sub-committee group. The survey was inaccurately labelled as "Racism in the Playground", and suggested that some pupils took all morning to complete the questionnaire. However, the adviser for multicultural education in the borough said that the survey was the only logical way teachers could assess pupils' attitudes. The survey provided teachers with vital information they could not obtain in any other way. The adviser went on to stress that the success of multicultural education depends heavily on the views of children.

The teachers were supportive of the initiative as far as the Press were concerned. The survey also gave currency to any new developments that I suggested. Once the teachers realised the extent of racist views of their pupils, they were more than willing to undertake some curriculum development work. This is highlighted in the range of subject areas that I was able to undertake at this school. Meetings between Head of Department and other teachers took place in English, Home Economics, Science and Mathematics as well as discussions with the pastoral teaching staff. My attendance at the Equal Opportunities Working Party continued and in due course we produced a document dealing with racist incidents which became school policy.

10 Institutional racism

...a conceptual framework for multi-cultural education can only become clearer if the issues of institutional racism and problems between dominant and subordinate groups are identified.

The evidence of institutional racism is so voluminous that I cannot hope to do more than provide a few examples. [1]

In the previous chapter, an in-depth account of the pupil questionnaire looking at the understanding of racism amongst white pupils was provided. Graphs, tables and comments supplemented the questions. I have not come across any other pupil survey carried out amongst white children looking specifically at the issue of "race".

This chapter is an attempt to arrive at a working definition of the term "institutional racism" to serve as a backdrop for the main conclusions concerning multicultural and antiracist education in all-white schools. It examines in some detail the history of the term, and provides a critique of the phrase. The chapter also serves to place into context the whole nature of structuralised racism and the long term effects on the educational sector with relation to equal opportunities. I would argue that it is not possible to fully understand antiracist education without a prior understanding of racism in the first place. Furthermore, since one of the major differences between multicultural education and antiracist education is that antiracist education critically looks at the structuralised racism within the school context in particular, and in society generally, it is pertinent to have an understanding of the nature of institutional racism for a full understanding of the arguments put forward in this book.

It is pertinent, then, to begin this discussion with the concept of racism because a clear understanding of the ideology of racism is essential if one is to appreciate the nature of institutionalised racism. Racist ideology may be conceived as being a belief system which provides a picture of the world in which individuals are classified as inferior/superior in terms of moral, intellectual or cultural worth, these being deterministically based on what are seen as racial origins. Contemporary forms of racist ideology have their roots in colonialism.[2] Racism is not a new phenomenon, it has existed ever since human beings began living in societies. In its simplest form, racism is the hatred of one race of people by another distinct group of people. For instance, the ancient Romans "hated" the Christians; while in the mid-Twentieth century, the Nazis despised the Jews. This chapter is primarily concerned with the racism in present day Britain and as such concentrates on the fact that colour plays an important role in the "hatred" between races.

Defining racism

Ruth Benedict was perhaps the first person to tackle the issue of defining racism in the Twentieth century. She defines racism as "a classification based on traits which are hereditary." [3] Racism is defined as "the dogma that one ethnic group is condemned by nature to congenital inferiority and another group is confined to congenital superiority".[4] (In the case of present day United Kingdom, the "superior" group is white while the "inferior" group is black.) Benedict is thus using scientific ideology to define the notion of racism, and goes on to state that racism is linked to class and therefore power. She maintains that racism was originally formulated in France in 1727 during the conflicts between the nobles and the monarchy as the nobles were exasperated by the growing demands of ordinary people. Kirp [5] traces the roots of racism in Britain to the nineteen century. For Lord Swann [6] the roots of racism begin with post-war immigration of black people. However, other writers have maintained that the notion of racism was present earlier. Indeed a cursory look at the literature of the Sixteenth century will show that there were racist attitudes to be found during the time of Queen Elizabeth I. However, what is of importance to us here is that during the Sixteenth century, racism was specifically linked to colour. This is made plain in the proclamation issued in 1601 licensing Casper Van Sanden to deport Negroes from England because of strife felt by the natives.[7] Both Jordan[8] and Mason[9] trace the origins of racial prejudice that is rampant in Britain today to the Sixteenth century.

Mason uses Shakespeare as a representative of the Sixteenth century to illustrate the notion that his contemporaries viewed Negroes, Amerindians and Asians as curiosity figures. In the *Tempest*, for instance, Shakespeare deals with the exotic; the shipwreck and the inhabitants of the island, although in part a feature of the playwrights imagination, had their origin in the "real" world - that is, in discoveries of different coloured people by the Spanish and English navigators. John Donne, the metaphysical poet and one time Dean of St Paul's in London and Shakespeare's contemporary, also uses the theme of shipwreck in his poem "The Storme".

In *Othello* the concept of "race", differentiated by colour, is made explicit. A tragedy - like *Othello* - is essentially concerned with feelings and emotions, the feelings raised in the audiences as they watch the action on the stage. In this case it is the feelings of prejudice against the black protagonist, Othello. We need not concern ourselves overtly here with the internal evidence in the play about the offspring of a mixed-race copulation producing a "beast". What is pertinent to the argument is that the racism prevalent in Britain today has its roots in the Sixteenth century.

Other writers maintain that the root of racism lies in the nineteenth century and draw attention to two works published independently in three different countries: Knox's *The Races of Man* (1850), Goineau's *Mankind* (1854).[10] These authors treated the notion of racism in a scientific manner - "Scientific racism" - and they based their theories on biological "evidence". Banton goes on to state that "as biological doctrine, racism is dead". He argues that discrimination is not based on the false notion of the superiority of whites, but on sociological considerations, namely one of easier assimilation. However, a news item on BBC television in May 1986 made explicit that the idea that of racism based on biological "evidence" is far from dead: on a discussion on why West Indian cricket bowlers were able hurtle the ball at great speeds, the news-team sought out a white medical doctor to "confirm" that this was because of the West Indian players' bone structure. The medical expert claimed that the length of their pelvic bones made it easier for them to bowl faster. Only people of African origin possessed this bone structure. Thus one can see that far from being dead, the notion of scientific (or biological) racism is very much alive. This is also a prime example of how the study of "race" is influenced by the personal values of research workers. Indeed, the whole debate of racism is made more complex because there are so many diverse definitions of the term. Banton represents the liberal school of race relations research and his use of "scientific" data in defining racism ignores the power relations which are an integral part of Benedict's definition quoted above. The notion of power will be dealt with more fully in the discussion of institutional racism.

In line with Banton, it is possible to use the word "race" to mean a group of people who define themselves (or are defined by other groups using physical characteristics, such as skin, eye or hair colour, as criteria. These physical traits are considered a determinant of social behaviour and moral or intellectual qualities, that is, the group is socially defined using physical criteria. Hartman and Husband[11] put it succinctly:

> Race in itself is a matter of no importance; it is a biological fact as peripheral to essential human nature as differences in height or eye colour. Race as a means of *classifying* (original emphasis) people socially, however, is important. That is another way of saying that race is important because people think it is important.

The advantages for white liberals in this use of the term lies in the way that once the existence of any trace of "biological" determinism is removed or repudiated, then the problem of racism as defined by den Berghe and Banton cannot be considered as racist. Thus racism, within this framework, is a convenient form of ideology. Or as Sivanandan argues, firstly, as Capitalism requires stratification on racist lines as a result of specifically economic requirements, and secondly, Capitalism requires racism as a justification for certain forms of political practice that may or may not correspond to economic requirements.[12] Thus, for Marxist theorists, racism usefully diverts the proletariat from arriving at a full understanding of their position in relation to the economic world and their position in the social hierarchy.

One can see from the above short discussion that there is no one agreed meaning of the word "racism" and this leads to the confusing array of meanings that are accorded the term by different writer. Indeed, there are as many meanings of the word "racism" as there are workers in the field.[13]

This brief outline shows the origin of racism (based on colour) in the Western world. One must not forget the slavery of black people because this period especially was used to justify the subjugation of Africans on the grounds of "race". Indeed, during the Nineteenth century black people were not considered as human beings - they were seen to be less than human, they were considered beasts, and they did not possess a soul. Using these three reasons it was argued that their enslavement was justified. Even after "scientific" knowledge had established that black

186

people were indeed human beings, the racist ideology came up with the notion that black people were inferior human beings. The thinkers of the nineteenth century turned to the Bible to support this view and alluded to the passage where God condemns the offspring of Ham as "savages". I now turn to the term "institutional racism".

Institutional racism in the United States of America

The term "institutional racism" was coined in the 1960s in America and gained rapid currency - especially among the middle-class and in academic circles. One of the major reasons for this was that, once and for all, the blame for the lowly status and poor life standards of the black people could be blamed on the "system". Institutional racism, by the mere phrase, took the blame away from individuals - now white people could be racist, intentionally or not, and still feel that the plight of black people had nothing to do with them. It was the "system", the status quo, which prevented black people from rising above the drudgery in which they found themselves. Stokely Carmichael and Charles V Hamilton[14] were instrumental in making the phrase popular, but it was theorised by such sociologists as Baron[15], Benokratis and Feagin,[16] Blauner,[17] Jones,[18] Knowles and Prewitt[19] and Wellman[20] and educationalist such as Baratz and Baratz,[21] Katz,[22] and Spears[23]. Carmichael and Hamilton differentiated between individual and institutional racism by stating that the latter was less overt, more subtle and associated with established and respected institutions in society.

> When white terrorists bomb a black church and kill five black children, that is an individual act of racism, widely deplored by most segments of society. But when in that same city, Birmingham, Alhabama, five hundred black babies die each year because of the lack of proper food, shelter and proper medical facilities, and thousands more are destroyed or maimed physically, emotionally, and intellectually, because of conditions of poverty and discrimination in the black community, that is a function of institutional racism.[24]

According to Carmichael and Hamilton it was the power which was located in the hands of the white people that made it so difficult to dismantle institutional racism.

For Jones[25] institutional racism specifically referred to the established laws, customs and practices which were systematically

187

reflected in American society and the consequences of this was not governed by the fact that individuals were not racist. It was the end result of the system of the particular institution that was important. So long as the practices and customs of the institution prevented black people from progressing within the structure, then that institution was racist, whether or not the individuals maintaining those practices had racist intentions. For Blauner,[26] institutional racism was concerned with unintentional and routine actions. Benokraitis and Faegin[27] provide a more detailed definition of the term:

> Institutional racism refers to the structure of inequality, (1) reflected in the racially based differential allocation of status, privileges and material rewards in numerous institutional sectors; and (2) shaped by the historically precipitated and currently persisting processes of subordination whose mechanisms primarily involve the imposition of conventional norms by often unprejudiced role players in the various institutional sectors, in a way which, though covert and usually unintentional, produces racially relevant consequences.

What are we to make of this initial response to the use of the term "institutional racism"? Firstly, it is obvious that all the writers who analyzed the term stressed the significance of racist ideologies in sustaining, initiating and justifying racial inequalities and the oppression of black people. However, the term as employed by these analysts does not denote an ideology - that came later - but refers to a number of other processes such as the active and pervasive anti-black attitudes white people and the policies designed to subjugate black people, so that they are unable to be an equal part of American society. Frequently, the words, racism and institutional racism, were used interchangeably and this necessarily led to confusion.

Secondly, the term institutional racism was not used in isolation as an explanatory concept. The racial oppression of black people was explained by a group of concepts of which institutional racism was one. The others included such concepts as internal colonialism, Franklin and Resnick[28] pointed out the similarities of urban ghettos and neo-colonial situations when they described the ways in which material necessities were imported from the outside, profits together with low paid black labour were exported and, "foreign aid", that is welfare, was received from the government. Blauner[29] extended this analogy - entry into the ghetto was, in his view, involuntary and forced. It was a result of the conquest of the colonisers who destroyed or transformed beyond recognition black values and life styles. The colonised were administered by the dominant white group who used racism as their main justification for social domination. This is not to say that the white working classes were not exploited. But there was one essential difference - whereas the black people were colonised, the whites were not.

Thirdly, as Carmichael and Hamilton pointed out "The core problems within the ghetto is the vicious circle created by lack of decent housing, decent jobs and adequate education....the pervasive cyclic implication of institutional racism." [30] Thus, we can see how the term "institutional racism" is used to describe the inter-relationships between different institutions and how these together reinforced racial inequality.

The fourth point to emerge from this approach is that emphasis was placed, rightly in my opinion, on the fact that white people benefitted from racism and the institutions which perpetuate the system. Wellman stated that racism constitutes "culturally sanctioned beliefs which, regardless of intentions, defend the advantages of the whites".[31] Walker[32] extends this further to point how discrimination is also of benefit to white people. Baron[33] shows how different small white groups benefitted in financial terms and, more importantly, also psychologically. Blauner could hardly disagree with this view and stressed that skin colour served "as a visible badge of group membership that facilitates the blockage of mobility" thus creating a division within the working class which effectively prevented the development of group kinship.[34] Cox[35] on the other hand maintains that it is members of the capitalist ruling class who benefit most from the perpetuation of racism. However, what he fails to realise is that all white people, regardless of class position, benefit because of the racism which is based on skin pigmentation and that whites would lose out if the racial inequalities were eliminated. Thus it is in the interests of all white people to try and preserve the status quo. Even those white people who have made every effort to rid themselves of their racist attitudes may fail to see how deep rooted these racist attitudes of white people being superior to black people really are.[36] Gibson makes the same point:

> There is a common, but mistaken, assumption in this country that racists are all people with ill will towards blacks. The phenomenon of racism extends, however, far beyond the frontiers of blind prejudice typified by organisations like the National Front; in fact, the worst offenders are often those with the very best of intentions. Such people do not call for the expulsion of black people, nor do

they proclaim openly that whites are more intelligent, civilised, clean, cultured, etc. They merely assume these things, though often without realising it. They even bend over backwards to be helpful to ethnic minorities, but their fundamentally patronising betrays the underlying racist attitude with which the system has imbued them.[37]

Lastly, the emergence in the 1960s of racism as a central analytical concept had important implications for political strategies. Allen argued that the focusing on racism took precedence and prevented a wider understanding of exploitation generally.[38] Marable has documented the forms of national and cultural nationalism which followed directly from the notion of racism as the central issue in the life chances of both white and black people.[39] Thus class alliances were avoided in the struggle for equality and opportunity and one group of people were able to benefit from the misfortunes of another group(that is, white people benefitted because black people suffered).

The above provides in a very sketchy manner the nature of institutionalised racism in the United States of America. However there are many similarities to be found in the situation in Britain as will be seen in the next section.

Institutional racism in the United Kingdom

In Britain Humphrey and John were the first writers to popularise the notion of institutional racism. They described the appalling situation black people faced in Britain and went on to stress that this was not merely as a result of individual prejudice or racism but ingrained in the institutions such as hospitals and schools. "Institutionalised racism - manipulating the bureaucratic system to outflank the unwanted - may not be as rampant in Britain as in America, but it appears vividly among planning and housing regulations".[40] However, I argue later in this chapter that institutional racism is just as rampant in the educational system.

Dummet [41] offered further evidence of the pervasive nature of racism on black people in Britain. She uses the same term of descriptive definition of the term, institutional racism, as Humphrey and John: "Institutions which effectively maintain inequality between members of different groups in such a way that open doctrine is unnecessary...Racist institutions, even if operated partly by individuals who are not themselves racist in their beliefs, (emphasis added) still have the effect of making and perpetuating inequalities".[42] Thus we can see how institutionalised racism, while beneficial to white people, effectively renders them blameless for the appalling situation of the black citizens of Britain. Allen[43] on the other hand maintains that institutional racism could be found in the relationships between immigrant (euphemism for black) and indigenous (meaning white) people, and in the wider sphere, between metropolitan and colonial societies. Here again the emphasis is on the consequences of these factors rather than on the intentions of individuals. Fenton provides a clear exposition of the term:

(a) Racism is not to be found in the ideal construct but in regular practices, rules and the enduring features of society,

(b) Racism as a belief or attitude is somehow masked but is nonetheless structurally evident in practice.

(c) It may even be conceded that racist attitudes are absent but the structure correlates - inequality, disadvantage and subordination - are still fashioned along racial lines.[44]

Space has limited me to an examination of just a small handful of examples of definitions of the term institutional racism, but there are many others.[45] What they all reveal is that the emphasis placed on consequences rather than individual actions are the same as in the case of the American usage of the term. Also, racism is seen as something beyond individual discrimination or prejudice against black people. But most important of all perhaps is the fact that the notion of institutional racism has become so popular that it is frequently used without clarifying its meaning.[46] A discussion of institutional racism in Education is best left until after an examination of the wider issues within British societal structure.

Institutional racism and the immigration of black people to the United Kingdom

In dealing with institutional racism in the context of Britain, there are two main threads which throw light on the matter. The first one concerns the laws which have been passed to restrict the entry of black people into Britain. The second one concerns the bussing policy introduced in the 1970s by several local education authorities, for example Hounslow and Leicester.

One can begin with the Nationality Act of 1984 which, though not debarring black people from work per se, had the effect of deskilling them - black workers were forced to take dirty, low paid jobs that white workers no longer wanted. This had the effect of segregating the workforce. As a result of the Nationality Act, racialism operated on a free market, not on the basis of avowed racialism but in the habit of acceptable exploitation.[47] Racialism operated under the name of "colour bar" in pubs, dance-halls, clubs, bars and other public places. The same colour bar deprived Asians and African-Caribbeans from decent housing. The result was that the black population and pooled their resources and bought their own property.

With the passing of the Commonwealth Immigrants bill in 1962, racism passed on from being a matter of free enterprise to being nationalised. The Act restricted admission of Commonwealth immigrants for settlement to those who had been issued with employment vouchers. In this way Britain could cream off the best professional people, such as engineers and doctors, from third world countries, thus depriving the countries of emigration of their most able workforce - their future leaders.[48] Discrimination was now institutionalised. Racism became respectable, sanctioned by government, it became acceptable. And the logic was impeccable: it was not colour that was the important factor, but numbers. It was reasoned that a fewer number of black people in Britain led to better race relations. Henceforth racism was institutionalised and racial discrimination was inhered in the structure of the state, both locally and nationally. One has only to look at some of the events in the year following the Commonwealth Immigrants Act to see how discrimination on colour lines was becoming more acceptable.

On 1 March 1968, the Labour Government passed the Kenyan Asian Act (incidently the longest debate to date in Parliament) barring Asians from entering the United Kingdom. The reason given was geographical not racial though of course it was the colour of the Asians' skin that prevented them from entering what many regarded as their "mother country", as their "second home" and legal right as British Passport holders. The 1962 Commonwealth Act did not apply to the Kenyan Asians as they were already British citizens by virtue of the fact hat they held British passports. However with the passing of the Kenya Asian Act, official racial discrimination was introduced into the British Immigration policy.[49]

The 1977 Immigration Act stopped all primary immigration of black people. Only "patrials" (euphemism for white Commonwealth citizens) had right of abode in the UK now.

The latest Immigration Act has been shown to favour certain peoples more than others. One does not have to delve deeply to realise that those not allowed in to Britain are black. The latest event in this sage is to introduce a visa system for certain selected countries, namely, Bangladesh, India and Pakistan. British (white) officials were posted in these countries so that applications by people wishing to join their families already settled in the UK can be turned down in the country of application. In September 1987, there was talk of five plane loads of immigrants and refugees from Bangladesh arriving at Heathrow, that the British Government introduced visa restrictions immediately. This is a clear example of overt institutional racism.

This brief and sketchy outline shows how racism has been institutionalised in British society. By passing laws, discrimination on colour grounds has become not only institutionalised but acceptable. And of course, the phrase itself absolves the (white) individual of any guilt.

The black feminist novelist and poet Alice Walker [50] gives a flavour of the present-day racism in the United States of America in her poem entitled "These days I think of Rebecca". The poem encapsulates, it seems to me, some of the issues which are pertinent to black people in America and Britain. The poem focuses on how the black people are still at the bottom of the heap, despite antiracism, civil rights or positive action.

Institutional racism and the education system

Now to turn our attention to institutional racism in the education system. Ben-Tovim[51] maintains, contrary to other researchers who believe that institutional racism constitutes the most important and only way to understand the operation of racism within the educational system,[52] that institutional racism operates in tandem with cultural, ideological, structural and organisational forms of racism. His argument is that institutional racism refers directly to such factors as "bussing" for the "immigrant child" (i.e. the black child), the "hidden curriculum" which propagates racist views, and the bias towards Eurocentric values in school textbooks. In October 1963, white parents in Southall demanded separate classes for their children on the grounds that the black pupils were holding back their children's progress. In December that same year, the Commonwealth Immigrants Advisory Council reported "the presence of a high proportion of immigrant children in one class slows down the whole class, especially where the immigrants do not speak English fluently."[53] In some local education authorities, such as Leicestershire, the black children were bussed to schools in rural areas, sometimes as far away as twenty miles distance, in order to arrive at a more "balanced" pupil intake. For these mainly Asian children the day began at 7.30 in the morning outside their local school where a local education authority school bus picked them up, and ended well after five o'clock in the evening. Part of the racism that is apparent is that the local education authorities did not think of bussing in white children to inner city schools. Similar patterns of discriminatory views and practice can be found in the field of employment.[54]

To return to Coard who was one of the first people to point to the over-representation of West Indian children in Educationally Subnormal schools (ESN schools) and their under-representation in academic sixth forms (they are often found to be doing non-examination courses at sixth form level), and under-representation in higher education. Coard [55] publicised the horrendous situation in ESN schools concerning the great over representation of West Indian children in these schools. His short book was a land-mark in the multicultural education movement and led to several LEAs re-evaluating their selection procedures for ESN schools. However, the situation has remained unchanged over the past twenty years, and black pupils are still underachieving. At least one white liberal author has described Coard's book as a "polemic",[56] thereby belittling Coard's important work. This after several LEAs had accepted Coard's findings and acted on them! This perhaps also highlights how racist views can be perpetuated by well-meaning white writers. Another fairly recent publication is Gibson's study of African-Caribbean children which will no doubt be dismissed as another polemic, a work not to be taken too seriously. As Gibson points out in his Introduction: "These research findings will no doubt be challenged and the methodology decried by those who have nothing better to do than snipe at the efforts of others without bothering to see what lessons can be learned." [57]

An indication of the power of institutional power is the fact that writers such as Kirp are taken so seriously. His thesis is that changes can occur in school on a basis of indirect action. This action is seen as being conducted in little doses (*Doing Good By Doing Little*, as the title of his book proclaims), and preferably without open mention of the changes taking place. Thus he can be seen to be taking a multicultural stance, whereas the more pro-active antiracist stance is to be preferred. Once one has accepted that there is a problem, i.e. of racism, then one can go about tackling it. If however, as Kirp maintains, things are to be changed so gradually that teachers will not notice the alterations, then the process will easily take us into the next century. With the rise of racist attacks in all parts of the country[58] and across Europe[59] and the political climate particularly in view of the high, and rising, rate of mass long-term unemployment, it is not practical to take the slow route as suggested by Kirp. As Tierney points out, Kirp's final analysis is that there is no solution to the [race] problem.[60] One can only hope that teachers will move away from the mere tinkering of the curriculum that has characterised multicultural education over the past twenty years, and declare a commitment to real overt change for time seems to be running out fast. The post 1986 riots and the recent events in Los Angles may be an indication of what the future may hold if antiracist practices are not adopted on a wide scale, particularly in all-white schools.

Attempts have been made by white people to understand that situation of black people in Britain and America. In London this has taken the form of the Metropolitan Police actively mixing with the black youth in an effort to learn British Jamaican. In America, a white man turned himself black in a "scientific experiment" to understand at first had what life might be like for a black man in the States.[61] As Griffin himself points out, this is really the experience of a first-class (white) citizen as a Negro in the South, and not the Negro's. The experiment was a brave undertaking, but very limited in scope because it only lasted for four weeks. And Griffin had the choice of turn himself white at will by not applying the black dye. No white person in Britain can really understand what it feels like to be hated because of one's skin colour, twenty-four hours a day, every day of one life. Perhaps all one can do is read black peoples accounts of their experience of racism in Britain and in America, in an effort to empathise with them.[62]

Saunders specifies four types of racism: individual, cultural, institutional and structural. So far as institutional racism is concerned, it is [usually] expressed covertly. For example, in schools various forms of grouping, such as setting, tracking, streaming and special classes and units may be called institutional racism in so far as they lead to a preponderance of, say, West Indian children in any group of lower attainment [63]. Saunders goes on to highlight how institutional racism manifests itself in the "hidden curriculum" - for instance, all role models (teachers, pupils, and so on) are white, ethnocentric testing materials which are biased in favour of the white majority pupils, and ethnographic teaching materials. All these factors are part of the biases found in school organisation. Thus we can see how certain practices lead to institutional racism within the education system - materials is particularly apparent in schools.[64] The same is true for higher education, but research has yet to be undertaken in this sphere.

Shallice[65] suggests that institutional racism accounts for the low number of black students being recruited into the teaching profession;

even when black teachers are found in schools, they are usually in the lower echelons of the profession's hierarchy;[66] the refusal of teachers to take seriously the State's laws on immigration and nationality particularly when child are actually removed from school classrooms by police and the general absence of an antiracist curriculum to enable greater understanding of the insidious nature of racism by pupils.

Institutional racism and the school curriculum

It will be useful at this point to see how institutional racism functions in schools. A good place to start is the curriculum. To take history as an example: this has traditionally been concerned largely with Britain and if other parts of the world are studied, it is through British eyes. For instance, the "discovery" of East Africa - "the Doctor Livingstone, I presume" syndrome was one that was propagated throughout the study of African history. Indeed, African history was not concerned with Africans at all but with white people who came to colonise the continent.[67]   None of the African civilisations were seen to be "developed" - for instance, no mention is made of the elaborate systems of government that the Nigerian tribes had organised. Indeed one of the greatest and oldest civilisations - that of Egypt - is not even considered an African civilization. Egypt is seen somehow to belonging to Europe and the people not considered African.[68] It is this blinkered vision that makes up part of the institutional racism in schools today. Traditionally, anything European was seen to be best - indeed, white is right - and anything different was seen as inherently inferior. Everything was compared by taking the European as the correct standard, as the norm. This is even true today where all subjects and things are compared with European counterparts. And usually the European model is taken to be the superior. A graphic example is to be found in the field of Architecture.[69] In the case of Britain, and other European countries such as Denmark and France, this attitude of superiority stems from the days of colonial conquest and rule.

Most school histories ignore the fact of economic conditions which influenced the rise of slavery. But to talk of slavery in purely colour terms would be a falsehood. The Romans had Christian slaves and the Greek traded in slaves. Colour was not the issue here - black leaders were just as likely to have white slaves. However, the ancient slavery was very different from the slavery which arose in the eighteenth and nineteenth centuries. The Greeks, for instance, did not see slaves as inferior human beings: the slaves had the option of buying their freedom, something that the black slaves were denied. The Greek slaves formed a particular rung on the social order and served a particular function in that order. Another main feature was that the slaves could rise above their lowly status and become slave owners in their turn. Failing this they were able to better themselves with learning - they were not left illiterate, but were treated as part of the family. Indeed, Aesop, the writer of fables who had a profound influence on most major English writers from Shakespeare down, was a slave of African parentage in a Greek household.[70]

Another myth about slavery that is taught in schools is that it was the white people who were the protagonists in the fight to abolish slavery. No mention is made of the constant "freedom riots" which the slaves organised in an effort to disrupt the hold slave owners had on them. The uprisings frustrated the plantation owners greatly and had a direct effect on the abolition of slavery. School books usually also ignore the economic factors which formed part and parcel of the abolition of slavery. It is no coincidence that just at the time that the slaves were becoming uneconomical, the British decided to abolish slavery. It is only by looking at slavery in the wider context of the socio-economic world that one can begin to understand the nature of history writing. School history teaching is biased towards the British point of view and does not present an objective world picture. This is just one example of how racism has become institutionalised in our school curriculum.

Just two factors of the history syllabus have been chosen for comment here; there are countless others. For example, the reference to the Indian "Mutiny", rather than a fight for independence. The same analysis as that applied to the history syllabus has been applied by local education authorities in their multicultural education documents to other subjects: they have all pointed out the need for a "world perspective".[71] Syllabuses generally fail to reflect the multi-racial nature of British society and this is just one aspect of how institutional racism functions in schools. The underlying effect of merely "tinkering" with the school curriculum is to preserve the status quo. In schools, as in all other educational establishments, it is imperative to re-assess the content of the whole curriculum for its relevance for twentieth century Britain. The GCSE examinations were an ideal opportunity to achieve a balanced curriculum, in terms of an antiracist education curriculum. But, to take the example of the English syllabus, the people in power have failed once again to make any positive changes.[72]

It will be useful at this juncture to provide a critique of the term "institutional racism". In this I follow Williams and Carter[73] and Troyna and Williams.[74] Current applications of the term differ in two important ways from the initial use. The initial use drew attention to the historical institutionalisation of racial inequalities and perpetuation of these inequalities by several interconnecting relationships of several institutions in urban settings. Now, however, the use is usually restricted to a single institution, such as a school. In this limited context the meaning of the term has become oversimplified because it has been reduced to a direct causal link between inequality and institution. There is an assumption here that ideologies are accepted from above and unconsciously absorbed by all white people just because they are white. Williams and Carter argue that "ideologies are actively taken up and reinterpreted by different groups for different purposes. Teachers do not accept stereotypes as a result of indoctrination but because in certain circumstances, and in various ways, they make "sense" in explaining their day to day experience." [75] However true this many be, one must recognise the influence of the media on the population generally, including teachers; comedy programmes, or the news item mentioned above, are presented in such a way that white people are made to feel "OK" about their attitudes to black people.[76]

The concept has taken on the role of being a descriptive term so that if there is evidence of discriminatory practices against black people, then "institutionalised racism" has taken place. Of course, as discussed above, inequalities occur in all spheres of society, from education establishments to factories. However, as educational institutions are the "training ground" for future generations then they must be singled out for special study. Further, what happens in schools is mirrored in colleges and universities and in factories, hospitals and all other institutions.[77]

Troyna and Williams [78] draw attention to the fact that examples of institutional racism are given from a societal level or from an individual level. As far as schools are concerned, this happens in singling out teachers' attitudes, expectations and stereotypes of black people which lead to and perpetuate racial inequality. Newsam's claim that "A "racist" institution is quite simply one in which discriminatory rules or systems apply and no one has either noticed or tried to remove them" [79] is seen by them as being overly simplistic. However, it is not possible to separate the two; institutions are made up of individuals who act in a discriminatory way, even if it is the "system" which forces them to act

198

in this way. The power to change institutions lies in the hands of individuals - and as we have seen, white individuals do not wish to alter the status quo as they have far too much to lose. As Sarup has pointed out, black people in this country form a special and oppressed section within the British working class; black people are a sub-proletariat, a new dark-skinned underclass beneath the white social order. black and immigrant workers suffer specific racial oppression over and above the normal oppression and exploitation experienced by all workers.[80] Thus it is in the interest of white workers and educators to try and diffuse the situation by suggesting that there is a dichotomy between institutions and individuals. However, it has been argued above, the two are inseparable.

Troyna and Williams conclude by asserting that it cannot be assumed that streaming, teacher stereotyping, the designation of catchment areas, the monocultural curriculum and so on, are causally related to each other or contribute straightforwardly to the generation of racial inequalities. Of course, they are all examples of injustices and should be removed as soon as possible from the educational stage. But their exact relationship to racial inequality can only be theorised not demonstrated empirically at the moment.[81] An attempt has been made to demonstrate from the single instance of institutional racism detailed above that it *is* possible to evaluate racial inequality in schools. Again, it is individuals who are the key actors in the function of institutional racism. And for Troyna and Williams to claim that it does not matter if the individuals are white or black is to ignore the "hidden curriculum". Another example of how white liberal educators have (perhaps unintentionally) tried to nullify the effects of racism on black people is provided by Jeffcoate.[82] He suggests that achievement in sport is just as valid as achievement in academic subjects. This is in response to conclusive evidence that African-Caribbean pupils are streamed into non-academic classes. Jeffcoate seems to be suggesting that teachers' attitudes and stereotyping is quite acceptable because black children are doing well at sports. But as every unemployed black (and white) youth knows, what Sivanandan has called not the unemployed, but the never employed,[83] it is academic qualifications which are the route to employment. Jeffcoat's analysis can be seen as being part of the methods by which institutional racism is effected.

Institutional racism and power

Racism, like sexism and other issues about oppression, necessarily has to do with power. And in present day Britain (and other countries such as Australia, Canada, New Zealand and United States of America) it is white people who wield the power at all levels of the social order. The above discussion has been confined to the power within the school system. The same is repeated in other educational establishments, including colleges and universities, as well as the employment field - the experience of a black female architect was highlighted earlier. What some educators have failed to realise is that institutional racism is not merely a set of rules which, when broken down, will enable inequality to disappear. It is not sufficient to stress that by changing individual attitudes one can change institutional racism. One must remember that racism in Britain is based on colour, with white people at the top and black people at the bottom. It is not simply a matter of class differences. It has been suggested that there a black middle class.[84] However, racism, in the guise of racial harassment, is experienced by *all* black people, irrespective of class. The Guardian reported the racial harassment meted out to Lenny Henry, the local press in Newcastle highlighted the racism faced by black footballers.[85] A more recent case involved the black MP for Tottenham, Mr Bernie Grant, who while travelling on British Rail was asked to move from a First Class Restaurant compartment to his Standard Class compartment as his ticket was deemed not to be valid for the First Class seat which he occupied.

The consciousness of black youth has changed over the past decade. Afro-caribbean and Asian youth are increasingly joining forces as they realise that they are at the brunt of racist attacks. They are beginning to acknowledge that their experience of racism has drawn them together, and are beginning to question the notion of divide and rule - who was it that first suggested that there was a difference between Asian and African-Caribbeans? Are not all black youth to be found together in the dole queues in all major cities? They know that education is note merely about "child-minding"; it is there to develop certain skills for use in the factories; to grade and discipline the workers. Racism is not simply the discriminatory attitudes of white people with whom black people come into contact, but rather a specific mechanism which reproduces the black labour force from one generation to another in places and position that are race-specific. In other words, black people experience a form of indigenous racism which has its roots in the real material conditions of existence.[86]

Hope for positive change lies in the hands of black youth who are becoming politicised and are voicing their views in no uncertain terms: "We're no longer immigrants but black British, and no power, whether by inducement, coercion or even the most extreme violence will deny us the right to enjoy full and equal British citizenship".[87] In parallel with the limited empowering of black youth, I would argue that the white youth has been greatly empowered as a result of the "disenfranchisement" of black youth. As stated earlier, what is of disadvantage to black children is of direct and proportional advantage to white children. The scientific notion of action and reaction would seem to apply in this case.

Summary

This is a wide ranging discussion on the nature of institutional racism. An historical development of the concept of institutional racism was described and also how the concept travelled from the USA to Britain in the 1960s. I also provided a critique of the term.

I see this chapter as central to multicultural education and antiracist education work in all-white schools. As mentioned in chapter two above, an understanding of institutional racism is crucial for an appreciation of multicultural education and antiracist education as initiatives in the area of "race" and education. The discussion here forms an integral part of the proposals put forward in the following chapter which draws together the salient points of the two projects and the future of multicultural education and antiracist education within the new National Curriculum.

Notes

1 The first quote comes from Gundara, J (1992) in Parker, K "The revelation of Caliban - "The black presence" in the classroom" in Gill, Mayor and Blair, *Racism and Education*; the second quote is from Rushdie, S (1982) "The new empire within Britain", New Society, 9 December 1982. Salman Rushdie gives further examples of institutional racism in this article.

2 Tierney (1982) *Race, Migration and Schooling.*

3 Benedict (1942) *Race and Racism*

4 ibid, p 97

5 Kirp (1979 *Doing Good by Doing Little*

6 Swann (1985) *Education For All*

7 see Hughes and Larkin ((1969) *Tudor Royal Proclamations 1588-1603* and Walvin (1972) *Black and White*

8 Jordan (1962) *Prospero's Magic*

9 Mason (1962) *Race Relations*

10 Banton (1979) in Verma and Bagley *Race, Education and Identity*

11 Hartman and Husband (1974) *Racism and the Mass Media*

12 Sivanandan (1976) *Race, Class and the State*

13 Mullard (1982) *Racism in Society and schools: History, Policy and Practice*

14 Carmichael and Hamilton (1967) *Black Power*

15 Baron (1969) "The web of Urban Racism"in Knowles and Prewitt (eds), *Institutional Racism in America*

16 Benokraitis and Feagin in Troyna and Williams (1986), *Racism, Education and the State*

17 Blauner (1972) *Racial Oppression in America*

18 Jones (1972) *Prejudice and Racism*

19 Knowles and Prewitt (1969) *Institutional Racism in America*

20 Wellman (1977) *Portraits of White Racism*

21 Baratz and Baratz (1970) "Early Childhood Intervention: the Social Sciences Base of Institutional Racism *Harvard Educational Review* 40, 1, 29-50 in Troyna and Williams (1986)

22 Katz (1978) *White Awareness*

23 Spears (1978) "Institutional Racism and the Education of blacks", *Anthropology and Education Quarterly*, 9, 2, 127-36

24 Carmichael and Hamilton (1967) op cit. See also Ginsburg (1992) "Racism and Housing - concepts and reality" in Braham, Rattansi and Skellington (eds) *Racism and Antiracism*, p 110 ff

25 Jones (1972) op cit

26   Baluner (1972) op cit
27   Benokraitis and Faegin (1986) op cit
28   Franklin and Resnic (1973) *Political Economy and Racism*
29   Blauner (1972) op cit
30   Carmichael and Hamilton (1967) op cit, p 156
30   Wellman (19770 op cit, pxviii
32   Walker (1985) *Horses Make a Landscape Look More Beautiful*
33   Baron (1969) op cit
34   Blauner (1972) op cit, p 37
35   Cox (1970) *Caste, Class and Race*
36   ILEA (1983) Anti-Racist Statement and Guidelines
37   Gibson (1986) *The Unequal Struggle*, p 105
38   Allen (1973) "The Institutionalisation of Racism", *Race* 15, July pp 99-105
39   Marable (1984) *Race, Reform and Rebellion*
40   Humphrey and John (1971) *Because they are Black*, p 112
41   Dummet (1973) *A Portrait of English Racism*
42   Humphrey and John (1971) op cit, p 131
43   Allen (1973) op cit
44   Fenton (1982) "Multi-Something Education", *New Community*, 10, 1, p 59
45   for instance, ILEA Guidelines (1983); as well as Newham Anti-Racist Statement (1985)
46   for instance, NUT (1986), Plashet School (London Borough of Newham) NUT Policy Statement (1983); Williams (1985) "Redefining institutional racism", *Ethnic and Racial Studies*, Vol 8, No 3
47   Sivanandan (1982) *A different Hunger*
48   see Parekh (1990) *Charter 90 for Asians*
49   Tandon (1984) *The New Positions of East Africa's Asians*
50   Walker (1985) op cit, pp 75/6
51   Ben-Tovim (1978) "The Struggle Against Racism", *Marxism Today*, July pp 203-13
52   see for example Mukerjee (1983) "Collusion, Conflict of Constructive Antiracist Socialisation", *Multicultural Teaching*, 1, 2, pp 24-5
53   quoted in Sivanandan (1982) op cit, 5
54   for instance, Wilson (1978) *Asian Women Speak Out*; and Wandsworth CCR (nd) *No Bloody Suntans*
55   Coard (1971), *How the West Indian child is Made Educationally Subnormal*

56   Kirp (1979) op cit, p 142, note 27

57   Gibson (1986) op cit, p 15

58   CRE, (1987), *Learning in Terror, Living in Terror*; Hesse, et al (1992) *Beneath the Surface: Racial Harassment*; Sheffield CRE (1988) *Because the Skin is Black*

59   see for instance Standing Conference on Racism across Europe (SCORE); *Searchlight*

60   Tierney (1982) op cit

61   Griffin (1983) *Black Like Me*

62   see for instance Braithwaite, Mohanti, Kapo, Cottle, Mehmood. As Klein (1994) points out: "Those of us born white cannot imagine what it is like to go through life knowing that as a black person, you are always open to being called to account for the suspicions held by whites." *Multicultural Teaching*, Volume 12, No 3, Summer, p 6

63   Saunders (1982) "Education for a new Community", *New Community*, 10, 1, pp 64-71

64   see for example, Eggleston, et al (1986) *Education for Some*

65   Shallice (1984), "Racism and Education" in ALTARF, *Challenging Racism*

66   see Patel, T (1986) for a discussion of this issue. See also, Hardy and Vieler-Potter, "Race, schooling and the ERA" in Gill, Mayor and Blair (eds) *Racism and Education*, p 109

67   see Rodney (1983) *How Europe underdeveloped Africa*

68   Paul (1975) *Mozambique, Memoirs of a Revolution*, p 14

69   Haque (1988) "The Politics of Space" in Grewal, et al *Charting the Journey*

70   Rogers (1972) *Great Men of Color*

71   see for example policy statements by Berkshire, Newham, ILEA

72   Umed (1986) "A Rage in Harlem", *Multicultural Teaching*, Vol 4, Summer

73   Williams and Carter (1985) " "Institutional Racism": New orthodoxy, old ideas", *Multicultural Education*, NAME

74   Troyna and Williams (1985) *Race, Education and the State*

75   Williams and Carter (1985) op cit, p 7

76   Hartman and Husband (1974), op cit

77   Eggleston, et al, op cit; Race Today Collective (1983) *The Struggle of Asian Workers in Britain*

78   Troyna and Williams (1985) op cit

79   quoted in Troyna and Williams (1985), op cit

80   Sarup (1982) *Education, State and Crisis*, p 96

81   Troyna and Williams (1985) op cit, p 57
82   Jeffcoate (1979, 1984); Jeffcoate and James (1982)
83   Sivanandan (1976) op cit
84   Brown (1985) "Britain's New Middle Class", *The Sunday Times Magazine*, October 27; Landry (1988), *The New Black Middle Class*
85   *Sunday Plus* Magazine, 5 December 1990, pp 8-10 (plus photographic feature on the front cover)
86   Sarup (1982) op cit, p 108
87   Ali (1980) *The Visible Minority*

11 Conclusion

Multicultural education is dying a slow death.[1]

A number of implications arise from the examination of curriculum development work and the extensive pupil questionnaire survey undertaken in the name of multicultural education and antiracist education in all-white schools that we have coursed through in the course of the foregoing discussion. We have seen in chapters eight and nine some of the initiatives undertaken through Education Support Grant projects in two local education authorities, located in different geographical areas - one in East London and the other in the North East of England.

I set out to show that a multicultural education approach is easier to implement than an antiracist one. However, during the course of my work in several schools - both primary and secondary - we have seen how teachers were willing only to conduct curriculum development work with their children at classroom level along multicultural education lines; on the whole, they were not prepared to take on an antiracist perspective for a variety of reasons. One possible reason may be that teachers felt threatened by the demands made of them by their (mis)understanding of antiracist education as exemplified in the case studies. Another reason may be the brutal attack heaped upon anti-racism by extreme right wing educationalists, the so-called anti-antiracists.[2] Throughout the history of multicultural education and antiracist education, the left has been identified as being the party most likely to make changes through curriculum development along multicultural education and antiracist education lines.

Mac an Ghaill, quoting Green, makes the following observation with regard to education and "race":

There is a common tendency in much educational writing on race to allow that critical slippage from "the problems encountered by" to the "problem of". Given the way in which the state frames the issues in terms of the "problem" posed by blacks rather than the problem of racism, it's little wonder that people should read state policies not as remedies for racism but as ways of dealing with blacks.[3]

If one examines critically the multicultural policies of the two local education authorities under consideration in this book, one begins to see how these are nothing more than glib statements without the inbuilt commitment to put them into action. I would argue that most local education authorities who boast multicultural policies publicise them purely as a public relations exercise - rather like the statement in job vacancies which claims that the company or authority is an equal opportunities employer. However, as we have seen, when I have tried to implement these policies in all-white schools, I have experienced passive toleration at best or outright hostility at worst. Several senior teachers in both local education authorities have made comments such as "the borough is wasting taxpayers money on this [Education Support Grant] project", or "we don't have any black children here, so I don't know why they have sent you to this school. It is not as if we need multicultural input."[4] I would argue that, in addition to the public relations function, multicultural policies are also designed to quell the dissatisfaction expressed by some teachers and most black parents. The local education authorities can place a hand on their heart and say: "We have a multicultural policy - what more do you want?" In the same way that the pupil questionnaire was seen by the teachers at school C as an end in itself, and as a delaying tactic to actual curriculum development work within the Education Support Grant project, so too, I would contend, have the multicultural policies become the ultimate goal so far as multicultural education at classroom level is concerned. It must be emphasised that I am referring to the all-white sector - the situation in multi-racial schools is different, but is not the concern of the present book.

Mac an Ghaill goes on to state that at the two institutions dealt with in the particular inner-city situation which he reported on, "the widespread evidence of black youths' resistance to schooling and the relatively higher levels of black youth unemployment, demonstrate the inadequacies of many multi cultural educational programmes to improve life-chances of black youth" showing clearly that multicultural education as educational philosophy is not working.[5]

208

Sivanandan demands an explicit antiracist approach when he states that "In the field of education...it is important to turn ethnicity and culturalism into anti-racism. But this involves not just the examination of existing literature for racist bias (and their elimination) but for the provision of antiracist texts...and not just an examination of curricula and syllabuses but of the whole fabric of education: organization and administration, methods and material, attitudes and practices of heads and teachers, the whole works."[6] As already noted, Gilroy calls for a move beyond multiculturalism and anti-racism.[7] I have already mentioned that now is the time to think about the alternatives, if there are any, to multicultural and antiracist education. My perspective on the role of multicultural education and antiracist education within the National Curriculum is discussed later.

Curriculum development

It will be useful at this juncture to pause and reflect on the effectiveness or otherwise of the case studies discussed earlier. One of the examples of multicultural education that we saw in the case studies, namely the Gujarati counting rhyme, is precisely at the level which teachers are willing to accept curriculum changes. Another example is the use of different menus around the world that we saw in school A under the development of the Home Economics second year [Year 8] syllabus. Unfortunately it has not been possible to include details of the lesson plans and children's work in any of the schools due to lack of space. However, when I have tried to encourage teachers to take on board antiracist work whereby the school staff would examine the institutional racism prevalent in society at large and present in schools in particular, the co-operation from teachers and head teachers has been conspicuous by its absence. This is graphically illustrated by the work which was planned and which I hoped to undertake in the Mathematics department at school B where the Head of Department, after prolonged meetings and several sessions spent observing lessons, was not able to commit himself to any work other than the Gujarati rhyming work which was discussed in the case studies. The head of department of Mathematics did, however, after lengthy discussions, tackle the issue of "Pascal's" triangle, which was in fact developed in China many centuries before Pascal.[8] An historical perspective was not followed in the course of this work, thereby missing the opportunity to give correct mathematical and historical facts. In all fairness, it must be said that the head of department did undertake some Indian *rangoli* patterns as symmetry work with the children as his curriculum development work encompassing a multicultural perspective. However, when it was suggested that we look at the Mathematics curriculum from an antiracist perspective, for example, the names used in text books which were mainly Christian names, he avoided tackling this by saying that the children were following a scheme of work already agreed by the department the previous year, and further that the children were being prepared for public examinations. Moreover, he claimed that he did not have the time required to devote to this exercise within the constraints of the planned scheme of work. Thus it can be seen that teachers are only willing to accept piece meal and minor changes to the curriculum in the name of multicultural education.

However, there have been some successes. For instance the material which was developed and used in the English Department at school A, and later at school C, was developed with an antiracist perspective. The Head of English department at this school was Anglo-Indian and considered herself to be black - this may have played a major factor in her acceptance of this material for use by all the first year [Year 7] classes in her department. However, it is significant to point out that it was her probationary teacher, straight out of teacher training college, who approached me in the first instance. This occurred after my initial introduction to the school staff at the beginning of the Education Support Grant project. The Head of Department was supportive of the probationary teacher, and once she saw the value of the Language module, adapted her work schedule to incorporate the antiracist module within her English syllabus for the whole of the first year.

Unity

I mentioned this as a case study because I find it ironic that in project which was funded for advisory teachers to work with white school children in the white highlands, one of the few avenues of work open to me as a black teacher in this borough was to produce a black edition of *Unity* which is a publication of Tyne and Wear Anti-Fascist Association (TWAFA) aimed at young people. This example highlights the marginalisation of multicultural and antiracist work in all-white areas. I would argue that it is the structuralised nature of British society, as discussed in the previous chapter, that is at the root of the marginalisation that I experienced in this borough.[9]

Race equality implications of the Education Reform Act 1988

Before I go on to discuss the impact of the latest draft proposals from School Curriculum and Assessment Authority (SCAA) which were published in May 1994, it will be useful to examine the implications of ERA on multicultural education and antiracist education as educational philosophies and practices.

The Education Reform Act 1988 established the National Curriculum for England and Wales and consisted of ten foundation subjects. English, Mathematics and Science were designated as core subjects. The other foundation subjects were: Art, Geography, History, Music, Physical Education and Technology, with a modern foreign language (that is, a European language) for pupils aged eleven and above. At the age of fourteen, some other options were available. For instance, students could drop art and music. They could drop either history or geography, or follow a short course in each, and they could either choose to follow short courses in technology or a modern foreign language. Although Religious Education was not part of the National Curriculum, all schools are required by law to teach it. At the time of writing, the indications are that from September 1994, sex education will become statutory requirement within the National Curriculum. It can be argued that the National Curriculum and National Assessment as established by the Education Reform Act 1988 has challenged teachers' assumptions of what their pupils can achieve and has, as a consequence, helped to raise standards. This aspect is only touched on here; the subject deserves a whole book in its own right.

The 1988 Education Reform Act is one of the many additions to the statutory framework within which educational services are delivered in this country. In this particular case, as the name itself implies, the legislation is aimed more at alteration of the education system rather than mere addition to the statutory powers. However, the Act needs to be seen in common with all legislation and must be understood in the historical and political context of which it is a product and in which it operates. In one sense, the present legislation can be seen as a reaction against the much criticised progressive educational initiatives of the 1970s and 1980s, namely multicultural education and antiracist education.

Local education authority structures

There are three main changes indicated by the Act: these are management relationships, opting out, and education officers and advisors. So far as management relationships is concerned the relationship between local authority education departments and schools is radically altered. The role of the local education authority has been much curtailed. For example, although most schools have taken on board and adopted the local education authorities existing policies on "race" and equal opportunities, the continuing impact at school level will depend to a large extend on the future goodwill of Governing Bodies who may not be supportive of multicultural education, let alone antiracist education initiatives. Also, in all-white areas black people will not be represented on Governing Bodies. In multiracial schools, there may well be a token black Governor, but s/he will find it very difficult to be in a position to affect changes, particularly at curricular level.

Opting out has been seen as a lucrative option by many head teachers because there are additional financial benefits to be gained, provided by Central Government. The possibility exists that there may arise in multiracial areas separate schools where the pupil intake is along racial lines. It is possible that black and ethnic minority parents will demand separate schools for their children in the same way that some parents opt for separate single sex schools for their daughters. The issue of separate Muslim schools was discussed in chapter two. The passing of the 1988 Act seems to enhance the chances of separate schools for Muslims. Although such schools are not deemed to be racially segregated, in that all Muslims, whether black or white, will be eligible to attend, in practice such schools may well become all-black schools.

The burgeoning Saturday schools which have grown up in various parts of the United Kingdom in the African-Caribbean community as well as the long established language schools in the Asian and Chinese communities seem to indicate that some black groups may prefer their schools to attend all-black schools. The case for extending the Saturday schools so that they become main stream opted out schools is one that needs addressing in greater detail.

So far as education officers and advisors are concerned, their role has changed to one of overseeing the implementation of the National Curriculum. The powers of the education officers and advisors is reduced to an advisory role only - they do not have any policy making power, which has been passed on to the school Governing Bodies. Further, this advisory role will have to be exercised in a co-operative rather than executive manner.

A fundamental change with far reaching consequences is in the establishment of local management of schools which will result in the reduction of the local education authority to a staffing agency. It is noteworthy that the Department for Education commissioned Coopers and Lybrand, an organisation rooted in the business world, rather than educationalists and those in the field of education to draw up an action plan for the education system. Theirs was the proposal for the local financial management of schools, together with the statement that "a new culture and philosophy" must enter our schools. That is, in essence, schools should become small companies and "the number of pupils within a school" is the "prime determinant of the need to spend". This has led to the creation of a "pupil-number driven schools" with the resultant change in the philosophy of the organisation of education. Thus the changes required are much wider than purely financial and should be recognised as such.[10]

Multicultural education, antiracist education and the National Curriculum

Circular 6, issued in October 1989 laid down some of the underlying philosophical implications for cross-curricular issues within the National Curriculum. It will be useful here to highlight relevant sections as they pertain to multicultural education and antiracist education in all schools in the England and Wales. Little would be gained by repeating some of the recommendations here as the Dearing Report and the new Draft Proposals have superseded the previous documents.

However, a discussion of the National Curriculum Document No 3, *The Whole Curriculum*, published in March 1990, is particularly relevant to the discussion here. The points made in Circular 6 were reiterated in Document No 3. The three aspects of cross-curricular elements in the National Curriculum were divided into dimensions, skills and themes.

Dimensions are defined "as a commitment to providing equal opportunities for all pupils, and a recognition that preparation for life in a multicultural society is relevant to all pupils, [and] should permeate every aspect of the curriculum....Equal opportunities is about helping all children to fulfil their potential. Teachers are rightly concerned when their pupils underachieve and are aware that educational outcomes may be influenced by forces outside the school's control such a pupil's sex or social, cultural or linguistic background."[11]

Skills are defined in terms of the following elements: communication, numeracy, study, problem solving, personal and social and information technology.

The National Curriculum Council identified five themes which, although by no means a conclusive list, seem to most people to be pre-eminent. It is reasonable to assume at this stage that they are essential parts of the whole curriculum. The five elements of themes are as follows: Economic and Industrial Understanding, Careers Education and Guidance, Health Education, Education for Citizenship and, finally, Environmental Education.[12] It was stressed that the themes "appear in a coherent and planned manner throughout the secondary curriculum in a form which ensures continuity and progression."[13]

The Dearing Report and its impact on multicultural education and antiracist education

The Dearing Committee

In April 1993, Sir Ron Dearing, the Chair of the National Curriculum and his Assessment Group, was invited to undertake a review of the National Curriculum and of the framework for assessing pupils' progress. Four main tasks were identified:

1.   The scope for slimming down the Curriculum.
2.   How the central administration of the National Curriculum and testing arrangements could be improved.
3.   How the testing arrangements might be simplified.
4.   The future of the ten-level scale for recognising children's attainments.

The interim report identified three issues which were deemed for further consideration and consultation.

1.   The future shape of the Curriculum for fourteen to sixteen year olds.
2.   The timetable for slimming down the Curriculum - whether streamlining should be introduced in all subjects simultaneously or over a period of time.
3.   The future grading of pupils' attainments based either on retention

214

of the existing ten-level scale with some improvements, or on a replacement.

Dearing pointed out that there is a need to respond to the many siddenness of talent which underlies the development of three broad educational pathways for post-sixteen education and training. These are:

1.   The "craft" or "occupational" that is equipping young people with particular skills and with knowledge directly related to a craft or occupation though National Vocational Qualifications (NVQs).
2.   The "vocational" a mid way path which is the academic and occupational leading to General National Vocational Qualifications (GNVQs).
3.   The "academic" leading to "A" and "AS" levels.

Dearing argues that the development of the three pathways for post-sixteen education raises the question of whether and, if so, to what extent, students aged between fourteen and sixteen should be able to follow a well-devised vocational course as one element in the broadly-based Curriculum. It is suggested that with full-time education and training post-sixteen becoming the norm, we should see the age of fourteen as a beginning of an education continuum from fourteen to nineteen, but one which does not commit the student prematurely to a narrow track.

Evidence from formal inspection, which was carried out by the Dearing Committee, has shown that the introduction of the National Curriculum has begun to produce improvements in the key subjects of English, Mathematics and Science. It is now up to schools to ensure that their Curriculum in key stage four enables schools to build on this foundation. The aim must be to equip all young people, and not to please those who are currently achieving little success in the core subjects, with the knowledge and skills they need to maximise in adult and working life. The answer lies, at least in part, in providing courses which engage and motivate the students concerned.

Dearing has placed great emphasis on the vocational aspects of the National Curriculum and it is fitting to discuss this issue here.

Vocational vs academic

As regards the academic and vocational pathway, Dearing recognises that it will be a challenge to establish how a vocational pathway in

215

particular, which maintains a broad educational component, might be developed over the next few years as part of a fourteen to nineteen continuum. As recognised such a pathway is already a feature in many European countries, and head teachers and others have clearly indicated their interest in the opportunities which these courses can offer to young people.

Only a small number of schools at present provide vocational qualifications pre-sixteen. However these courses might provide a foundation for progression to post-sixteen education with qualifications such as General National Vocational Qualifications (GNVQs) and National Vocational Qualifications (NVQs) and, in particular, for the academic the A/AS grades as appropriate. In making selections for the future, schools will need to pay particular attention to the possibilities for progression to post-sixteen education and training and the public acceptability of the qualifications they offer. It is hoped that the application of the School Curriculum and Assessment Authorities' (SCAA) responsibilities for the approval of qualifications for use in key stage four will provide a mechanism to support this. Thus it can be seen that the recommendations of the Dearing report will have lasting impact on post-sixteen education.

Even before the publication of the Dearing Report, the days of multicultural education and antiracist education were numbered, chiefly through the gradual withdrawal of Section 11 funding which has been the mainstay of multicultural education and antiracist education work in multi-racial schools. In addition to the activities along multicultural lines, Section 11 of the Local Government Act 1966 has been used by multi-racial boroughs to fund bilingual teaching support and foster better relationships between schools and parents. It appears likely that most Section 11 funding will come to an end by March 1995. Although multi-racial schools will still be able to bid for money from a new single regeneration budget, the global amount is £100m. The National Union of Teachers described this figure as "totally inadequate".[14] Doug McAvoy, the union's general secretary, pointed out that Section 11 funding had been cut from £130m last year to £110m for 1994/5. He went on to say that "The Government has also reduced its contribution from 75 per cent to 57 per cent this year, a cut of 18 per cent. Next year it plans to cut it to 50 per cent. Few authorities have been able to make up the shortfall this year. As a result that 18 per cent cut has been closer to 25 per cent."[15] In addition to the eventual withdrawal of Section 11 funding, I would contend that the publication of the Dearing Report is the beginning of the end for multicultural education and antiracist education as we know them.

It is recognised that by age fourteen, students are developing particular interests and preferences and the curriculum needs to reflect this diversity. Those who are least well-served by the current arrangements may, to varying degrees and in different ways, give limited commitment and poor progress. This is vitally important for the future needs of students who are entering post-sixteen education.

There are some important recommendations of new approaches to education between the ages of fourteen and nineteen which include the extension of vocational options. This will mean that apart from the three core subjects of English, Mathematics and Science, the other time spent on the other foundation subjects could be divided between the "academic" and "vocational". It must be emphasised that the National Curriculum was never intended to occupy the whole of the school time. The prevailing view, when the Education Reform Bill was before Parliament, was that it should occupy some 70 to 80 per cent of the time leaving the balance for use at the discretion of the school. It was argued that a margin for use at the discretion of the school is needed in the interests of providing the best possible education for pupils. It provides scope for the school to draw upon particular strengths in its teaching staff, to take advantage of learning opportunities provided by the local environment, and to respond to the needs and enthusiasms of particular children.

Dearing points out that the raising of educational standards has been a constant theme in the representations which were received by the Committee. There was evidence from the Adult Literacy and Basic Skills Unit that substantial numbers of young adults do not have the literacy and mathematical skills which they need if they are to function confidently in a rapidly changing world. Achievement of the national education and training targets will depend heavily on students being numerate and literate.

One of the aims of the revamped National Curriculum is to seek to develop the talents of all students; which recognises the multi-faceted nature of talent; and which accepts that we have for too long had too limited a concept of what constitutes worthwhile achievement.

A second language other than English

The importance of the modern foreign language, that is a European language, is stressed on the assumption that today's young people may need to pursue part of their career in any part of the world. It is suggested that Britain's economic prosperity will also depend increasingly on our relationships with our trading partners in both Europe and the wider world. In addition, it makes no sense to start a subject at age eleven and drop it at age fourteen. Thus this would have implications for post-sixteen education in terms of all students learning another European language in addition to English.

The recommendations ignore the fact that there are a substantial number of children in this country whose first language is neither English nor another European language, and thus no recognition is given to their mother tongue. Further, their mother tongue, and by extension their cultural background, is given no currency in post-16 education. With the concept of a federal Europe gaining currency, children with a European mother-tongue, for example Italian children in Peterborough, will have a higher status placed on their home language, while children with an Asian or an African mother-tongue will be made to understand in no uncertain terms that their language, and by extension their culture, has no value in present day Europe.

SCAA Draft proposals

I now turn to the recently published draft proposals for the subjects which were discussed in the case studies. At the time of writing, these draft proposals had just been published by the School Curriculum and Assessment Authority and it has not been possible to carry out extensive criticism on the content of the documents. I mention here the English, Information Technology and History draft proposals for several reasons. The English proposal has been singled out to see if the antiracist language module I developed during the Education Support Grant projects would still be applicable given the new constraints, and as a teacher of English, I am interested in the use or non-use of world literature. The Information Technology document highlights the plight of Home Economics as a subject - you will recall that Home Economics had been designated a non-subject status as a result of the Education Reform Act 1988 and the introduction of the National Curriculum. With the publication of the draft proposals the fate of Home Economics has been sealed. I have briefly highlighted the draft proposals for History because of the controversy that it has caused with the Secretary of State for Education, John Patten's call for a study of British history at key stage

1. Needless to say, there is no mention of Peters' projection in the Geography draft proposal. There are of course a range of different perspectives which have been developed since the Arnos Peters projection.[16]

Draft proposals for English

There is no mention in this document to antiracist education. There are, however, a few references to cultures other than "British". Even "traditional" stories are either from Britain or Western Europe; stories from the Bible are recommended. No mention here of other traditional stories, for instance the great Indian myths, nor any other religious books, such as the Koran.[17] This is covered at Key Stage 2 as mentioned below.

A mere three lines are devoted to "stories from a range of cultures" which is one way for multiculturalists to include the study of books by black writers.[18]

Under the sub-heading "Selection of Literature" there is a mention of texts drawn from a variety of cultures and traditions, although the works recommended are on the whole by Western, and more specifically, English, writers. The inclusion of Greek, African-Caribbean and Welsh "myths, legends and traditional stories" indicates the narrowness of the English curriculum.[19]

Draft proposals for Information Technology

Information Technology has been separated from Design and Technology and now appear as separate documents. It is significant to note that a single page is devoted to Home Economics within the Design and Technology draft proposals. Further, at Key stage 3, the study of food becomes optional. This is a great loss for Home Economics as this is one area where multicultural education and antiracist education curricula work is possible, as we saw in the case studies. Most people are aware of the "multicultural bread" topic - the use of flour and water by people from different cultural groups making a myriad range of products - from the many kinds of bread to *chappatis* and *naan*. Work such as this will give way to the more prescriptive articles.

In a recently published book on science and technology in the primary school, Bently and Watts devote a whole chapter to equal opportunities issues.[20] However, their focus is mainly on gender issues (needless to say, they did not examine the specific area affecting black girls - that is, race and gender oppression). Antiracism and multiculturalism are allocated seven small paragraphs - two of which are a quote from an agriculturist from Ghana who talks about saving a whole pile of plastic bags under his bed which he had collected every time he went to the supermarket while living in Europe. This is used to highlight the "throwaway" life we lead in the West. Reading this, I found it hard to work out what this had to do with multicultural education and antiracist education. (In all fairness, Bently and Watts state that they had used the quote to illustrate the notion of appropriate technology.) I would hope that the model I have proposed below would act as a catalyst to avoid such misuse of the terms multicultural and antiracist. Further, that an antiracist perspective would be an integral part of the whole text and not devoted a minor section in a chapter.

Draft proposals for History

It is worth mentioning in passing the History proposals and the controversy raging following the call for the study of British history at key state 1 by John Patten, the Secretary of State for Education. Primary teachers are already lamenting the disappearance of such favourite topics as the Egyptians. Perhaps now is the time to raise the question regarding British history - from whose perspective? Can British history not be studied from a black and feminist perspective? Such a move would place antiracist education at the heart of this subject.

The North/South divide

Alistair Bonnett maintains that antiracist educational ideology is geographically, as well as historically specific and contains within itself the potential for its own radical or reactionary transformation. His article stems from interviews conducted between 1978 and 1988 with antiracist teachers who positioned themselves in the forefront of the education for race equality debate.[21]

Significantly, all twenty-five of Bonnett's sample of antiracist teachers had either taught or been brought up in more multiracial localities, twenty suggesting that this experience was important in initiating their commitment to anti-racism. He argues that in Tyneside such a multicultural/antiracist vanguard has emerged and, by defining anti-racism solely in reformist, individual and consensus-seeking terms, has been able to incorporate as emphasis on racism into liberal-educationalist ideology. Some of the comments that were repeatedly expressed by Bonnett's cohort group were as follows:

- multiculturalism is part of anti-racism; I'd see it being the overall philosophy and anti-racism as the urgent needs system
- anti-racism is more anti-prejudice than politics...it's certainly nothing to do with social revolution!
- racism is people's prejudice, it's their ignorance that requires a good education in human tolerance and inter-understanding [sic][22]

Bonnett concludes that teachers in Tyneside, because of the different geographical and historical contexts, adopt a "softly softly", non-confrontational, approach to the issue of racism.[23] This would suggest that Bonnett see anti-racism as being confrontational in approach.

Bonnett suggests that the Tyneside teachers did not regard multiculturalism as simply dated or reactionary but as a necessary component of anti-racism. Although the liberal culturalist approach to race equality was seen as "not tackling the root structural and institutional causes of racism" all twelve teachers interviewed stressed that it "has a role to play" in Tyneside since "pure" anti-racism, it was felt, would be dismissed locally as "something alien, some trendy, London "loony left" nonsense."

I would agree that one cannot "go ramming racism down people's throats who...aren't better off than blacks. In fact to not talk of class but only of race would be sheer folly" and "antiracist politics up here has got to come out of people's own experiences of inequality; without that broad perspective we're just indulging ourselves."[24] However, I would argue that this is true whether one is in London or the North East or anywhere else in the country.

Moreover, I would suggest, having worked on Education Support Grant projects in London and Tyneside, that Bonnett's conclusions do not fit into my own lengthy experience working on multicultural education and antiracist education in all-white schools. We have seen in the chapter on case studies, how materials developed in London were used, without modification in Tyneside. I would disagree with Bonnett, that because of the different geographical locations of schools, different approaches need to be developed. Rather, I would argue that if multicultural education and antiracist education, as educational philosophy, if sound enough, would stand up to examination whatever that location of the school, whether all-white or multi-racial, whether primary or secondary sector.

Feminism and racism: parallels and differences

I have deliberately placed the discussion of feminism and disability at the end of this concluding chapter, not because these issues are not of paramount importance, but in the hope and belief that they will remain with you once you have finished the book.

In the same way that feminism is seen as a struggle to end sexist oppression[25] antiracist education can be seen to be challenging racist oppression, which, I would argue, a multicultural education approach does not do.

Further, I think a discussion of feminism throws some light on the nature of racism as found in the United Kingdom at present. I would contend that there are some parallels that need to be drawn between the two movements to highlight the complexity of antiracist eduction which needs to be seen in a holistic way if it is to be meaningful and effective, particularly in all-white schools.

As bell hooks (she does not use the upper case in her name) contends, many contemporary feminist activists argue that eradicating sexist oppression is important because it is the primary contradiction, the basis of all other oppressions. Racism as well as class structure is perceived as stemming from sexism. Implicit in this line of analysis is the assumption that the eradication of sexism, "the oldest oppression", "the primary contradiction" is necessary before attention can be focused on racism and classism. Suggesting a hierarchy of oppression exists, with sexism in first place, evokes a sense of competing concerns that is unnecessary....Since all forms of oppression are linked in our society because they are supported by similar institutional and social structures, one system cannot be eradicated while the other remain intact. Challenging sexist oppression is a crucial step in the struggle to eliminate all forms of oppression.[26] Antiracist education enables the education of pupils to be seen in a holistic way, whereas multicultural education can draw false differences between the various cultures that are an integral part of multi-racial Britain.

Discussing the women's movement, which did not take on board the issue of black women's position within that movement, bell hooks writes: "Frequently, white feminists act as if black women did not know sexist oppression existed until they voiced feminist sentiment. ...They do not understand, cannot even imagine, that black women, as well as other groups of women who live daily in oppressive situations, often acquire an awareness of patriarchal politics from their lived experience, just as they develop strategies of resistance....[27] In the same way, I would

222

argue, white pupils in all-white schools do not, in some cases are unable to, necessarily make links with the experiences of their black peers, both female and male, in other schools and the experience of oppression faced through racism. This is most apparent in all-female groups of school children, where black female pupils face the double oppression of "race" and gender - and where their white peers do not see the effects of multiple oppression. Privileged feminists have largely been unable to speak to, with, and for diverse groups of women because they either do not understand fully the inter-relatedness of sex, race, and class oppression or refuse to take this inter-relatedness seriously.[28]

The focus of much multicultural education development has been at the level of changing attitudes rather than addressing racism in a historical and political context. Antiracist education would address the underlying institutional racism. As Toni Morrison writes: "Those (white women) who could afford it gave over the management of the house and the rearing of children to others. (It is a source of amusement even now to black women to listen to feminist talk of liberation while somebody's nice black grandmother shoulders the daily responsibility of child rearing and floor mopping, and the liberated one comes home to examine the housekeeping, correct it, and be entertained by the children.)   If Women's Lib needs those grandmothers to thrive, it has a serious flaw."[29]

What arises from the foregoing discussion on feminism is that we need to look at multicultural education and antiracist education in a holistic way. In the past, as demonstrated in chapter one, we saw the division between multicultural education and antiracist education as compartmentalised within the education system. Multicultural education and antiracist education were very much separate from the mainstream, did not form part of the whole curriculum, if at all. Multicultural education and antiracist education were meant to be cross-curricular, but in fact ended up by being treated as an added extra in certain subject areas only - particularly in the arts and humanities sections of the curriculum. In English, for instance, as we saw in the case studies, multicultural education meant including books by and about black people, without real discussion about the nature of publication, authorship, class system which prevented working class children from reading certain books because they lacked the reading skills needed for the texts.

Language use

It is pertinent, I think, to mention the power of language and how ingrained the language we use can and does hinder our understanding and appreciation of sexism, and by extension racism.

The following example is taken from the editorial introduction to Shireen Motala's article "Training for Transformation revisited" in *Multicultural Teaching* and is written by the editor, Gillian Klein, an active antiracist.

> This article by a black researcher at a traditional white liberal university identifies the needs for and dilemmas around positive action. Her observations on the role of *black and women researchers* (emphasis added) in shaping the intellectual inquiry are widely relevant....[30]

I want to examine here the phrase "black and women researchers" in some detail. Although I recognise that Klein might maintain that my reading of the phrase is perhaps over sensitive or misunderstood, or that this was not what she implied, nevertheless the fact remains that this is the particular meaning I assigned to the phrase. The article in question is written by a black female researcher, the phrase "black and women" I would suggest implies that there are two categories of researchers - black (male and female) and women (white). Unless we liberate and emancipate ourselves and free our minds from mental slavery, to borrow Bob Marley's famous phrase, racism and sexism will continue to be a force in our lives. I would have preferred the more explicit phrase "black female and male, and white female" researchers. Am I reading something into this that was not intended? Am I playing around with semantics? I think not - language is a powerful tool - and can, and does, oppress. It is part and parcel of power structure of racism and sexism. The models I described of multicultural education and antiracist education in chapter two are essentially power models.

As bell hooks points out:

> In much of the literature written by white women on the "woman question" from the 19th century to the present day, authors will refer to "white men" but use the word "woman" when they really mean "white woman". Concurrently, the term "blacks" is often made synonymous with black men.[31]

Racism is not reported on a regular basis in national newspapers, as it was during the 1980s. This does not mean that racism, and its daily manifestations on the streets, racially motivated attacks on black people are on the decline. Hesse, et al detail the racial harassment faced by the black inhabitants of Waltham Forest, a London borough.[32] No one black is immune to racism - not even black stars such as Lenny Henry who is married to a white woman. *The Guardian*, in their "birthday" column reported that racists had "daubed NF in shit above his front door - another kind of recognition."[33]

Another example that springs to mind is the German tennis star Boris Becker and his black partner who was the butt of racist attacks a couple of years ago. That racism is rampant in Britain is an undisputed fact. Journals such as *Searchlight*, and organisations such as Standing Conference on Racial Equality in Europe (SCORE) publicise regular occurrence of racist attacks on black people on a Europe-wide basis. Arthur Ashe, the black tennis player stated, when he contracted Aids through a blood transfusion that racism, for him, was a tougher issue than Aids. He said: "You're not going to believe this, but living with Aids is not the greatest burden I've had in my life." He went on to say that facing racism, which included sitting at the rear of the bus as a boy and attending a segregated school, was far more trying. Just before his death, he said that "even now it [racism] continues to feel like an extra weight around me".[34]

I highlight these few examples of overt racism in an effort to show that antiracist education needs to be seen in a particular context. Underlying all the work in the two Education Support Grants projects was the latent, and sometimes not so latent, racism that I experienced as a black teacher in all-white schools.

As nearly fifty per cent of the ethnic minority population of the United Kingdom live in London, it is not surprising that there are no one hundred percent all-white schools in London.[35] Although there are many which have less than the cut-off five per cent to make them "all-white" for the purposes of Education Support Grant projects. I would estimate that some eighty per cent of schools in the United Kingdom are one hundred per cent all-white - the majority of the primary schools in the rural areas of "Tyneside" borough were one hundred percent all-white, although the secondary schools had maybe eight to ten black pupils on their roll.

Disability and "race"

I now turn to an area which has generally been ignored by teachers, educationalists and academics - that of disability as it affects black people. Disability is rarely included in discussions of oppression. I now work in the disability field and have been made aware of the specific battles that black disabled people face in their fight for equal rights and equal services. Also, I am on the management committee of a Section 64 project aimed at improving services to hard of hearing people from a black and ethnic minority background at the Royal National Institute for Deaf People. This particular project was funded through Section 64 of the Health Services and Public Health Act 1968. The main objective of the Section 64 grants is to help enable the provision by voluntary organisations of services which contribute ti the effectiveness of the National Health Service.[36] The contacts that I have established from black disabled people in these two roles seem to me pertinent for an inclusion of the "race" and disability debate here - in the hope that this issue will have a higher profile in the future on discussions of "race" and education. Disability is not just at the level of access by wheelchair users.[37]

Increasingly, black disabled people, both male and female, have been put in an untenable position - they do not "fit" into any category: the disability field has not addressed their needs, and neither has the "race" lobby. I know of groups of visually impaired and hard of hearing black people who have had to form networks and support groups because their issues are raised at neither disabled nor race fora. Indeed, black disabled people have been asked to state their alliance - whether to the disabled movement or the race movement. Black disabled women are in a most difficult position, because the white and black feminist movements have not included disability as an issue worthy of inclusion in their discussions. Oppression is not so clear cut - one does not suddenly become "black" and forget that one is dependent on a guide dog for mobility, or that one is a woman.

Kirsten Hearn, a member of *The Tokens* which is a five-piece singing/Signing [sign language] group, writes about her experience as a blind lesbian. She rightly questions the notion of the single issues movement which is unwilling to take seriously the fact of multiple oppression. She states that "Black disabled people have been marginalised in the Disability Movement because tackling racism from within and outside is not given sufficient priority."[38]

One of a few examples of disability organisations taking on board the issue of "race" is the article by Mansourian taking up the flag for library provision for people from a non-English speaking background with disabilities. This article is confined to providing material in languages other than English to visually impaired people. It is interesting to note that this work is based in Australia.[39]

Mention was made earlier to the taped version *Unity* which was an effort to reach visually impaired young people, both black and white.

The vast subject of disability, education and race merits a book in its own right.

Antiracist education is aborted

I began this chapter with the statement that multicultural education was dying a slow death; through the discussions and deliberations in the course of this book, particularly chapters eight and nine, the case studies, I am forced to conclude that antiracist eduction, at least in all-white areas, has been aborted. This conclusion has been reached by actual classroom practice over a long period of time. Time and again I have tried to implement an antiracist perspective in the schools I have worked in - but because of institutional factors and lack of commitment form head teachers and senior teachers, this has not been possible.

We have seen above the gradual reduction of Section 11 funding from the Home Office and the eventual total withdrawal of this source of funding which has been the mainstay of multicultural education perspectives in multi-racial areas. According to the criteria, all-white areas are of course not eligible for Section 11 funding.

One of the reasons why antiracist education has been aborted may be that as it grew out of a critique of multicultural education as discussed in chapter five. Further we saw how multicultural education was based on the false premise of white culture being superior to black culture. We saw how multicultural education developed after the ad-hoc practices which were designed to meet the needs of newly arrived immigrant children from the New Commonwealth in the 1960s and 1970s. In this case practice came before policy. However, for antiracist education policy came before practice, which is a sound basis for educational innovation. However, I would maintain that when the premise is based on a false notion, it is not surprising that the theory of antiracist education, which grew out of the false, mistaken philosophy of multicultural education, is failing in schools.

I set out to show that an multicultural education approach was easier to implement than an antiracist education one. We have seen in the case studies how this is the case - teachers are reluctant to agree to more than piecemeal, superficial changes at curriculum level. I suspect the recommendations of the Dearing Report will made any initiative along multicultural education or antiracist education lines practically impossible to implement - particularly in all-white schools. I think that the case studies discussed in chapter eight, as well as the model proposed here can be operationalised by all teachers in all schools, whether all-white or multiracial. Because at the heart of it, the educational philosophy of antiracism remains constant, and is based on a sound footing.

As already mentioned earlier there is a reluctance for teachers and educationalists to accept a world or global perspective, which would form the cornerstone of an antiracist perspective. There is also a reluctance to incorporate an antiracist education perspective across the whole school as an institution. The case studies illustrated some minor changes in one or two curriculum areas along a multicultural education perspective. However, when suggestions were made that the whole school take on board an antiracist perspective, which would include mid-day supervisors, cleaners, the kind of menu offered during the school lunch break, and so on, then an antiracist education perspective was not supported.

The implementation of the National Curriculum along the recently published proposed guidelines can be restrictive - we have seen how it was impossible to conduct antiracist education work in the Mathematics Department at school B in the case studies. It is likely that the National Curriculum will be used, indeed is already being used, by teachers avoid using an egalitarian approach in their teaching. New social orders are established gradually, and the struggle for an antiracist perspective will be gradual and protracted. But we must not give up hope.

I have not had the opportunity to discuss the pedagogical methods of each approach. However, I would like to stress that there is no occasion for the "neutral" teacher. Schools are places full of inequality - a teacher cannot fully devolve his/ her power to the pupils. There may be more child centred and collaborative teaching in an antiracist education approach, but the power structure remains. Even in a free, democratic and "liberal" school such as A S Neill's Summerhill, there are power structures between the teachers and the taught.[40] And we have seen how the models of multicultural education and antiracist education are essentially power models. Equality - or more properly - oppression - is embedded in power relationships. Although in some instances, the teacher is as much a learner as the pupils, it is the teacher who sets the agenda and decides the curriculum - sometimes because of external

228

pressures, such as the National Curriculum.

I hope that the arguments presented in this book will be addressed by all teachers, not just the committed minority. To acknowledge that we need to move beyond multicultural education and antiracist education, as Paul Gilroy advocates, is not to admit defeat in the face of extreme pressures from external forces. As Gillian Klein points out, in this country, the politically driven changes have been rapid in the field of education.[41] We should think about the ways of moving beyond multiculturalism and anti-racism - if only because, as we have seen, it is becoming increasingly difficult to maintain these approaches at class room level. In all-white schools, where the development of multicultural education and antiracist education has been slow and short-lived, ways of incorporating an antiracist approach to the National Curriculum are doubly important and urgent. In the same way that the new SCAA recommendations call for "English across the curriculum" [42] (this is not a new development) I would advocate an antiracist approach across the National Curriculum.

The way forward

There is space within the National Curriculum, in meeting the needs of a linguistic minority, namely the Welsh. There is special allocation for the teaching of Welsh as a mother tongue. However, this facility is not offered to all linguistic minority children attending British schools. Also, I would argue that if there is space for such major allocating of resources for Welsh, then we have to find ways to argue for more space, not only in terms of financial resources, but in terms of political commitment, for multicultural education and antiracist education across the National Curriculum. And this would include the study of one's mother tongue if this were not English. In such a scenario, the place of Standard English remains intact.

To reiterate, multicultural education is dying a slow death and antiracist education has been aborted. This is not to say that there isn't a place for an antiracist perspective within the National Curriculum as already noted. Political will and financial commitment from central government are required to instill an egalitarian approach to teaching and learning in all schools, but particularly all-white schools to ensure that the citizens of the future will be well rounded and so that some of the social problems we have today may be eradicated.

I know there will be committed teachers, as there always have been,

229

in multi-racial schools who will endeavour to "bend the rules" and include a multicultural education and perhaps an antiracist education approach in their teaching and learning materials. Interested teachers have always found ways to work around guidelines. For instance, recognising that sitting public examinations are a disadvantage to some pupils, some teachers developed a hundred per cent course work component as an alternative to an examination paper, thus negating the actual taking of examinations. In the same way, committed teachers will no doubt find ways to include black writers, both male and female, within the English Draft Proposals. However, I would hope that all teachers, committed multiculturalists and antiracists or not, will endeavour to teach the National Curriculum from and antiracist, egalitarian perspective. This need not necessarily cost money, often the advance only requires a different perspective and self-education.

What I envisage with the revamped National Curriculum is beautifully illustrated by a metaphor used by the playwright and novelist Dennis Potter in reference to the monarchy and the British Tourist Board. "They [the British Tourist Board] are becoming more effective not in selling products but in selling the whole culture in which they are embodied, like bits of fruit in a cake, the whole cake becomes a fruit cake."[43] In the same way I envisage a National Curriculum, applicable in all schools across the land, which is littered right through with bits of antiracist perspectives so that the National Curriculum becomes an antiracist national curriculum.

Notes

1   Bagley C (1992) *Back to the Future*
2   for example, Flew (1987) *Power to the Parents* and Lewis (1988) *Anti-Racism: A Mania Exposed*
3   Ghaill M (1988) *Young, Gifted and Black*, p 151
4   at a recent conference, Herman Ouseley, the Chair of the Commission for Racial Equality, made the same observation. Even in the early 1990s, people are still articulating the reason for non-action with the phrase "We have no problem here [because there are no black people]". The conference was organised by the London Research Centre and held at the St Thomas' Hospital on Friday 15 July 1994.
5   op cit
6   Sivanandan A (1983) "Challenging Racism: Strategies for the 80's" in *Race and Class*, Vol XXV, No 2
7   Gilroy P (1990) "The end of anti-racism", *New Community* Vol 17, No 1, pp 71-83; also in Donald and Rattansi (1992)
8   Joseph G (1992) *The Crest of the Peacock: Non-European Roots of Mathematics*, p 197 ff
9   see Bonnet (1993) *Radicalism, Anti-Racism and Representation*
10   Cooper and Lybrand (1988) *Local Management of Schools*
11   *The Whole Curriculum*, (1990) p 2
12   ibid, pp 4 - 6
13   ibid, p 6
14   *Education*, 1 July 1994, p 6
15   ibid
16   see for example Mundell (1993) "Maps that shape the world"
17   Draft Proposals for English (1994) p 11
18   ibid
19   ibid, p 14
20   Bently and Watts (1993) *Information Technology in the Primary School*, pp
21   Bonnett (1990) "Educational Ideology in London and Tyneside", *Oxford Review of Education*, p 159. The same arguments are repeated in *Radicalism, Anti-Racism and Representation* (1993)
22   ibid, p 263
23   ibid
24   ibid
25   hooks (1984), *From Margin to Center*, p 24 Similar arguments are put forward by hooks in *Ain't I a woman* (1992) and *Yearning*

(1991)

26 ibid, pp 35 - 36
27 ibid, p 10
28 ibid, 14
29 in Hooks, op cit, p 50
30 Gillian Klein (1994) *Multicultural Teaching*, Vol 12, No 3, Summer
31 hooks (1992) *Ain't I a woman?* p 140
32 Hesse, et al (1992) *Beneath the Surface: Racial Harassment*
33 *The Guardian*, 28 August, 1990
34 *The Voice*, 23 June, 1992
35 Herman Ouseley (1994) Foreword to *London's Ethnic Minorities* (London Research Centre), p 1
36 Health Service Guidelines, issued by NHS Management Executive. Form HSG(94)4, dated 10 February, 1994
37 See Patel, K (nd) (1991) "Education and Training" in *Race and Disability - a dialogue for action* (GLAD), pp 13 - 16
38 Hearn (1993) "Putting our own house in order"
39 Mansourian (1994) "Multicultural Library Services for People with Disabilities", *Link-Up*, June 1994, pp 14-16
40 Neill (1976) *Summerhill* for an account of the Neill's philosophy
41 Klein (1994), *Multicultural Teaching*, op cit, p 47
42 Draft Proposals for English (1994) p
43 Potter (1994) *Seeing the Blossom*, p 69.

Appendix 1:
Policy documents

Multicultural policy of "Tyneside"

Education in a Multi-racial, Multi-cultural Society

"Tyneside" Local Education Authority recognises that the problem of racism is as serious in predominantly white areas, as it is where there are more people of ethnic minority origin. It is made worse by the activities of groups who encourage racial hatred and who particularly target their propaganda at young white people in areas like the North East. The borough of "Tyneside" being no exception in these matters, it is important that schools and the college acknowledge that racist attitudes will be communicated to and by their students, either unconsciously or deliberately, but that in either case, they should be challenged. Schools and the college should be aware that it is possible to unintentionally reinforce these attitudes if staff and students are not helped to identify racism in its overt and covert forms and to apply consistent counter measures and strategies where it occurs.

The curriculum and ethos of the school should be developed in ways which enable students of all ages to share a commitment to oppose racism alongside all forms of injustice, harassment and abuse, which generally complement and reinforce one another. This means that racism, sexism, classism, ageism, discrimination against the disabled, the handicapped, those with exceptional needs, against different nationalities or religious groups should be seen as interrelated and equally important issues, while acknowledging the specific ways in which each operates and needs to be addressed. To that end, the LEA uses the term Education in a "Multi-racial, Multi-cultural Society", intending culture to embrace gender culture, class culture and any group culture. The curriculum should reflect and value the multi-racial, multi-cultural nature of British and world society, actively encouraging positive, appreciative attitudes to the differences between races, cultures and nationalities, while acknowledging the similarities which link and can unite them. All aspects of learning should take account of ethnic and cultural diversity, the different perceptions and experience of the world that this shapes, and the contribution this makes to the development of the local national and international communities. The attitudes and values which affect the way people respond to racial and cultural differences should be examined, so that students of all ages can understand how those attitudes and values are formed, and how they affect the information, treatment and provision people receive. In this context, schools and the college should examine and develop the content, scope and nature of their curriculum, and the books, materials, resources, teaching and learning strategies and structures which support it. Young people should learn how to identify the images and attitudes which are being conveyed to them through books and other media as well as the patterns of behaviour they around them. This should help them to make their own judgements and come to their own considered opinions.

It is clear that, in order to successfully implement a policy for Education in a Multi-racial, Multi-cultural Society, the whole school methods should reflect its aims, in terms of the philosophy, relationships, social and working environment which are created. Teaching and ancillary staff all need to be trained accordingly, and parents should be involved in policy and curriculum development with them. It is essential, in the light of the findings of recent reports, that children are partners in the policy development process, if it is to be seen by them as something to which contribute, rather than something imposed upon them. Everyone in schools and the college should believe they share the responsibility to ensure that no student is disadvantaged or feels excluded or harassed because of race, nationality, religions, culture, gender, class, age, disability or exceptional need.

Where there are pupils from different ethnic or cultural backgrounds, schools should take fully into account the importance of those pupils learning to speak, read and write English to a level of competence which is equal to that which they would expect or hope for from any child. It is equally important that schools value all languages and dialects, recognising bilingualism as a positive asset by encouraging the use of mother tongue, writing and display in more than one language, and making similar provision for the valuing of regional dialect alongside standard English.

Multicultural policy of "London"

The June resolution

On 1st July 1982, the Council adopted the following policy for education in the Borough:

> "To demonstrate through a policy statement and ensuing action, that the education service in the London LEA
>
> - Welcomes cultural and linguistic diversity
> - rejects and opposes racism and concerned to promote equality of opportunity, racial justice, and good relationships between all groups".

This policy is known as the "June Resolution" as it was recommended by the Committee for Education and the Arts in June, 1982. It is emphasised that the resolution refers to all aspects of the service, to all persons involved in the service, and to all educational establishments, whatever their cultural, racial or ethnic composition.

Education for a multicultural society

In adopting this statement, the Council is responding to changes in philosophy, which have occurred due to an increased understanding of the nature of our multicultural society, over the past two or three decades. In addition the Council has a legal obligation to comply with the requirements of the Race Relations Act, 1978 which are:

a)   to eliminate unlawful racial discrimination: and
b)   to promote equality of opportunity and good relations between persons of different racial groups.

Our perspective of education for a multicultural society is based on these concepts and places them within a framework of cultural pluralism, acknowledging and valuing cultural and linguistic diversity. We believe that this is the only framework within which our ultimate goals are likely to be achieved. In accepting that society is enriched by the presence of diverse cultural groups, we reject the treatment and perceptions of any group as inferior, by whatever processes, and however unconsciously and unintentionally. Such a position is wholly unacceptable.

235

In order to give practical effect to the policy stated in the June Resolution several different kinds of action are needed. These will involve one or more of the following principles.

a) Promoting an understanding of, and commitment to, the ideals of the policy.

b) Developing a positive response to the cultural and linguistic diversity of our community through all aspects of the curriculum and school life.

c) Identifying and removing all forms of discriminatory practice, whatever the source and however unintentional.

d) Improving communication and relationships between schools, parents and the communities.

    i) by involvement of parents and the communities in education

    ii) by promoting support for education by the communities

e) By promoting full implementation of the Council's stated policy of equal opportunity in all appointments.

f) Monitoring and evaluation of the implementation of the policy.

All action should be judged in the light of these principles.

Areas for action

This section identified general areas for attention in each of the main division of the Council's education service. More detailed and specific aspects will emerge as practical policies are developed.

a) Schools and other educational establishments

The staff of all educational establishments are required to consider the meaning of the policy and decide what further steps they need to take. It should be made publicly clear that no form of racism is acceptable. Any appraisal which is sufficiently thorough to be meaningful would encompass all aspects of the life of the establishment, including the following:

- The inclusion in all school policy documents of an endorsement of the June Resolution
- general ethos and atmosphere
- language and the whole curriculum, including books and materials, and choice of examination syllabuses
- extra-curricular activities
- teaching methods and approaches
- class and school organisation, including arrangements for school meals, i.e. special dietary requirements
- testing and assessment
- consultation and relationships with parents and the communities
- racialist behaviour and organisations
- appointment and staff development at all levels
- monitoring and evaluation

b)   The Education Department

The Education Department must be similarly systematic and thorough in order to fulfil its duties and obligations in accordance with the policy. The list is not exhaustive but must include the following aspects:-

- in-service training of employees of the education department
- appointments
- the development of an Agreed Syllabus in Religious Education which takes account of the religious diversity in our society
- allocation of resources
- Section 11 Staffing and the development of support services
- monitoring and evaluation

Appendix 2:
Teacher produced materials:
An equal opportunities approach

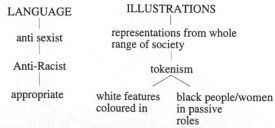

LANGUAGE
|
anti sexist
|
Anti-Racist
|
appropriate

ILLUSTRATIONS
|
representations from whole
range of society
|
tokenism
⌒
white features   black people/women
coloured in   in passive
                        roles

TOKENISM - An Anti Racist approach need not remain tokenist when
considered within the context of the whole school, the Borough and other
LEA's. Multi-racial illustrations, for instance, remain tokenistic if they are
the only example the children come across. But if in a school, all subject/
curricular areas take an Anti-Racist approach into consideration, and if in
the Borough other schools too are involved, then tokenism is negated. It is
helpful to remember that nationality and internationally other educationalists
are carrying out anti-racist/ anti-sexist work.

PUPILS

TEACHER PRODUCED
MATERIAL

AUDIO-VISUAL
MATERIALS

FABRICS,
etc

RESOURCES

MAPS
AND
POSTERS

EQUIPMENT

BOOKS
illustrations
date of publication

TEACHER/S

Appendix 3:
Pupil evaluation sheets and graph

An example of pupil evaluation questionnaire

Can you please say which of the activities we covered this half term you most enjoyed? Were there any activities you disliked? Try to give reasons. Do not write your name on the questionnaire.

1   Signs and signals

2   Hieroglyphics/codes

3   Language quiz

4   Chinese writing

5   Written Standard English

6   Black/White words

Thank you

Evaluation of replies on Languages work

There were 19 replies to the survey.

1) *Did you enjoy our work on languages?*

The replies were:
Yes	10
No	7
No reply	2

Those who enjoyed the work said that it was because it was something different, or that it made a change form English; it was interesting to learn a different language, and to learn about code; and that it was interesting to learn how people communicate.

Those who didn't enjoy it said that they had not understood all of it, or that they prefer to work than to listen for a long time.

2) *Did you learn anything about language which you did not know before?*

The replies were:
Yes	9
No	2
No reply	8

Most of the replies emphasised that they had learnt about the origins of words which they had thought were purely English, and also that they had learnt about hieroglyphics and codes.

3) *Which bits of the work did you most enjoy?*

(Some pupils ticked two or three boxes).
Signs and signals	8
Hieroglyphics/codes	11
Language quiz	5
Chinese writing	3
Written standard English	6
Black/White words	6

4) *Which bits of the work did you least enjoy?*

(Some pupils ticked two or three boxes).

Signs and signals 4
Hieroglyphics/codes 2
Language quiz 5
Chinese writing 3
Written standard English 8
Black/White words 8

5) *Would you like to do further work on languages?*

The replies were: Yes 6
No 2
No reply 11

Those who said "yes" thought it had been interesting, and taught them about the origin of English words. Those against said "It gets Mudly" and it was quite "boaring."

The data for this questionnaire has been transfered on to a graph for ease of reference and analysis. See next page.

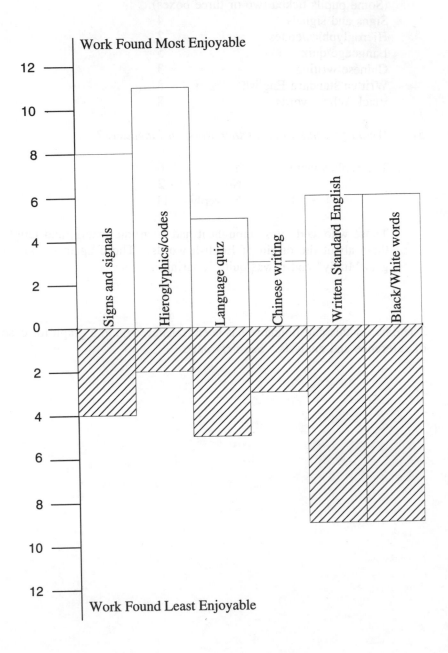

An Example Of Pupil Evaluation

244

Appendix 4:
Examples of Pro formas

Pro forma for "Tyneside"

Record of visit made by Advisory teacher

Teacher/s involved

Place

Date and Time of visit

Duration of visit

Purpose of visit

Main contact/link with place of visit

Staff &/or students involved

Ground covered

Style of visit

Process

Outcomes

Key factors/issues emerging from visit

Response from parties involved

Agreed/recommended follow up

Any further comments

Pro forma for "London"

School

Purpose

Contact person/s

Brief note on discussion

Action taken

Appendix 5:
Pupil and staff questionnaires

Pupil survey questionnaire

This survey is being carried out in order to enable the school to help every pupil to achieve his/her best. Answer all of the questions truthfully. Your answers will be treated in confidence.
DO NOT WRITE YOUR NAME

1.   What is racism?

_____

_____

2.   Have you ever suffered racism in this school?

Once   ☐

Many Times   ☐

Never   ☐

3.   If yes, was this because of your: Colour   ☐

                                         Religion   ☐

                                         Race   ☐

                                         Language   ☐

                                         Country of Origin ☐

4. Describe one incident. DO NOT GIVE NAMES

_____

_____

_____

5. Did you tell anyone about this? DO NOT GIVE NAMES.

(Tick Boxes) Parent ☐   Tutor ☐

Uncle ☐   Teacher ☐

Brother ☐   Head Teacher ☐

Sister ☐   Deputy Head ☐

Friend ☐   Dinner Staff ☐

6. Was anything done about it? DO NOT GIVE NAMES.

_____

_____

7. Were you satisfied with the result?   YES/NO

Explain your answer. _____

_____

_____

8. Do you know anybody who has suffered racism in school?   YES/NO

9. If yes, explain what happened. DO NOT GIVE NAMES.

_____

_____

250

10. If you did not report these incidents, please explain why.

_____

_____

_____

11. Have you witnessed racist incidents outside school?YES/NO
     Explain your answer.

_____

_____

_____

_____

12. If you were to witness a racist incident in school, what would you
     do?

_____

_____

_____

13. Do you think that the school should teach children to read and
     write the language of their parents.   YES/NO
     Explain your answer.

_____

_____

_____

14. Should all pupils be given an opportunity to learn a non-European language? **YES/NO**
    Explain your answer.

    _____

    _____

    _____

15. Do you think letters should be sent home in the language of the pupils' parents? **YES/NO**
    Explain your answer.

    _____

    _____

    _____

16. Do you think we should celebrate all religious festivals, as is done for Christmas and Easter? **YES/NO**
    Explain your answer.

    _____

    _____

    _____

17. Would you like teachers to use examples of other countries and cultures in lessons? **YES/NO**
    Explain your answer.

    _____

    _____

    _____

18. (a) Do people in school make enough effort to pronounce your name correctly?   **YES/NO**

    (b) How do you feel about this? _____

    _____

19. Have you ever discussed your cultural/religious beliefs with:
    (a) Your teacher?   **YES/NO**
    (b) Your class?   **YES/NO**
    (c) Your friends?   **YES/NO**

20. Do teachers expect you to do well?   **YES/NO**

    Explain your answer. _____

    _____

21. There are some Black and Asian teachers in school. Do you think it would be better if there were more?   **YES/NO**

    Explain your answer. _____

    _____

22. How would you describe yourself? (Please tick)
    (a) *Ethnic origin*

    AFRICAN   ☐ CHINESE   ☐

    (state country _____)   CYPRIOT   ☐

                                      GREEK   ☐

    AFRO-CARIBBEAN   ☐ IRISH   ☐

                                      TURKISH   ☐

ASIAN: BANGLADESHI ☐

EAST AFRICAN ☐ MIXED RACE ☐

INDIAN ☐ (please specify

_____)

PAKISTANI ☐

OTHER ☐

BRITISH: BLACK ☐ OTHER European ☐

WHITE ☐ OTHER ☐

OTHER ☐ (please specify

_____)

(b) *Homes languages*

BENGALI ☐ HEBREW ☐

CHINESE ☐ ITALIAN ☐
(please specify _____) PUNJABI:

Urdu Script ☐

CREOLE ☐ Gurmuki Script ☐
(please specify _____) TURKISH

ENGLISH ☐ URDU ☐

GREEK ☐ OTHER ☐

GUJARATI ☐

(c) *Religion*

BUDDHIST ☐

CHRISTIAN ☐

HINDU ☐

JEWISH ☐

MUSLIM ☐

RASTAFARIAN ☐

SIKH ☐

NONE ☐

OTHER ☐
(please specify _____)

23. If you have anything else to say about racism, write it here.

_____

_____

_____

Thank you for your help

Staff survey (teaching and non-teaching)

1   What is racism?

2   What do you understand by the term "institutional racism?"

3   Have you studied the Borough's statement on multicultural/ anti-racist education?

4   Does your teaching take into account the Borough's anti-racist policy?

5   What do you think are the most important reasons for the school to have an anti-racist policy?

6   Have you witnessed racist incidents in school:

   a   Between pupils and staff
   b   Between staff and staff
   c   Between non-teaching staff and pupils
   d   Between teaching staff and non-teaching staff.

7　　Have you developed links with the wider community of the school?

8　　Do you have any further comments about racism?

Appendix 6:
Reports of pupil questionnaires

Report on 1st year survey: No 1

1)   All the pupils seemed to understand what racism was, although a few talked about "people who are different" without mentioning that it usually meant on the grounds of race or religion.

2)   Only 3 of the class said they had suffered racism, on "many times" and the other two, once only, while the remaining 19 said they had never experienced it.

3)   The 3 pupils who had suffered racism said that it was on the grounds of country or race.

4)   These incidents all consisted of name-calling.

5)   One pupil had not reported the incident, one had told a friend, and another had told a parent and sister.

6)   Nothing was done in any of these cases.

7)   One child said he was not satisfied because nothing had been done by his parents, the others left this answer blank.

8)   Once again, most of the class had come across racial incidents: 18 said that they had, as against 4 who said they had not.

9) All the incidents seem to have involved verbal abuse (this includes one child being teased for their Welsh accent and another being called a "Scottish bastard"), apart form one in which "pople go round with dog bones after this girl".

10) No-one at all said that they had reported these incidents: 6 left the space blank, while the other 16 included the following reasons for doing nothing:

"I didn't want to get involved/it was none of my business" (3)
"I couldn't be bothered"
"I was afraid to"
"Nobody was hurt or upset"
"My friend didn't want me to tell anybody" (2)
"I did not because she did not mind she was used to it and it was really none of my business"
"He said he was OK"
"My friend seemed to be controled and took it in and didn't say a thing"
"I thought she had said something"
"He said something to the teacher"
"I didn't know who to tell"
"She says it will only make the people worse nobody can stop them"
"I feel hurt and I didn't like telling people that I have been called a name."

11) Asked whether they had witnessed racist incidents outside school

14 said they had not
7 said they had
1 did not reply

The incidents were mainly name-calling, although one involved throwing mud at someone.

12) On the question of what action they would take if they witnessed a racist incident in school, the answers varied. Of those who said they would report it:

        2 would tell their mother
        1 would tell a teacher/the Headmaster
        1 would tell a friend
        3 would tell someone/someone older/the nearest person

Of the rest, 2 said they would ask the person if they wanted it reported, and 2 others said they would tell the person to stop and then tell a teacher.

        3 said they would do nothing
        1 said the person should deal with it themselves
        4 left the answer blank.

13)   Most of the class thought that children should be taught to read and write the language of their parents.

        16 said yes
        4 said no
        2 didn't know

The reasons for saying yes included the possibility that the family might visit their country of origin, their parents might not be able to understand them, and "We get our language so other people should learn they language". Of those opposed to the idea, 3 said that they should accept English and 1 that they should go back to their own languages. 4 said they didn't know.

14)   The majority of pupils (13) thought that they should have the opportunity to learn a non-European language - in case you go there to live or on holiday, it could help you to get a job - while 5 were against it: there is enough to learn already, we should stick to our own languages. 4 said they didn't know.

15)   Most pupils (16) thought that letters should be sent home in the language of the pupil's parents: they felt that this would help them to understand what was happening, and that it was especially important if the letter was of a private nature. Only 6 said "no", on the grounds that it would cause too much work for the school, or that they if they lived here should speak English.

261

16) Slightly more of the class (12) were against celebrating all religious festivals than were in favour (9), with one "don't know". One of those in favour said "so as not to be racialist": reasons against included the arguments that they were nothing to do with us, or that there would be too many - "other wize we would not have any normal school days".

17) Most of the class (17) thought that using examples from other cultures was a good idea, as it might help you to get a better job, you might go and live there, or we should learn more about the world we live in. 5 were against, 3 of them saying that they just wanted to learn about this country.

18) On the question of whether people in school made enough effort to pronounce pupils' names correctly, 10 said "yes" and 12 said "no". 5 of these didn't mind, 3 said they got a bit cross if it went on too much and one said they were "discusted".

19) On the question of discussing religious and cultural beliefs with teacher, class or friends, the breakdown is as follows:
a) teacher   Yes   1   No   17   No response 4
b) class   Yes   1   No   18   No response 3
c) friends   Yes 12   No   9   No response 1

20) The class was virtually unamimous on the questions of teachers' expectations of them they all said teacher expected them to do well, apart from one who said "yes and no" (it depends on the teacher).

21) Most of the class were against having more Black or Asian teachers: only 3 were in favour and 15 against, with 4 "don't knows". The reasons against included the fact that they were more difficult to understand or spoke too fast, that there were enough already, or that it should go by their work rather than their colour: those in favour said "There are lots of coloured children" or "I could talk to them in my language and discuss things."

22) a) **Ethnic origin**

British white	18
Black/white	1
Greek	1
Pakistani	1
Canadian	1

b) **Home language**

English	20
Greek	1
English/Urdu	1

c) **Religion**

Christian	13
Home	7
Muslim	1
Christian/Rastafarian	1

23) 9 pupils did not make any comment on racism, the 13 who did included the following:

"The problem is not taken seriously enough" (3)
"Racism is overdone just because their different colour or race"
"Some Pakis will always say there gonna take over ther world and I think they should go back to there own countrie" (2)
"I think the borough is spending too much money on special races"
"Most people in our school think rascism is all 1 way (white rascist to black) but I think black people are rascist to white as well" (2).

Report on 1st year survey: No 2

1) All 22 pupils understand what racism is - most used the same phrase "taking the micky out of someone because of their colour or race."

2) 16 pupils said they had never suffered racism, 5 said they had experienced it many times, and 1 said only once.

3) Of the 4 pupils who had suffered racism, 3 said that it was on the grounds of colour or race and the other did not give a reason.

4) About 1/3 of the class (7 children) described a racist incident (including one who had taken part in one); all but 2 involved sneering, laughing or name-calling, and the other 2 had been pushed around or said that "people cross their fingers when they see me coming."

5) Only one of these did not report it to anyone, the others told either a parent, other relative, a friend or their teacher.

6) 3 said that nothing was done, in another case the teacher had a word with them, another 1 said action was taken without specifying what it was and 1 did not reply.

7) 3 said that they were satisfied with the result, 1 said "no", 1 said "not really" and the other 2 did not reply.

8) In answer to the question whether they knew anybody who had suffered racism at school, 18 said "yes" and 4 said "no".

9) Almost all the racism described was verbal - taking the micky, name-calling or being teased. Of the rest, one gave no details and the other said that her had hit someone.

10) 11 pupils did not reply to the question as to why they did not report incidents that they knew about at school, and 3 said that the person involved had reported it themselves. The other reasons are as follows:

"I left it to him because he may of not wanted miss to know"

"I thought they...would sort it out for themselves"
"I was friends with the person who was racilist"
"I was afraid of getting beaten up"
"It was not my friend"
"I did not think it was fair to her"
"Because it was nune of my bisnis"
"I didn't think it was bad enough"

11) When asked whether they had witnessed racist incidents at school,

> 8 said they had
> 12 said they hadn't
> 2 did not reply

12) Asked what they would do about racist incident witnessed at school,

> 14 said they would tell a teacher or the Head Teacher
> 5 would do nothing
> 1 said he would "egg the victim to grass on him" or "make him/her apologise"
> 2 did not reply

13) Most of the pupils (18) thought that the school should *not* teach children to read and write the language of their parents. Only 4 thought they should and 1 of these said that it should be in their spare time. Several said that their parents should teach them, others thought that it would lead to confusion or that because they were in England now they should concentrate on English.

14) Pupils were divided roughly half-and-half over the teaching of European languages: 12 thought they should be taught "in case you visit the country" or "to teach them why you get teased." 10 said "no" because they were of no use later, they had enough to learn already, or they should learn only European languages.

15) With reference to sending letters home in the parents' language, only 8 were in favour of this while 14 (nearly twice as many) were against. 3 pupils said they should learn English, while others thought they might know enough English already.

16) 17 pupils were against celebrating all religious festivals, and only 5 in favour. Reasons included "why should we learn about that" or "they don't celebrate ours."

17) 14 pupils were in favour of teachers using examples from other countries and cultures, and half of these said "So we can learn about other countries." 6 replied "no" and 2 were non-committal.

18) With reference to the correct pronunciation of pupils' names,

14 said that people did not make enough effort
7 said they did not (1 said they were upset, and 1 was very upset)

19) Most pupils said they had not discussed their religious or beliefs with their teachers. The breakdown is as follows:

a) teacher   8   No   3   Yes   No reply   11
b) class   10   No   3   Yes   No reply   9
c) friends   10   No   5   Yes   No reply   7

20) 11 Pupils think teachers have a high expectation of them:

5 think that they don't
6 don't know

21) In response to whether there should be more Black and Asian teachers in school, more replied "no" than "yes" (11 as against 8) with 3 don't knows. A Jamaican pupil said "It shos the teacher are not NF". 3 pupils said that it would put white people out of a job.

Report on 1st year survey: No 3

1) The vast majority of pupils understand what racism is and can identify it.

Understood	18	"When you don't like someone because of their colour, religion etc".
Unsure	1	"Racism is a way not to co-operate with others. And it's giving a bad expression."
No response	2	

2) About 1/3 of the pupils said they had suffered racism.

Once	5
Many times	2
Never	13
No response	1

3) Most pupils who suffered racism in school believe this was because of their colour. The breakdown is:

Colour 5
Race 2 (1 pupil ticked both "colour" and "race").
No response 1

4) Of the 7 pupils who said they had suffered racism, 4 felt they could not give a description of an incident; the other 3 said they had been verbally abused. It is interesting that 6 of the pupils who said they had *not* suffered racism described racist incidents: verbal abuse, "throwing bricks through windows" and "throwing petrol bombs through letter boxes"; physical abuse, stabbing.

5) Of the 7 who said they had suffered racism, 2 said they'd reported it to their relatives and 2 that they'd reported it to a teacher/tutor in addition to telling their relatives/friends. The other 3 didn't report the incident to anyone. 3 of the passive observers said they had told their relatives/friends about what they had witnessed.

6) Most pupils who reported the incident said no action was taken.

7) Of the 7 pupils who said they had suffered racism, 3 were satisfied with the result; one wasn't; while the other 3 did not respond.

8) In answer to whether the pupil knew of anybody who had suffered racism in school, 15 did compared with 3 who did not. 3 did not reply.

9) A vast majority of the pupils said that the racism suffered by someone they knew was verbal abuse. One said a Jewish boy had his hat taken off his head.

Verbal abuse   13
Physical abuse   1
No response   7

10) Most said they did not want to get involved and thus they did not repeat these incidents to anyone. 2 pupils said "we new the teachers already new".

11) Asked whether they had witnessed racist incidents outside school,

8 said they hadn't
7 said they had
6 did not respond

12) About 3/4 of the pupils (16) said they would report the incident to a teacher, some said they would only report the "serious" incidents such as physical abuse. They would "ignore" racist name-calling.

13) About 1/2 of the pupils thought the school should *not* teach the children to read and write the language of their parents. Reasons given varied from "No, their parents should teach them their language", "because teachers are only paid for English. The parents should teach that languag" to "No, why bother, I say keep your own language at home."

Of those who said "Yes", on pupil gave the reason as "Because if they come from another country to England they might go back there". (Positive - for a holiday, say).

14) The majority (17) though pupils should be given an opportunity to learn a non-European language. 2 replied "No" and 2 did not respond.

15) An equal number of pupils (7 each) thought that letters should/should not be sent home in the language of the pupils' parents. 3 pupils said "Yes" and "No"; 1 was undecided while 3 did not respond.

16) The vast majority (12) of the pupils thought that only Christmas and Easter should be celebrated. 6 said that they wanted other religious festivals celebrated. 3 did not respond. One pupil said "I think, as this being a Christian country, they should celebrate Christmas."

17) In response to the use of examples about other countries and cultures in lessons, pupils responses were as follows:

10   Yes
4   No ("Because it is our country")
7   Did not respond or did not know.

18) The results as to whether staff in school make sufficient efforts to pronounce pupils' names correctly were:

9   Yes
6   No   "Because they find it boring to learn"
            "Fed up with it"
            "It's OK, I don't really mind"
5   No response
1   "Yes" and "No" -   "It does not worry me too much
                          but I don't like my name wrong on
                          important paper."

19) Most pupils said they had not discussed their religious or cultural beliefs with their teachers. The breakdown is:

a) teacher   12   No   5   Yes   4   No response
b) class   13   No   3   Yes   5   No response
c) friends   10   No   7   Yes   4   No response

20) With regard to whether teachers have a high expectation of pupils, 13 said they thought teachers expected them to do well ("because they are not racism" and "all teachers expect everyone to do well"). 2 answered "No" and 6 did not respond.

21) In response to whether there should be more Black and Asian teachers in schools, most pupils (9) just wanted a "good" teacher of any cultural background. 4 though here should be more Black and Asian teachers; 8 did not respond.

22) a) **Ethnic origin**

Black British	1
White British	13
Mixed race	1 (Australian/West Indian)
No respond	6

b) **Home languages**

English	12
English/Jamaican dialect	1
English/Greek dialect	1
English/Spanish	1
No response	6

c) **Religion**

Christian	7
None	5
Greek Orthodox	1
No response	8

23) "I think why dose skin cause so much trouble?" (Black British)
"I think that other people should not juje other people by they outside but by how nise they are." (White British)
"No I just think it's silly"
"I think Racist People are Ignorant and I myself think it is a sin to be racist." (Mixed race)

2 of the questionnaires in this group were left completely blank, so they are included in the "No respons" section each time.

1)   Most of the children seemed to understand that racism meant taking the mickey or name-calling, although 2 left it at that and did not mention that it was on the grounds of race or colour.

2)   No-one in the class has suffered racism at school, 18 replied "No" and the other 5 were left blank.

3-7) Not applicable.

8)   14 of the class (nearly 2/3) had come across racist incidents, while 7 answered "No" and 2 were left blank.

9)   All the racist incidents involved name-calling or verbal abuse, apart from 1 in which someone was spat at and punched in the face.

10)   Only 2 pupils said they had reported these incidents, of the others:

          2 thought the victim had dealt with it themselves
          2 were afraid of the consequences
          1 thought it would make things worse
          7 were left blank

11)   7 pupils said that they had witnessed racist incidents outside school, while 9 said they had not and 7 did not reply. The incidents which were described all involved racial abuse.

12)   of the 23 pupils, 8 did not reply to the question on what they would do if they witnessed a racist incident in school. Of the remaining 15,

          6 would try to help in some way by intervening of getting
               someone to come straight away
          5 would tell a teacher
          3 would go and tell someone (unspecified)
          1 would keep away.

13)   Asked whether children should be taught the language of their parents, 12 said "yes" and 4 said "no", with 7 not replying. Of those in favour, some felt that it would help the children with their school work or generally to communicate with others, and one said "So they can go back to their country where they belong"; those against said that it was the parents' job, or that it was too much trouble interfering into another culture.

14)   Nearly 2/3 of the pupils thought that they should be able to learn a non-European language: 14 said yes, 5 said no and 4 did not reply. Some felt that it would be helpful if they visited or worked in the countries concerned or for exams, and on said "So they won't feel left out."   On the other hand, comments against included "There's no point if we live in England"; "they may not enjoy it and it would encourage people to take more of a mikey"; "it would encourage racism"; "it is not their own country...its stupid to learn...you are nothing to do with it."

15)   With reference to letters being sent home in the parents' language, 13 were in favour, 7 were against it, and 3 did not reply. Most of those in favour thought it would help them to understand things better or make them feel at home, another said "they would enjoy knowing that their child is learning their language." Most of those against thought that they should learn their English, one said, "Because if you live in England you can read English (well most can)."

16)   On the question of celebrating religious festivals other than Christmas and Easter, 6 said "yes", 6 said "no" and the other 11 did not specify. Some liked the idea of more holidays or thought it would be more fair "as they have to observe ours", while others said "they can do that in there own country" or "not our religion."

17)   8 pupils were in favour of teachers using examples from other countries, while 6 were against the idea and 9 did not respond.

Those in favour thought we should learn more about other countries, others thought they had enough to learn already and 2 thought it would encourage racism - "they laugh and find it funny."

18) On the question of peoples in school making enough effort to pronounce the pupils' names correctly, 7 though they did, 5 thought they didn't and 11 did not respond. No-one expressed any strong views on the subject.

19) The figures for pupils discussing their religious and cultural beliefs with others is as follows:

Teacher	2	Yes	11	No	10	No response
Class	3	Yes	10	No	10	No response
Friends	5	Yes	7	No	11	No response

20) No-one in the class thought that their teachers did not expect them to do well; 11 said that they were expected to do well while 12 did not know or did not reply.

21) More than half of the class (14) expressed no opinion on the question of having more Black or Asian teachers in school: 5 were in favour - "coloured people would feel more at home" - while 4 were against - "more whites are unemployed", "they're taking over".

22) **Ethnic origin**

British White	14
Sikh	1
Other European	1
Blank	7

Language

English	11
Italian	2
Urdu	1
English/Other	1
Blank	8

Religion

Christian	11
Rastafarian	1
Sikh	1
Other	1
None	4
Blank	5

23) Only 4 pupils made any comment on racism, these were as follows:

"It's just stupidness and silly"
"It's stupid"
"Send all the blaks home expet nurse and docters"
"Sod all the pakis send em back up there trees" (this pupil claimed to be Rastafarian).

1) All the children seem to have a rough idea of what racism is, although one or two just say it's name-calling without specifying that it should be on the grounds of race or colour. Several children mentioned that racism can be black against white as well as white against black.

2) 18 of the pupils have never experienced racism: of the remaining 4, 2 have suffered it many times and 2 on one occasion only; the latter 2 give not details of the incident.

3) With reference to the 2 pupils who have suffered racism many times, 1 said that he was called ginger-nut and the other that he was called names on the grounds of his colour, religion, language and country.

4) The incidents both consisted of verbal abuse.

5) The first pupil did not tell anyone, and the other told a friend.

6) Nothing was done.

7) Neither made any comment on whether they were satisfied with the result.

8) 9 of the class said that they had witnessed a racial incident, 12 said that they had not and 1 did not reply.

9) All the incidents consisted of verbal abuse (including one person being called fat).

10) None of the 9 pupils who had seen an incident in school had actually reported it, for the following reasons:

   1 didn't see it for themselves
   2 couldn't be bothered
   3 said that the person involved didn't want them to
   2 said the person was caught in the act
   1 was afraid of getting into trouble with the people concerned

11) Asked whether they had witnessed racist incidents outside school,

4 said yes
16 said no
2 did not reply

12) If they were to see a racist incident in school, the action children would take is as follows:

12 would report to the Head/Deputy Head/Year Head/teacher
1 would report it to someone (unspecified)
2 would ask the victim if they wanted it to be reported
2 would tell their friends
1 would tell the police
3 would not get involved
1 did not reply

13) Most of the pupils did not think that children should learn the language of their parents: 15 said "No", 6 said "Yes" and 1 did not reply. Reasons varied as to why it was not a good idea; several said that everyone should be treated the same, 2 said that they might try to forge letters (for instance to get out of PE), others thought "if their parents had wanted them to speak and behave in that language, they would not be in this country."

14) Slightly more than half of the class thought it would be a good idea to learn a non-European language: 12 were in favour as against 10 who opposed it. Once again they mentioned the possibility of moving to or visiting the country concerned, or the fact that it might help with employment prospects. Those against said it would be too complicated or confusing, you wouldn't need it, or "Why can't we just learn our own language?"

15) More of the pupils were against the idea of sending letters home in parents language (12) than were in favour of it (12) with 1 not replying. As usual a few pupil said that they should learn our language.

16) About 3/4 of the class (16) were against the idea of celebrating other religious festivals as well as Christmas and Easter, as against 6 in favour. The latter thought that we should understand each

others' religions, or that black people should have fun as well; but others said that there would be too many holidays and too much time off school, "they don't celebrate ours", it's nothing to do with us, and "the Mums would be spending out a lot on food."

17) In response to the question about the use of examples of other cultures in lessons, the replies were as follows:

11 said yes
10 said no
1 did not reply

Some felt that this would be a waste of time, or that "lessons would be even more boring."

18) Twice as many pupils were satisfied with the school's efforts to pronounce their names correctly (15) as were dis-satisfied (7), but no-one seemed particularly bothered about this issue.

19) Most pupils do not seem to have discussed their religious or cultural beliefs with their teacher, class or friends. The breakdown is as follows:

Teacher	Yes	4	No	16	No response	2
Class	Yes	4	No	16	No response	2
Friends	Yes	4	No	16	No response	2

20) On the question of teachers' expectations of their pupils, the results were:

13 felt that they were expected to do well
6 did not think so
3 did not reply

Pupils said that you came to school to learn, or that they want you to get a good job.

21) The majority of the class (13) had no strong opinion on the question of more black and Asian teachers in school; only 3 were in favour and 6 were against. One pupil said "It helps teach children that white is not the only race", while 2 said that it was

fair as it was at the moment as there are some of each; 1 felt that black or Asian teachers were sometimes harder to understand.

22) a) **Ethnic origin**

British White	20
Pakistani	1
Blank	1

b) **Language**

English	18
English/Urdu	1
Blank	3

c) **Religion**

Christian	8
Muslim	1
None	7
Other	2
Blank	4

23) 7 pupils made a comment in the last section, and they are as follows:

"I think it is horrible that some people should call people horrible names they should be sorry for themselves I don't know how the could call people names."

"Every person in this world is human no matter whether they are black, white or purple with orange spots on we are all human beings."

"I don't like coloured people's breath."

"Everybody should have equal opportunities, no matter what colour, religion, language or country of origin, we are all human after all."

"You have to just take what is thrown at you. You just have to take it and take these things calmly."

"I think that it is unkind that other people are treated badly."

"I think it is unfair to tease people about their colour, country, religion etc."

1st Year survey: summary of results

110 surveys were returned, of which 2 were completely blank. Some of the rest had large parts of the survey uncompleted, so some of the results have been worked out twice: once as a percentage of the actual answers and once as a percentage of the whole, including the blanks.

1) *What is racism*

Virtually every child knew that racism involved unpleasant behaviour from one person to another, although in a few cases they had not mentioned that it was specifically on racial grounds.

2) *Have you ever suffered racism in this school?*

Never	80.8%	Never	76.4%
Once	9.6%	Once	9.1%
Many times	9.6%	Many times	9.1%
No response	5.4%		

3) *On what grounds?*

This cannot be quantified as most of the pupils either gave more than one reason or gave no explanation at all.

4) *Describe one incident*

Again there is insufficient explanation in these answers, but the impression is that almost all the incidents involved verbal rather than physical behaviour, although there are a few examples of this as well.

5) *Did you tell anyone about this?*

Of the incidents described, 60% were reported. (12 out of 20).

6) *Was anything done about it?*

In 10 of these 12 cases, nothing was done. (10 out of 12).

7) *Were you satisfied with the results?*

[Figures in this section should be treated with caution, as some of the incidents referred to are not described in sufficient detail, or answers are omitted altogether. This makes it impossible to quantify this answer].

8) *Do you know anybody who has suffered racism in school?*

Yes	71.2%	Yes	67.3%
No	28.8%	No	27.3%
No response	5.4%		

9) *If yes, explain what happened*

Once again, this is difficult to quantify because answers to 9) do not always follow on from answers to 8). However, it seems clear that most of the incidents were verbal rather than physical.

10) *If you did not report these incidents, please explain why*

Not everyone answered this question, but the reasons which were given for not reporting an incident can be broken down into the following groups:

Thinking someone else/the victim had done so	26%
Didn't want to get involved/"none of my business"	24%
Told not to by the victim	20%
Didn't think it mattered	10%
Fear of the consequences	10%
Embarrassment	2%
Friends with the aggressor	2%
Didn't know who to tell	2%
Other	4%

11) *Have you witnessed racist incidents outside school?*

No	64.5%	No	54.5%
Yes	35.5%	Yes	30.0%
No response	15.5%		

12) *If so, what would you do?*

Of those who replied, the breakdown is as follows:

Tell a teacher/Head Teacher	51%
Do nothing	15%
Tell someone (unspecified)	9%
Ask the person if they wanted it reported	8%
Tell them to stop	8%
Tell a friend	3%
Tell a member of the family	2%
They should deal with it themselves	1%
Tell the police	1%
Other	2%

13) *Should children learn the language of their parents?*

No	55.2%	No	48.2%
Yes	44.8%	Yes	39.1%
No response	12.7%		

14) *Should pupils learn a non-European language?*

Yes	68%	Yes	61.8%
No	32	No	29.1%
No response	9.1%		

15) *Should letters be sent home in the language of the parents?*

Yes	53.5%	Yes	48.2%
No	46.5	No	41.8%
No response	10.0%		

16) *Should we celebrate all religious festivals?*

No	66.3%	No	57.3%
Yes	33.7%	Yes	29.1
No response	13.6%		

17) *Should teachers use examples of other countries and cultures?*

Yes	65.9%	Yes	54.5%
No	34.1%	No	28.2%
No response	17.3%		

18) *Do people make enough effort to pronounce your name correctly?*

Yes	59.8%	Yes	50%
No	40.2%	No	33.6%
No response	16.4%		

19) *Have you ever discussed your cultural or religious beliefs with:*

Your teacher

No	81%	No	58.2%
Yes	19%	Yes	13.6%
No response	28.2%		

Your class

No	82.7%	No	60.9%
Yes	17.3%	Yes	12.7
No response	26.4%		

Your friends

No	61.2%	No	47.3%
Yes	38.8%	Yes	30.0%
No response	22.7%		

20) *Do teachers expect you to do well?*

Yes	84.1%	Yes	62.7%
No	15.9%	No	11.8%
No response	25.5%		

21)   *Should there be more Black and Asian teachers in school?*

No	62.7%	No	33.6%
Yes	37.3%	Yes	20.0%

No response/
Don't mind 46.4%

22)   *Ethnic origin*

There are 7 children of non-European language - 6.4% of the total.

Home language

There are 6 children speaking a non-European language - 5.5% of the total.

Religion

There are 2 Rastafarians, 2 Muslims and a Sikh - 4.5% of the total.

[Again, these figures could be considerably higher if all the forms had been completed].

Report on 4th year survey

All the 4th Year pupils have been treated together and not as separate classes. Out of 83 questionnaires, 70 have been completed and 13 left.

1)   *What is racism?*

Most of the pupils defined this in some way as being discriminated against or otherwise ill-treated - being picked on, called names, treated with violence, and so on - because they are different in some way, either by race or culture.
"Racism is a colour problem because if you are white black people think you are against them because of there colour"; "where a person from one culture makes another culture feel inferior"; "when something is said or done against a person without reason" (Pakistani pupil).

2)   *Have you ever suffered racism in this school?*

Never	55
Once	1
A few times	1
Many times	6
Blank	7

3)   *If yes, was this because of:*

Colour	2
Religion	1
Language	1
Colour/religion	1
Religion/race	1
Colour/race/country	1
Colour/race/religion/language/country	1

4)   *Describe one incident*

Most of the incidents involved name-calling; one child was hit and called a Yid, another was made to kiss someone's feet under threat of being beaten up. One child wrote: "I was sitting in my car when a group of boys shouted "Paki go home". They threw a

half-eaten Mars bar through the open window". Another said:
"This boy was throwing rubber bands around at me, when I told
the teacher. Then in my next lesson him and his friends called me
racist names."

5) *Did you tell anyone about it?*

> Told member of family/friend   3
> Told member of staff at school   0
> Told both   4
> Told no-one   1

6) *Was anything done about it?*

> Yes   2
> No   5
> No reply   1

7) *Were you satisfied with the result?*

Most of these pupils said that they were not satisfied: "it didn't
change anything", "telling him off wouldn't make him not do it
again", "I was just told not to worry about it.

8) *Do you know anyone who has suffered racism in school?*

> Yes   38
> No   27
> Blank   5

9) *If yes, explain what happened*

> Name-calling and abuse 30
> Physical ill-treatment   6
> No details   2 (Total 38)

Examples: "A boy called someone a dirty Paki and kicked them
over", "A child said something to a teacher (Asian)"

10) *If you did not report these incidents, please explain why*

Reasons included the following:

> Self-preservation
> Victim asked me not to
> It was know about already/teacher dealt with it
> Didn't think it was serious enough
> Nothing to do with me
> Because I was being racialist

11) *Have you witnessed racist incidents outside school?*

Yes	37
No	29
Blank	4

These incidents include a great deal of name-calling and racial abuse and a lot of physical abuse too, although this is by blacks against whites as well as the reverse. Incidents include abuse of black footballers and bananas being thrown onto the pitch; a girl being teased because it's against her religion to watch East Enders; abuse of shopkeeper, and muggings. "I've seen skinheads beat up Asians and football hooligans kick in blacks"; "a few boys were taking the micky out of an Indian boy they were telling racist jokes and singing racist songs". One pupil commented: "Often I see people putting people of different races down, letting white people etc get way with things black people etc couldn't. Also some people tend to blame black people for incidents and crimes more so than they do white people."

12) *If you were to witness a racist incident in school, what would you do?*

Nothing	20
Don't know/blank	5
Something	45 - made up as follows:

Get a teacher/someone else	16
Encourage the victim to report it	3

Watch/join in	3
Try to stop it	11
Report it if it was serious	3
Depends on the victim/how bad it is	8
Nothing, they might deserve it	1

One child admitted that "Although I'm not racist I haven't got enough guts to try to defend the coloured person in case anyone turns against me."

13) *Should the school teach children to read and write the language of their parents?*

Yes	11
No	52
Don't know	7

Reasons include the following:

In favour -   the children should know about their origins they might want to visit their own country it would be easier to read their religious books it should only be if they want to.

Against -   they are in England so they should speak English (18)
their parents can teach them (12)
too many languages would be taught (9)
the children would be teased/singled out (4)
"It is up to the parents...I would refuse to speak an Asian language in school."

14) *Should all pupils be able to learn a non-European language?*

Yes	54
No	13
Don't know	3

Reasons in favour include the following:

> You might visit another country (6)
> You might emigrate (2)
> You would have more change of getting a job abroad (2)
> Because Europe isn't the whole world (1)
> So you could understand more about other people (1)

Those against said:

> It would be a waste of time
> They should do it outside school if they want to (4)
> We live in England/they should learn English like the rest of us
> We're only likely to visit countries in Europe

15) *Should letters be sent home in the parents' language?*

> Yes   20
> No   47
> Don't know   3

Those in favour said:

> Not all parents can understand English (15)
> It would be polite to use their English (2)
> It might be something the child shouldn't read
> English parents get letter in their own language, so why shouldn't the others?
> Only if parents cannot speak English

Reasons against include:

> They should be able to speak and read English (28)
> There would be problems with secretaries, typewriters, etc (7)
> Too much hassle, waste of time and money (5)
> The parents might be embarrassed/insulted (2)
> It wouldn't make any difference if the parents could speak English (2)

Most Black people's parents speak English - it's only Asians
who don't
The child could translate for them
If the parents can't read English then it should be they who
are at school

16) *Should we celebrate all religious festivals?*

Yes   11
No   51
Don't know   8

Those in favour said:

It would help children of other festivals feel at home (2)
Their religions are special to them like ours are to us (2)
It's interesting to learn about
We'd get more presents/more time off
It's sort of racism if we don't

Reasons against included:

We'd always be on holiday (13)
Let people celebrate their own festivals but not make
everyone join in
You should just celebrate your own (7)
It would be impossible - there are too many (3)
It's wrong to believe in more than one religion (2)
I don't care about other festivals - only the ones in my own
religion (2)
"If they was really worried about there festivals then they
should not have come over here in the first place."
They should have one massive festival for everyone
It's not our religion/they don't celebrate ours
"If Asians, Jews and Rastafarians want to celebrate their
own occasions let them do it in their own country."

17) *Should teachers use examples of other countries and cultures in lessons?*

> Yes   36
> No   16
> Don't know   13
> we do already   5

Reasons in favour:

> you could learn more (18)
> it would be more interesting (9)
> if it was relevant/not boring (3)
> it can help to stop racism (2)
> it's not fair if teachers just use our
> own language

Reasons against:

> we should only do it in RE
> it would be boring/irrelevant
> we shouldn't be compared with other countries because it is
> a liberty
> "they do it too much now, it gets on my nerves. This is
> England, not India they are either guests or immigrants to
> the country so they should fit into our way of living a best
> they can"
> everyone would just laugh at first, then get bored
> "it is boring and who wants to know about them anyway"

18) *Do people make enough effort to pronounce your name correctly?*

> Yes   37
> No   23
> Don't know   10

Reactions to this varied, a few said they were angry or annoyed but most said that they didn't really worry. One pupil said, "Nobody should worry, in England most names are easily pronounced so people don't worry to waste time spending ages trying to pronounce a name they've never heard of."

19) *Have you ever discussed your cultural or religious beliefs with*

    a) *Your teacher*   Yes   11
                                    No   50
                                    Blank 9

    b) *Your class*   Yes   9
                                    No   51
                                    Blank 10

    c) *Your friends*   Yes   29
                                    No   35
                                    Blank 6

20) *Do your teachers expect you to do well?*

        Yes   51
        No   2
        Don't know   17

One of the children who replied "No" added the comment: "Many" teachers think Black people are more stupid."

Those replying "Yes" gave reasons such as:

        so we can get a job
        because that's their job
        they want you to pass exams
        they want the best for you
        if you're clever they expect you to work hard
        all teachers should
        they expect every pupil to do well.

21) *Would it be better if there were more Black and Asian Teachers?*

        Yes   11
        No   33
        Don't know   26

Answers in favour included:

> It would stop racist complaints
> There would be more people to go to if there were any unpleasant incidents
> "Racist people could talk to them and get used to the more"
> Not enough at the moment - schools shouldn't be full of white teachers
> Black and Asian pupils would feel better and more secure

Those against included the following:

> "I'm sick and tired of Pakis that can't teach"
> A lot of white pupils are against them
> Some of the foreign teachers can hardly speak any English
> "Most Asian teachers that we have cannot speak good English and don't earn respect for themselves"
> They can't control classes
> You can't understand them - it's not worth them being there
> White people should be offered jobs before immigrants
> "They would end up leaving because of the racism, then we'd have to get used to another new teacher."
> "I would rather have a English lesson taught by an Englishman."
> Pupils will only take the micky and make their lives a misery
> "The ones we've got we can just about understand them"
> "I think that Asian teachers are difficult to understand"
> "You can't make out what they are saying as some of them can't speak English that well"
> "I don't (mind) if there were more black teachers but Asian teachers don't make good enough teachers and I can't understand their pronunciation of English. Their voices give me a headache."
> "You must be joking! Can't understand a word they are saying, so it would be worse, and you would not learn anything."

Some of the "Don't knows" commented as follows:

> I don't think Black teachers are different

292

The important thing is their teaching skills

Black and white should be equal

You shouldn't employ someone because they're Black

Teachers are all the same

The question is racist - most teachers are equal

It depends if they're strict enough

We should only have Black teachers who have been raised in England

It might increase racism; it might decrease it

"I'm not bothered what colour the teachers are. And I find that white teachers have more control over us than Asians."

22) *How would you describe yourself?*

    a) *Ethnic origin*

White	63
Black	2
Israeli	1
Mixed race	1
Indian	1
African/Pakistani	1
Afro-caribbean	1

    b) *Home languages*

English	66
Hebrew	1
Hindi/Persian	1
English/Gujarati	1
English/Swahili	1

    c) *Religion*

Christian	41 (including 7 non-practising)
Jewish	4 (including 1 parents only)
Muslim	3
Atheist	1
None	17
Blank	4

23) *Anything else to say about racism?*

There were 42 replies, (15 if them racist) and 29 forms left blank.
Here is a selection of the comments.

"I think this survey is silly and there are more black and pakis in
this country than white."
I don't feel any hate towards Blacks 50% of my friends are black.
I just don't like Pakistanis and all Asians. I have about 3 Asian
friends but in the street when I pass Asian familys I feel some hate
towards them'.
"I'm not racist but hate black and other colour when there together
in gang (survey is silly)."
"Black people make arguments all the time. fights etc but <u>some</u> I
think are really nice. Asian people have too many children and are
housed faster than white familys."
"I am not racist but when the foreigners come over here from their
home country and start demanding equal rights I think they should
go back to their own country."
"The law on it is unfair we have a police pamphlet through our
door and it suggested that if a white person picks on a black person
they can be nicked for racial harassment but if it is vice versa it
wouldn't be the case."
"Poverty breeds rascism. It's not the immigrants fault it's the
politicians who promised them work when they got here. I think
the worse act ever passed was the Race act. I also think Britain
should start repatriation."
"I think that racism is terrible. But people who have moved to our
country should try to fit in with our language. I don't like it when
ethnic minorities campaign for equal rights because they get them
already. Everyone gets the same from the state, ethnic minorities
are not being deprived of anything!"
"If coloured people want to live in England they should do things
the English way, ie speak English and do what the English do,
although as it's their religion they should celebrate their religious
events if they want to."
"I like most black people just like I like most white people but I
can't understand most ASIANS especially when they are treated
somewhat better than English whites. My sister is white and she
is constantly picked on by other pupils teachers do nothing about
this but if she was a paki those pupils would be in serious trouble.

I have been turned racist against Asians because they are made a fuss of by our stupid Loony Left council!! There is a family of Pakis which live near me they live in what USED TO BE VERY clean a pleasant house but since they moved there they have degraded the area. Its disgusting then the council give them money to do their windows get new ones but not to white people!"

"I don't mind them living here but when they start to try and bring all their religions into the country it annoys me very much (eg killing animals the Halal way because of religion if they don't like our meat keep their hands of our animals, shops where they rent videos for Asians). This annoys me because they are living in England they should speak English be able to learn English. If it was the other way round I would expect to learn their language to live."

"I don't mind blacks are chinese but I don't like pack because they've nicked all our jobs and they smell."

"Blacks are fine, but pakis smell and have all our corner shops and I wish they would sod off home."

"I think everyone has racism in them even if they don't realise it."

"There always has been racism and whatever measure are taken, there always will be."

"I find this racist. It is like a big campaign to feel sorry for minority groups so that you can give them preferential treatment. This is wrong because minority groups are not ashamed of what they are. They should be left alone and they will blend into society without any fuss. All the do-goods busy-bodies make it harder for everyone."

"I get annoyed at the fact of people making a big thing about deliberately employing someone because they are black so the employer doesn't look racist. The person who is best suited for the job ie best qualifications, reliability, trust should get the job."

"I feel sorry for people who are racist because they are ignorant and need help."

"Why is being black or brown a crime?"

"I think people should not be nasty to other races because like us they are only human the other difference is your colour!!"

"Some people are very narrow-minded especially the older generation but I think that in years to come racism will gradually die out and people will understand more."

"I think everyone should be equal...not to look up or down on somebody until you have found out what the person is like underneath the skin. People should be judged individually."

"I don't think there is any need for racism, I get on well with black people as well as I get on with white people."

"I think racism is horrible, just because a person is different on the outside it doesn't mean they're that different inside. The worst kind of people are the racist ones who are obviously nasty inside even though they're not so different on the outside."

"I think racism is childish and shows how immature racists are."

"Racism don't bother me cos if your black your black and if your white your white so your bound to get racist comments so is it worth worrying about."

"I am against racism. But sometimes I must admit sometimes I accidently say racist things."

"I think it'll never go away."

"We all have to remember that we can not condemn one set of people just because of a bad experience with one person."

"I see blacks just the same as whites but with a colour. My brother was mugged and nearly stabbed by a crowd of blacks but I haven't gone of of them because of that."

"I don't like racism, it isn't nice and I don't see why it happens, we have to learn to except other as they try to except us."

Appendix 7:
Percentage tables

Below are tables which give the percentages for responses to the pupil survey questionnaires which were administered to the first and fourth year pupils at school B in London. There were a total of 110 pupils in the first year who took part in the questionnaire; and 83 in the fourth year. This is very much a qualitative evaluation, rather than a quantitative evaluation.

Q 2   Have you suffered racism in this school?

	Never	Once	Many times	No response
1st years	80.8	9.6	9.6	0
4th years	66	1	7	26

Q 3   If yes, was this because of colour or race?

	Colour	Race	No response
1st years	23.81	9.52	66.67
4th years	2	4	94

Q 5   Did you tell anyone about it?

	Family	Staff	No-one	No response
1st years	9.53	9.53	14.29	66.65
4th years	3	0	1	96

Q 6   Was anything done about this?

	Yes	No	No response
1st years	16	83	1
4th years	2	6	92

Q 8   Do you know anyone who has suffered racism in school?

	Yes	No	No response
1st years	67.3	27.3	5.4
4th years	45.78	32.53	21.69

Q 11   Have you witnessed racist incidents outside school?

	Yes	No	No response
1st years	30	54.5	15.5
4th years	44.58	34.94	20.48

298

Q 12 If you were to witness a racist incident in school, what would you do?

	Tell staff	Do nothing	Tell someone else	No response
1st years	51	15	34	0
4th years	19.28	24.10	34.94	21.68

Q 13 Should children learn the language of their parents?

	Yes	No	No response
1st years	39.1	48.2	12.7
4th years	13.25	62.65	24.10

Q 14 Should pupils learn a non-European language?

	Yes	No	No response
1st years	39.1	48.2	12.7
4th years	65.06	15.66	19.28

Q 15 Should letters be sent home in the language of the parents?

	Yes	No	No response
1st years	61.8	29.1	9.1
4th years	24.10	56.63	19.27

Q 16 Should we celebrate all religious festivals?

	Yes	No	No response
1st years	29.1	57.3	13.6
4th years	13.25	61.45	25.30

Q 17 Should teachers use examples of other countries and cultures?

	Yes	No	No response
1st years	54.5	28.2	17.3
4th years	49.40	19.28	31.32

Q 18 Do people make enough effort to pronounce you name correctly?

	Yes	No	No response
1st years	50	33.6	16.4
4th years	44.58	27.71	27.71

Q 19a Have you ever discussed your cultural or religious beliefs with your teachers?

	Yes	No	No response
1st years	13.6	58.2	28.2
4th years	13.25	60.24	26.51

Q 19b Have you ever discussed your cultural or religious beliefs with you class?

	Yes	No	No response
1st years	12.7	60.9	26.4
4th years	10.84	61.45	27.71

Q 19c   Have you ever discussed you cultural or religious beliefs with your friends?

	Yes	No	No response
1st years	30.0	47.3	22.7
4th years	34.94	42.17	22.89

Q 20 Do teachers expect you to do well?

	Yes	No	No response
1st years	62.7	11.8	25.5
4th years	61.45	2.41	36.14

Q 21 Should there be more Black and Asian teachers in school?

	Yes	No	No response
1st years	20.0	33.6	46.4
4th years	13.25	39.76	46.99

Q 22 What is your ethnic origin: defined in terms of Black or White?

	Black	White
1st years	6	94
4th years	10	90

Bibliography

All books published in London unless stated otherwise

Abudarham S (1987) *Bilingualism and the Bilingual* (NFER-Nelson) Windsor

Ahmad B (1990) *Black Perspectives in Social Work* (Venture Press) Birmingham

Access to Information on Multicultural Education Resources (1992) *Photocopiable resources to support the multicultural dimension of the National Curriculum* (AIMER) Reading

Ali A (Ed) (1980) *The Visible Minority* (Hansib Publishing)

Allen S (1973) "The Institutionalisation of Racism", *Race* No 15, July pp 55-105

Allport G (1979) *The Nature of Prejudice* (Addison Wesley)

All London Teachers Against Racism and Fascism (1984) *Challenging Racism* (ALTARF)

Amin K, Fernandes M and Gordon P (1988) *Racism And Discrimination in Britain* (The Runnymede Trust)

Assistant Masters and Mistresses Association (1973) *Our Multicultural Society: The Educational Response* (AMMA)

303

Anwar M (1979) *The Myth of Return, Pakistanis in Britain* (Heinemann)

Arora R and Duncan (1986) *Multicultural Education* (Routledge)

Babatunde (nd) *Ndidi's Story* (Pan-African Institute) Manchester

Bagley C (1992) *Back to the Future* (NFER) Slough

Ball S (1987) *The Micro-Politics of the School* (Methuen)

Ball W & Troyna B (1989) "The Dawn of a New ERA?" in *Educational Management and Administration* (British Educational Management and Administration Society)

Banks and Lynch J (1986) *Multicultural Education in Western Societies* (Holt, Rinehart and Winston)

Banton M (1970) "The Concept of Racism" in *Race & Racism* Zubaida S (Ed) (Tavistock)

Banton M (1977) *The Idea of Race* (Tavistock)

Baratz and Baratz (1970) "Early Childhood Intervention: the Social Science Base of Institutional Racism", *Harvard Educational Review* Vol 40, No 1, pp 29-50 in Troyna and Williams (1986)

Barker M (1985) *The New Racism* (Junction Books)

Baron H M (1969) "The Web of Urban Racism" in Knowles and Prewitt, *Institutional Racism in America* pp 134-176

Barton L and Walker S (Eds) (1983) *Race, Class & Education* (Croom Helm)

Bash L, Coulby D and Jones C (1985) *Urban Schooling* (Holt Rienhart Winston)

BBC Education (1990) "A Roof Over Our Heads" in *Mosaic* (BBC)

Begum N (1990) *Burden of gratitude: women with disabilities receiving personal care* (Social care practice centre/University of Warwick)

Coventry

Begum N (1992) *Race & Disability Research Project* (Race Relations Unit, Waltham Forest)

Bently D and Watts M (1994) *Primary Science and Technology* (Open University Press) Buckingham

Ben-Tovin G (1978) "The Struggle Against Racism: Theoretical and Strategic Perspective", *Marxism Today*, July pp 293-313

Ben-Tovin G, Gabriel J, Law I and Stredder K (1986) *The Local Politics of Race* (MacMillan)

Benedict R (1983) *Race and Racism* (Routledge & Kegan Paul)

Benokraitis N and Feagin J (1986) *Institutional Racism*

Benyon J (1984) *Scarman and After* (Pergamon Press)

Bhatnagar J (1981) *Educating Immigrants* (Croom Helm)

Bicknell M (1986) *Books to break barriers* (ODEC)

Biott C (1991) *Semi-Detached Teachers: building support and advisory relationships in classrooms* (Falmer Press)

Blauner R (1972) *Racial Oppression in America* (Harper and Row) New York

Boggs J (1968) *The American Revolution: Pages from a Negro Worker's Notebook* (Modern Reader) New York

Boggs J (1970) *Racism and the Class Struggle: More pages from a Black Worker's Notebook* (Modern Reader) New York

Bonnett A (1990) "Educational Ideology in London and Tyneside" in *Oxford Review of Education*, vol 16, no 2, pp 255-67

Bonnett A (1993) *Radicalism, Anti-Racism and Representation* (Routledge)

Borthwick A, Dunn D, Naguib M and Parsons A (1988) *Planning NAFE* (Further Education Unit)

Bourne J (1987) "Homelands of the Mind" in *Race & Class* Vol XXIX No 1 (Institute of Race Relations)

Brah A (1992) "Difference, Diversity and differentiation" in Donald and Rattansi *"Race", Culture and Difference*

Brah A (1992) "Women of South Asian origin in Britain - issues and concerns" in Braham, Rattansi and Skellington *Racism and Antiracism*

Braham P, Rattansi and Skellington R (Eds) (1992) *Racism and Antiracism - Inequalities, Opportunities and Policies* (Sage/Open University)

Braithwaite E R (1962) *To Sir With Love* (New English Library)

Brandt G (1986) *The Realisation of Anti-Racist Teaching* (Falmer Press)

Bridges L (1994) "Tory education: exclusion and the black child", *Race and Class*, Vol 36, no 1, pp 33 - 48

Brown C, Barnfield J and Stone M (1990) *Spanner in the Works* (Trentham Books) Stoke-on-Trent

Brown M (1985) "Britain's New Middle Class", *The Sunday Times Magazine*, 27 October

Bryan, Dadzie and Scafe (1985) *The Heart of the Race* (Virago)

Bulkin E, Bruce Pratt M and Smith B (1984) *Yours in Struggle* (Long Haul Press) New York

Bullock (1975) *A Language for Life* (HMSO)

Burgess R G (Ed) (1985) *Strategies of Educational Research: Qualitative Methods* (The Falmer Press)

Burgess R G (Ed) *The Ethics of Educational Research* (The Falmer

Press) Barcombe, Lewes, East Sussex

Burt S (1987) *Multicultural and Antiracist Policies*, Unpublished PhD thesis, University of London

Carmichael S and Hamilton C (1967) *Black Power* (Penguin) Harmondsworth

Carrington B and Short G (1989) "Policy or presentation? The psychology of anti-racist education", *New Community*, Vol 15, No 2, pp 227-240 (CRE)

Cartwright R (1987) "No problem here - Multicultural Education in the All White School" *Multicultural Teaching* Vol V, No 2, pp 10-12

Cashmore E and Troyna B (1982) *Black Youth In Crisis* (George Allen & Unwin)

Cashmore E and Troyna B (1990) *Introduction to Race Relations* (Falmer Press)

Centre for Contemporary Studies (1981) *Unpopular Education* (Hutchinson)

Chinweizu (1987) *The West and the rest of us* (Pero Press) Lagos, Nigeria

Chivers T (1987) *Race And Culture* (NFER-Nelson)

Coard B (1971) *How the West Indian Child is Made Educationally Subnormal in the British School System* (New Beacon Books) Reprinted 1991

Cocking L (1986) *Multi-Ethnic Education Review* Vol V, No 1 (ILEA)

Cohen L and Cohen A (Eds) (1986) *Multicultural Education: A Source book for teachers* (Harper and Row)

Cohen L and Manion L (1980) *Research Methods in Education* (Croom Helm)

Cohen P and Bains H (1988) *Multi-Racist Britain* (Macmillan)

Cole M (1989) *Education For Equality* (Routledge)

Commission for Racial Equality (1977) *Housing Choice and Ethnic Concentration* (CRE)

Commission for Racial Equality (1983) *Code of Practice* (CRE)

Commission for Racial Equality (1987) *Living in Terror* (CRE)

Commission for Racial Equality (1987) *Racial Attacks* (CRE)

Commission for Racial Equality (1988) *Learning in Terror* (CRE)

Commission For Racial Equality (1989) *Local Authority Contracts and Racial Equality* (CRE)

Commission for Racial Equality (1989) *From Cradle to School* (CRE)

Commission for Racial Equality (1990) *Schools of Faith: Religious schools in a multicultural society* (CRE)

Commission for Racial Equality (1991) *Code of Practice* (CRE)

Committee of Inquiry into the Education of children from Ethnic Minority Groups (1981) *West Indian children in our schools* (cmnd 8273) (HMSO)

Confederation of Indian Organisations (nd) *Information Booklet* (CIO)

Cottle T J (1978) *Black Testimony* (Wildwood House)

Cox B (1991) *Cox on Cox* (Hodder and Stoughton)

Cox O (1970) *Caste, Class and Race* (Monthly Review) New York

Craft M (1984a) *Education and Cultural Pluralism* (Falmer Press)

Craft M (1984b) "Education for Diversity" in *Education and Cultural Pluralism* Craft M (Ed) (Falmer Press)

Dabydeen D (ed) (1985) *The Black Presence in English Literature* (Manchester University Press) Manchester

Daniel W (1969) *Racial Discrimination In England* (Penguin) Harmondsworth

Davis A (1982) *Women, Race and Class* (The Women's Press)

Davis G (1982) "Racism and the School Curriculum, Past and Present" *Multicultural Teaching* Vol 1, No 1

Day M and Marsland D (1978) *Black Kids, White Kids: What Hope?* (Regional Training Consultative at Brunel University)

Department of Education and Science (1965) *The Education of Immigrants* Circular 7/65

Department of Education and Science (1974) *Educational Disadvantage and the needs of Immigrants* cmnd 5270 (HMSO)

Despard A (1986) "We Have No Problems Here: teaching English in schools with no ethnic minorities", *Multicultural Teaching*, Vol 4, No 2, pp 30-34

Dhondy F, Beese B and Hassan L (1981) *The Black Explosion in British Schools* (Race Today Publications)

Dixon B (1977) *Catch Them Young 2* (Pluto Press)

Dodgson P and Stewart D (1981) "Multiculturalism or Anti-Racist Teaching: A Question of Alternatives", *Multiracial Education* Vol 9 No 3

Doherty S (1984) "Anti-Racist Teaching Policies" in *Education for a Multicultural Society* Stalker-Welds M (Ed) (Bell and Hyman)

Donald J and Rattansi A (Eds) (1992) *"Race", Culture and Difference* (Sage/Open University)

Donbrow M (1972) *They Docked At Newcastle* (Moriah Press) Jerusalem

Dufour B (Ed) (1990) *The New Social Curriculum* (Cambridge University Press) Cambridge

Dufour B (1990) "The New Social Curriculum: The Political, Economic and Social Context for Educational Change" in Dufour B (1990) *The New Social Curriculum*

Dufour B (1990) "Multicultural and anti-racist Education: Education for a Just Society" in Dufour B (Ed) *The New Social Curriculum*

Dufour B (1990) "Curriculum Change and Organisation: The Place of the New Social Curriculum within the National Curriculum" in Dufour *The New Social Curriculum*

Dummet A (1973) *A Portrait of English Racism* (Penguin) Harmondsworth

Education Services (1991) *Anti-Racist Guidelines* (London Borough of Haringey Council)

Eggleston J, Dunn D and Anjali M (1986) *Education for Some* (Trentham Books) Stoke-on-Trent

Epstein D and Sealey A (1990) *Where it really matters* (Development Education Centre) Birmingham

Fenton S (1982) "Multi-Something Education" *New Community*, vol 10, No 1, pp 57-63

Fergusen M (1987) *The History of Mary Prince* (Pandora Press)

Field F and Haikin P (1971) *Black Britons* (Oxford University Press)

Flew A (1987) *Power To The Parents* (Sherwood Press)

Flew A (1986) "The Wayward Curriculum" in Dennis O'Keeffe (Ed) *A Cause for Parents' Concern* (The Social Affairs Unit)

Forde F, Hall L and McLean V (1988) *The Real McCoy* Bookplace/ ABLSU)

Francis M (1984) "Anti-Racist Teaching: General Principles" in *Challenging Racism* ALTARF

Franklin R and Resnik S (1973) *Political Economy and Racism* (Holt, Rinehart and Winston) New York

Fryer P (1984) *Staying Power* (Pluto Press)

Fryer P (1988) *Black People in the British Empire* (Pluto Press)

Gaine C (1987) *No Problem Here* (Hutchinson)

Gaine C and Pearce L (1987) *Antiracist education in White Areas: Conference Report* (NAME, West Sussex institute of Higher Education)

Gibson A with Barrow J (1986) *The Unequal Struggle* (Centre for Caribbean Studies)

Gilbert D (1984) "Multicultural Mathematics" in *Education for a Multicultural Society* Straker-Welds M (Ed) (Bell & Hyman)

Gill D and Levidow L (1987) *Anti-Racist Science Teaching* (Free Association Books Ltd)

Gill D, Mayor B and Blair M (Eds) *Racism and Education - Structures and Strategies* (Sage/Open University)

Gillborn D (1990) *"Race", Ethnicity and Education - Teaching and Learning in Multi-Ethnic Schools* Unwin Hyman

Gilroy P (1982) "Steppin' Out in Babylon - Race, Class and Autonomy" in *The Empire Strikes Back* (CCCS/Hutchinson)

Gilroy P (1987) *There Ain't No Black In The Union Jack* (Hutchinson)

Gilroy P (1990) "The end of anti-racism", *New Community* Vol 17, No1, pp 71-83 (CRE) also in Donald and Rattansi (1992)

Gold L (1978) *X: a fabulous child's story* (Daughters Publishing Co) New York

Gordon P (1988) *Race in Britain - a research and information guide* (The Runnymede Trust)

Gordon P and Klug F (1986) *New Right, New Racism* (Searchlight Publications)

Grant C (1992) *Research & Multi-Cultural Education* (Falmer Press)

Greater London Association of Disabled People (GLAD) (nd) (1991) *Race and Disability Conference* (GLAD)

Green (1982) "In Defence of Anti-Racist Teaching: A Reply to Recent Critiques of Multicultural Education" in *Multiracial Education* Vol 10, No 2

Grewal, et al (Eds) (1988) *Charting the Journey* (Sheba Feminist Publishers)

Griffin J H (1983) *Black Like Me* (Granada)

Grudgeon E and Woods P (1990) *Educating All: Multicultural Perspectives in the Primary School* (Routledge)

Gundara J, Jones C and Kimberley K (Ed) (1986) *Racism, Diversity and Education* (Hodder & Stoughton)

Hall S (1978) "Racism and Reaction" in *Five Views of Multiracial Britain* (CRE)

Hall S (1980) "Teaching Race" in *Multiracial Education* Vol 9, No 1; also in *Early child Development and Care*, Vol 10, 1983

Halstead M (1988) *Education, Justice and Cultural Diversity* (Falmer Press)

Haque S (1988) "The Politics of Space: The Experience of a Black Woman Architect" in *Charting the Journey*, Grewal, et al (Eds)

Hartman H (1979) "The Unhappy Marriage of Marxism and Feminism" in *Capital and Class* No 8 (Summer)

Hartman P and Husband C (1974) *Racism and the Mass Media* (Davis-Poyner Ltd)

Hatcher R (1985) & Shallice J (1983) "The Politics of Anti-racist Education" in *Multiracial Education*, Vol 12 No 1

Hearn K (1993) "Putting our own house in order", *Disability Issues*, July/August 1993

Hercules T (1989) *Labelled a Black Villain* (Fourth Estate)

Hesse B, Rai D, Bennet C and McGilchrist P (1992) *Beneath The Surface: Racial Harassment* (Avebury), Aldershot

Holly D (1974) *Education or Domination?* (Arrow)

Home Affairs Committee (1986) *Bangladeshis in Britain* (HMSO)

hooks bell (1984) *Feminist Theory: from margin to center* (South End Press) Boston, USA

hooks bell (1991) *Yearning: race, gender and cultural politics* (Turnaround)

hooks bell (1992) *Ain't I a Woman* (Pluto Press)

Hopkins C and Antes R (1990) *Educational Research* (F E Peacock Publishers Inc) Itasca, Illinois

House of Commons Home Affairs Committee (1981) *Fifth Report from the Home Affairs* Committee Session 1980-81: Racial Disadvantage, Vol 1 (HMSO)

Hubah L (1984) "The Position of Black Teachers in this Society" in *Challenging Racism* (ALTARF)

Hughes J L and Larkin J F (1969) *Tudor Royal Proclamations, 1588 - 1603* (Yale University Press) New York
Humphrey D and John G (1971) *Because They're Black* (Penguin) Harmondsworth

Hunter B (1984) "Institutional Racism - LEA Action needed" in *Challenging Racism* ALTARF

Husband C (Ed) (1982a) *Race in Britain* (Hutchinson)

Husband C (1982b) "Race, the Continuity of a Concept" in *Race in Britain* Husband C (Ed) (Hutchinson)

Inaebnit S (1988) *Theory and Practice of Dance in Education from a Gender viewpoint*, unpublished PhD thesis, University of London

Indian Workers' Association (1987) *The Regeneration of Racism* (Indian Workers Association)

Inner London Education Authority (1981) *Education in a Multi-Ethnic Society, An Aide-memoir for the Inspectorate* (ILEA)

Inner London Education Authority (1983a) *Race, Sex and Class, 1 Achievement in Schools* (ILEA)

Inner London Education Authority (1983b) *Race, Sex and Class, 2 Multi-Ethnic Education in Schools* (ILEA)

Inner London Education Authority (1983c) *Race, Sex and Class, 3 A Policy for Equality* (ILEA)

Inner London Education Authority (1983d) *Race, Sex and Class, 4 Anti-Racist Statement and Guidelines* (ILEA)

Jeffcoate R (1979) *Positive Image* (Writers and Readers Publishing Cooperative)

Jeffcoate R (1985) *Ethnic Minorities in Education* (Harper and Row)

Jeffcoate R and James A (Eds) (1981) *The Schoolroom in the Multicultural Society* (Harper and Row)

Jones J M (1972) *Prejudice and Racism* (Adison Wesley) New York
Jordan P (1962) *Prospero's Magic: Some Thoughts on Class and Race* (Oxford University Press)

Joseph G (1992) *The Crest of the Peacock: Non-European Roots of Mathematics* (Penguin)

Joseph G, Reddy V and Searle-Chatterjee M (1990) *Eurocentrism in the social sciences* (institute of Race Relations)

Kapo R (1981) *A Savage Culture* (Quartet)

Katz J (1978) *White Awareness: Handbook for Anti-Racism Training* (University of Oklahoma Press) Oklahoma

Katz W (1987) *The Black West* (Open Hand Publishing Inc) Seattle, WA.

Keddie N (Ed) (1973) *Tinker, tailor....the Myth of Cultural Deprivation* (Penguin) Harmondsworth

Kincheloe J L (1991) *Teachers as Researchers: Qualitative inquiry as a path to Empowerment* (Falmer Press)

Kirp D L (1979) *Doing Good by Doing Little* (University of California Press) Berkeley

Klein G (1982) *Resources for multicultural education* (Longman)

Knowles C and Mercer S (1992) "Feminism and Antiracism: an exploration of the political possibilities" in Donald and Rattansi *"Race", Culture and Difference*

Knowles L and Prewitt K (eds) (1969) *Institutional Racism in America* (Prentice Hall) Eaglewood Cliffs

Knowles M (1992) "The issue of Moslem schools", *Education*, 1 May

Kumar A (1988) *The Heartstone Odyssey* (Allied Mouse)

Landry B (1987) *The New Black Middle Class* (University of California Press) Los Angeles, California

Lawrence E (1981) "White Sociology, Black Struggle" in *Multi-Racial Education*, Vol 9, No 3

Lax L (1984) "Anti-racist Policies" in ALTARF (1984) *Challenging Racism*

Leeds Commission for Racial Equality (1987) *Racial Harassment in Leeds* (CRE)

Leicester M (1991) *Equal Opportunities In School: Social Class, Sexuality, Race, Gender and Special Needs* (Longman)

Leicester M (1989) *Multicultural Education From Theory to Practice* (NFER-Nelson) Windsor

Leicester M and Field J (1990) "Anti-racist post-initial education: reform after the Act", *New Community*, Vol 16, No 3, pp 417-423 (CRE)

Lewis R (1988) *Anti-Racism A Mania Exposed* (Quartet Books)

Lindsay L (1985) *Racism Science Education and the Politics of Food* (ALTARF)

Little A (1978) "Schools & Race" in *Five Views of Multiracial Britain* (CRE)

Little A and Willey R (1981) *Multi-ethnic Education: The Way Forward Schools Council* Pamphlet 18 (Schools Council)

Lindsay L (1984) "Quinton Kynaston School" in *Challenging Racism* ALTARF

London Research Centre (1994) *London's Ethnic Minorities* (LRC)

Lynch J (1983) *The Multicultural Curriculum* (Batsford)

Lynch J (1989) *Multicultural education in a global society* (Falmer Press)

Mac an Ghaill M (1988) *Young, Gifted and Black* (Open University Press) Milton Keynes

MacDonald I, Bhavani R, Khan L and John G (1989) *Murder in the Playground* (Longsight Press)

Machiavelli N (1993) *The Prince* (Wordsworth Editions Ltd) Ware, Hertfordshire

Mahony E (1987) "Race Training in an All-White School" *Multicultural Teaching* Vol V, No 2, p 9

Mahoney T (1988) *Governing Schools: Powers, Issues and Practice* (Macmillan Education)

Maitland S (1989) *Multicultural Inset* (Trentham Books) Stoke-on-Trent

Mansourian, B (1994) "Multicultural Library Services for People with Disabilities", *Link-Up*, June (National Library of Australia) Canberra

Marable M (1984) *Race, Reform and Rebellion: the Second Reconstruction in Black America 1945 - 1982* (Macmillan)

Mason P (1962) *Race Relations* (Oxford University Press)

Massey I (1991) *More than Skin Deep: developing anti-racist multicultural education in schools* (Hodder and Stoughton)

McFarlane S (1988) Education for racial equality: simply "Good Practice?" in *Better To Light A Candle, Perspectives No 39* (University of Exeter) Exeter

McLean B and Young J (1988) *Multicultural Anti-Racist Education* (Longman Group)

Mehmood T (1983) *Hand on the Sun* (Penguin) Harmondsworth

Miles R (1982) "Racism & Nationalism in Britain" in *Race in Britain* Husbands C (Ed) (Hutchinson)

Miles R and Phizacklea A (1979) *Racism and Political Action in Britain* (Routledge & Kegan Paul)

Miles R and Phizacklea A (1984) *White Man's Country* (Pluto Press) Modgil S, Verma G, Mallick K and Modgil C (1988) *Multicultural Education* (Falmer Press)

317

Mohanti P (1985) *Through Brown Eyes* (Oxford University Press) Oxford

Morrell F (1989) *Children of the Future* (Hogarth Press)

Morris M & Griggs C (1988) *Education-The Wasted Years?* (Falmer Press)

Mukerjee T (1983) "Collusion, Conflict or Constructive Antiracist Socialisation" *Multicultural Teaching* Vol 1, No 2, pp 24-5

Mullard C (1980) *Racism in Society and Schools: History, Policy and Practice* (Centre for Multicultural Education) Occasional Paper No 1

Mullard C (1982) "Multi-racial Education in Britain: From Assimilation to Cultural Pluralism" in *Race, Migration and Schooling,* Tierney J (Ed)

Mullard C (1984a) *Anti-Racist Education: The Three O's* (National Association for Multi-Racial Education)

Mullard C (1984b) "The Three R's: Rampton, Racism and Research" in *Race, Education and Research: Rampton, Swann and After* (Centre for Multicultural Education and the Thomas Coram Institute, University of London, Institute of Education)

Multicultural Curriculum Support Group (1991) "Women in Focus" in *Equal Opportunities*, No 6 (London Borough of Haringey Education Service)

Mundell I (1993) "Maps that shape the world", *New Scientist*, 3 July, pp 21 -23

Murray N (1992) "Columbus and the USA: from mythology to ideology" in *Race and Class* Vol XXXIII No 3 (Institute of Race Relations)

Nanton P (1989) "The new orthodoxy: racial categories and equal opportunity policy", **New Community**, Vol 15, No 4, pp 549-564

National Anti-Racist Movement in Education (1985) NAME on Swann (NAME) Walsall
National Curriculum Council (1990) *The Whole Curriculum* (NCC)

National Union of Teachers (1978) *All Our Children* (NUT)

National Union of Teachers (1981) *Initial Response to the Rampton Committee Report*, Press Release 17 June 1981 (NUT)

National Union of Teachers (1992) *Anti-racist Curriculum Guidelines* (NUT)

Neill A (1976) *Summerhill* (Penguin) Harmondsworth

Newcome R (1990) "Education for Multi-Ethnic England at One Devon School" in *The Struggle is My Life, Perspectives* No 42 (University of Exeter) Exeter

Newham Monitoring Project (1991) *The Forging of a Black Community* Newham Monitoring Project/Campaign Against Racism and Fascism

Nixon J (1981) *A Teachers' Guide to Action Research* (Grant McIntyre)

Nixon J (1985) *A Teacher's Guide To Multicultural Education* (Basil Blackwell)

Northamptonshire Education Department (1986) *Multicultural Education* (Northamptonshire County Council)

O'Keeffe D (Ed) (1986) *A Cause for Parents' Concern* (The Social Affairs Unit)

Oliver M (1993) *The politics of Disablement* (Macmillan)

O'Sullivan T, Hartley J, Saunders D and Fiske J (1989) *Key concepts in communication Key Concepts* (Routledge)

Osler A (1989) *Speaking Out* (Virago Press)

Oswell J (1988) *The Divided Kingdom* (Constable)

Page A and Thomas K (1984) *Multicultural Education and the All-White School* (University of Nottingham)

Palmer F (1986) *Anti-Racism An Assault On Education And Value*

319

(Sherwood Press)

Parekh B (1978) "Asians in Britain: Problem or opportunity?" in *Five Views of Multi-Racial Britain* (CRE)

Parekh B (1985) "The Gifts of Diversity", *The Times Educational Supplement*, 29-3-85

Parekh B (1988) "Some Thoughts on Multi-Cultural Education" in *Better To Light a Candle*, *Perspectives* No 39 (University of Exeter) Exeter

Parekh B (1990) *Charter 90 For Asians* (CIO)

Parker K (1992) "The revelation of Caliban" in Gill, Mayor and Blair *Racism and Education*

Parmar P (1981) "Young Asian Women: A Critique of the Pathological Approach" in *Multiracial Education*, Vol 9 No 3

Patel K (1991) *Development Workers Conference* (Royal National Institute for the Blind)

Patel N (1990) *A "Race" Against Time* (The Runnymede Trust)

Patel T (1986) *The Position of Black Teachers in Post War Britain* Unpublished BEd Thesis (North London Polytechnic, now the University of North London)

Patterson S (1963) *Dark Strangers: a study of West Indians in London* (Penguin) Harmondsworth

Patterson S (1989) "Informal odysseys" *New Community*, Vol 15, No 4, pp 629-635 (CRE)

Pen Green Family Centre (1990) *Learning to be Strong* (Changing Perspectives Ltd)

Phillips-Bell (1981) "Multicultural Education: What is it?" in *Multicultural Teaching*, No 10, No 1, Autumn

Potter D (1994) *Seeing The Blossom* (Faber and Faber)

Prasher U and Nicholas Shan (1986) *Routes or Roadblocks?* (The Runnymede Trust)

Preston J (1990) "Widening the Brief:A Somerset County Perspective", *The Struggle Is My Life, Perspectives* No 42 (University of Exeter) Exeter

Race Today Collective (1983) *The Struggle of Asian Workers in Britain* (Race Today Publications)

Rae J (1989) *Too Little Too Late?* (Collins)

Rafferty J (1990) "Black, Beautiful and Baffling" in *Plus Magazine* (December 5)

Reeves F & Chevannes M (1983) "The Ideological Construction of Black Underachievement" in *Multiracial Education*, Vol 12, No 1

Rex J (1970) "The Concept of Race in Sociological Theory" in *Race & Racism* Zubaida S (Ed)

Rex J & Tomlinson S (1979) *Colonial Immigrants in a British City* (Routledge and Kegan Paul)

Richardson R (1989) "Materials, resources and methods" in Cole, M (ed) *Education for Equality*

Richardson R (1985) "Each and Every School: responding, reviewing, planning and doing", *Multicultural Teaching,* Vol 3, No 2, Spring

Richardson R (1990) *Daring To Be A Teacher* (Trentham Books) Stoke-on-Trent

Richardson R (1992) "Race policies and programmes under attack: two case studies for the 1990s in Gill, Mayor and Blair *Racism and Education*

Richmond A (1955) *The Colour Problem* (Penguin) Harmondsworth

Roddick A (1991) *Body and Soul* (Ebury Press)
Rodney W (1983) *How Europe Underdeveloped Africa* (Bogle L'Ouverture Publications)

Rogers B (1983) *52%* (The Women's Press)

Rogers J (1972) *Great Men of Color (Volumes 1 and 2)* Macmillan Publishing Co) New York

Rosen Harold (1974) "Language and Class" in Holly D *Education or Domination?*

Rutstein N (1988) *To Be One: A Battle Against Racism* (George Ronald)

Said E (1993) *Culture and Imperialism* (Chatto and Windus)

Sarup M (1982) *Education, State and Crisis* (Routledge and Kegan Paul)

Sarup M (1991) *Education and the Ideologies of Racism* (Trentham Books) Stoke-on-Trent

Saunders P (1990) *Social Class and Stratification* (Routledge)

Saunders M (1981) *Multicultural Teaching: A Guide for the Classroom* (McGraw and Hill)

Saunders M (1982) "Education for a new community", *New Community*, Vol 10, No 1, pp 64-71

Scott S (1985) "Feminist Research and Qualitative Methods: A Discussion of Some of the Issues" in Burgess (Ed) *Strategies of Educational Research: Qualitative Methods*

Select Committee on Race Relations and Immigration (1973) *Education* (HMSO)

Select Committee on Race Relations and Immigration (1977) *The West Indian Community* (HMSO)

Shaik M (1990) "Putting Multicultural Education on one School's Agenda", *Perspectives* No 42 (University of Exeter), Exeter

Shallice J (1984) "Racism and Education" in *Challenging Racism* (ALTARF)

Shan S (nd) Report of first year of ESG project in Birmingham (Birmingham LEA) Birmingham

Sharma C (1975) Homeopathy and Natural Medicine (Turnstone Press Ltd) Northampton

Shaw K (1988) "And What About The National Curriculum?" in *Better To Light A Candle, Perspectives* No 39 (University of Exeter), Exeter

Short G and Carrington B (1992) Towards an antiracist initiative in the all-white primary school: a case study" in Gill, Mayor and Blair *Racism and Education*

Sivanandan A (1976) "Race and Class and the State: the Black Experience" in *Race and Class*, Vol XVII, No 4

Sivanandan A (1977) "The Liberation of the Black Intellectual" in *Race and Class*, Vol XVIII, No 4

Sivanandan A (1978) "From Immigration to Induced Repatriation" in *Race and Class*, Vol XX, No 1

Sivanandan A (1981) "From Resistance to Rebellion: Asian and Afro-Caribbean Struggles in Britain" in *Race and Class*, Vol XXIII, Nos 2/3

Sivanandan A (1982) *A Different Hunger* (Pluto Press)

Sivanandan A (1983) "Challenging Racism: Strategies for the 80's" in *Race and Class*, Vol XXV, No 2

Sivanandan A (1985) "RAT and the Degradation of Black Struggle" in *Race and Class*, Vol XXVI, No 4

Smith D (1977) *Racial Disadvantage in Britain* (Penguin) Harmondsworth

Smith D and Tomlinson S (1989) *The School Effect: A Study of Multi-Racial Comprehensives* (Policy Studies Institute)
Smith J (1989) *Misogynies* (Faber and Faber)

Solomos J (1989) *Race relations research and social policy: a review of some recent debates and controversies* (Centre for research in Ethnic Relations, University of Warwick) Coventry

Solomos J, et al (1982) "The Organic Crisis of British Capitalism and Race: The Experience of the Seventies" in *The Empire Strikes Back*, (CCCS/Hutchinson)

Spears A K (1978) "Institutional Racism and the education of Blacks" *Anthropology and Education Quarterly*, Vol 9, No 2, pp 127-36

Stenhouse L (1977) *An Introduction to Curriculum Research and Development* (Heinemann)

Stenhouse L, Verma G K, Wild R D and Nixon, J (1982) *Teaching About Race Relations* (Routledge and Kegan Paul)

Stone M (1981) *The Education of the Black Child in Britain* (Fontana)

Stone S (1985) *Mitthu the Parrot* (Luzac and Co)

Stradling R, Noctor M and Baines B (1984) *Teaching Controversial Issues* (Edward Arnold Ltd)

Straker-Welds M (ed) (1984) *Education for a Multicultural Society* (Bell and Hyman)

Street-Porter R. (1978) *Race, Children and Cities* (The Open University Press) Milton Keynes

Swain J, Finkelstein V, French S and Oliver M (1993) *Disabling barriers - enabling environments* (Open University/Sage)

Swann Lord (1985) *Education for All: A Brief Guide* (Department of Education and Science) (HMSO)

Swann Lord (1985) *Education For All* (Department of Education and Science) (HMSO)

Syer M (1982) "Racism, Ways of Thinking and School" in *Race, Migration and Schooling*, Tierney J (ed) (Holt, Rhinehart and Winston)

Tandon Y (1984) *The New Positions of East Africa's Asians* (The Minority Rights Group)

Taylor F (1974) *Race, School and Community* (NFER-Nelson) Windsor

Taylor M (1981) *Caught Between - A Review of Research into the Education of Pupils of West Indian Origin* (NFER Nelson) Windsor

Taylor M and Hegarty S (1985) *The Best of Both Worlds..?* (NFER-Nelson) Windsor

Taylor M (1988) *Worlds Apart?* (NFER-Nelson) Windsor

Taylor M (1992) *Equality after ERA* (NFER) Slough

Taylor W (1990) "Multi-cultural education in the "white highlands" after the 1988 Education Reform Act", in *New Community*, Vol XVI, No 3, pp 369-378 (CRE)

Tierney J (1982a) *Race, Immigration and Schooling* (Holt, Rinehart & Wilson)

Tierney J (1982b) "Race, Colonialism and Migration" in *Race, Migration and Schooling Tierney* (ed) (Holt, Rhinehart & Wilson)

Thompson E P (1980) *The Making of the English Working Class* (Penguin) Harmondsworth

Tirrell P (1990) Networking: A Note in "The Struggle is my Life", *Perspectives* No 42 (University of Exeter) Exeter

Tomlinson P and Quinton M (Eds) (1986) *Values across the Curriculum* (Falmer Press)

Tomlinson S (1983) *Ethnic Minorities in British Schools* (Heinemann)

Tomlinson S (1987) "Towards A D 2000" in *New Community*, Vol XIV, Nos 1 and 2 (CRE)

Tomlinson S and Coulson P (1988) *Education for a Multi-Ethnic Society* (University of Lancaster)

Tomlinson S (1990) Multicultural Education or Educational Nationalism in "The Struggle Is My Life", *Perspectives* No 42 (University of Exeter) Exeter

Tomlinson S (1990) *Multicultural Education in white schools* (Batsford)

Tompson K (1988) *Under Siege: Racial Violence in Britain Today* (Penguin) Harmondsworth

Townsend H E R (1971) *Immigrant Pupils in England: The LEA Response* (NFER) Slough

Townsend H E R & Brittan E (1972) *Organisation in Multiracial Schools* (NFER) Slough

Troyna B (1990) "Reform or deform? The 1988 Education Act and racial equality in Britain", *New Community*, Vol 16, No 3, pp 403-416 (CRE)

Troyna B and Carrington B (1990) *Education, Racism and Reform* (Routledge)

Troyna B and Hatcher R (Eds) (1992) *Racism in children's lives* (Routledge)

Troyna B and Williams J (1986) *Racism, Education and the State* (Croom Helm)

Umed K (1986) "A Rage in Harlem" *Multicultural Teaching*, Vol 4, No 2

Van den Berghe P (1984) "Race Perspective Two" in Cashmore E (Ed) *Dictionary of Race and Ethnic Relations* (Routledge and Kegan Paul)

Van Sertima I (1983) *Blacks In Science* (Transaction Books)

Verma and Pumfrey (eds) (1988) *Educational Attainments* (Falmer Press)

Visram R (1986) *Ayahs, Lascars and Princes* (Pluto Press)
Wade B and Souter P (1992) *Continuing to think: The British Asian Girl* (Multilingual Matters) Clevedon

Walker A (1985) *Horses Make a Landscape Look More Beautiful* (The Women's Press)

Walvin J (1972) *Black and White* (Penguin) Harmondsworth

Wandsworth Council for Community Relations (nd) *No Bloody Suntans* (London Borough of Wandsworth CCR)

Warnock M (1988) *A Common Policy for Education* (Oxford) Oxford

Wellington W (1986) *Controversial Issues In The Curriculum* (Basil Blackwell)

Wellman D (1977) *Portraits of White Racism* (Cambridge University Press) Cambridge

Whitehead W (1980) *Different Faces* (Pluto Press)

Whyld J (1990) "Gender Education: Challenging Sexism in Education" in Dufour B (Ed) *The New Social Curriculum*

Williams J (1985) "Redefining Institutional Racism", *Ethnic and Racial Studies,* Vol 8, No 3

Williams J and Carter B (1984) "Institutional Racism: new orthodoxy, old ideas", *Multicultural Education* (NAME) Derby

Worswork C (1982) *Roots of Racism* (Institute of Race Relations)

Wright C (1992) "Early education: multiracial primary school classrooms" in Gill, Mayor and Blair *Racism and Education*

Wright P (1987) *Spycatcher* (William Heinemann) Australia

Young R (1992) "Racist society, racist science" in Gill, Mayor and Blair *Racism and Education*